Praise for previous editions of

" . . .
thr

"He
scr
and
bik

Help Us Keep
This Guide Up to Date

Every effort has been made by the author and editors to make this guide as accurate and useful as possible. However, many things can change after a guide is published—establishments close, phone numbers change, facilities come under new management, and so on.

We would love to hear from you concerning your experiences with this guide and how you feel it could be made better and be kept up to date. While we may not be able to respond to all comments and suggestions, we'll take them to heart, and we'll also make certain to share them with the author. Please send your comments and suggestions to the following address:

The Globe Pequot Press
Reader Response/Editorial
Department
P.O. Box 480
Guilford, CT 06437

Or you may e-mail us at:

editorial@globe-pequot.com

Thanks for your input, and happy travels!

SHORT BIKE RIDES® SERIES

Short Bike Rides®

in Eastern Massachusetts

THIRD EDITION

BY
HOWARD STONE

The
Globe
Pequot
Press

Guilford, Connecticut

Copyright © 1982, 1988, 1991, 1994, 1997, 1999 by Howard Stone

Short Bike Rides is a registered trademark of the Globe Pequot Press.

Cover design by Saralyn D'Amato-Twomey
Cover photo: Chris Dubé
Text design: Lisa Reneson

Photograph on page 274 courtesy of the Massachusetts Department of Commerce and Development, Division of Tourism. All other photographs courtesy of the author.

Library of Congress Cataloging-in-Publication Data
Stone, Howard, 1947–
    Short bike rides in Eastern Massachusetts / by Howard Stone.
— 3rd ed.
    p.   cm.   — (Short bike rides series)
    ISBN 0-7627-0434-9
    1. Bicycle touring—Massachusetts Guidebooks. 2. Massachusetts Guidebooks. I. Title. II. Series
GV1045.5.M4S766   1999
796.6'4'09744—dc21   99–25250
                                                              CIP

Contents

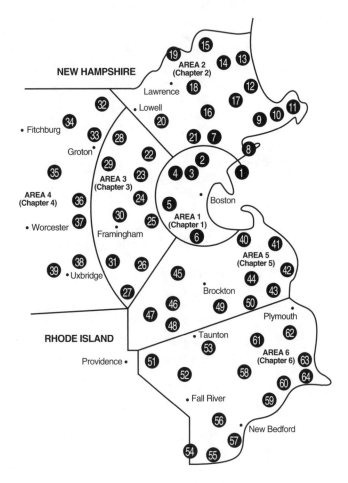

The numbers on this map refer to rides in this book.

Acknowledgments

This book could never have come to fruition without a lot of help. My wife, Bernice, provided continual encouragement, support, and late-night snacks. Many members of the Narragansett Bay Wheelmen kept me company while I was researching the rides by providing good cheer, taking notes, and patiently putting up with endless hours of backtracking and rechecking intersections. Dominique Coulombe, my supervisor, allowed me to work flexible hours so that I could take advantage of the daylight to research the rides. Jeanne LaFazia helped me interpret the intricacies of the laws of Massachusetts. Carla Kerber helped me type the manuscript. Dozens of local residents told me about hidden back roads and interesting places to see. I would also like to thank Kevin and Anita Clifford for putting me up overnight at various times.

Some of the photographs were supplied by the Massachusetts Department of Commerce and Development, Division of Tourism, which allowed me to look through its photo collection and choose scenes that would best capture the various landscapes of the state.

A few of the rides were originally mapped out as a whole or in part by the following members of the Narragansett Bay Wheelmen, to whom I extend my thanks:

Bill McIlmail, Ride 59   Phil Maker, Ride 52
Ed Ames, Ride 54   Steve McGowen, Ride 56
Chick Mead, Ride 60   Wes Ewell, Ride 57

Preface to the Third Edition

The third edition of *Short Bike Rides in Eastern Massachusetts* covers the same area as the second edition. The region west of Worcester and Fitchburg is covered in the companion volume *Short Bike Rides in Western Massachusetts*. The material in this book is arranged in the same basic format as the earlier edition, with an introductory description, a map, and point-to-point directions for each ride. The directions are more concise, but with no loss of clarity, and I've shown more connecting roads on the maps. Many of the rides have been modified slightly to improve scenery and safety or to avoid badly deteriorated roads. I have rerouted several rides from a counterclockwise to a clockwise direction in order to maximize right turns and minimize left turns.

Introduction

This book is a guide to bicycling in the portion of Massachusetts within reasonable commuting distance of Boston, covering the area between the Cape Cod Canal and a north–south line just east of Worcester and Fitchburg. The region, along with the sections of Rhode Island and New Hampshire just over the state lines, offers ideal cycling. Massachusetts is blessed with an impressive network of thousands of back roads, most of them paved but not heavily traveled. Beyond the built-up metropolitan areas, which compose a very small percentage of the state, the landscape is rural enough to give the cyclist a sense of remoteness and serenity, and yet the nearest town, village, or grocery is never more than a few miles away. The terrain is refreshingly varied for a relatively small state.

East of Boston lies the seacoast, one of the state's most scenic features. Most of the Massachusetts coast is beautiful and relatively unspoiled, with smooth, sandy beaches, windswept dunes, and extensive salt marshes. Outside Boston is a broad belt of affluent suburbs with gracious homes and estates surrounded by acres of gently rolling, open land. Southeast of Boston, toward Cape Cod, is a landscape of cranberry bogs and scrub pine. Beyond the metropolitan area, as the land becomes genuinely rural about 25 or 30 miles outside the city, lie lake-dotted forests, rolling apple orchards, and old mill villages.

Bicycling is an ideal way to appreciate the New England landscape's unique intimacy, which is not found in most other parts of the United States. The back roads turn constantly as they hug the minute contours of the land, forcing your orientation down to a small scale. Every turn and dip in the road may yield a surprise—a weathered barn, a pond, a stream, a little dam or falls, a hulking old mill right out of the Industrial Revolution, a ragged stone wall, or a pasture with grazing cattle or horses. Most of the smaller town centers are architectural gems, with the traditional stately white church and village green flanked by the town hall, a handsome brick or stone library, and graceful old wooden homes.

Geography of the Region

Not counting Cape Cod, Massachusetts is basically a rectangle that extends upward and downward at its eastern edge. The eastern side of the rectangle is notched inward by the C-shaped cup of Massachusetts Bay, with Boston lying at the innermost point. The area covered by this book measures about 90 miles from north to south and 60 miles from east to west.

In general the region is fairly flat with an occasional hill. Most of the rides traverse at least one or two hills, sometimes steep or long enough that you'll want to walk them. Yet no hills are long enough to be really discouraging, and for every uphill climb, there's a corresponding descent. The large majority of the hills you'll encounter are less than half a mile long, the steepest portion limited to a couple of hundred yards or less.

Culturally Massachusetts has a long and proud history, beginning with the Pilgrim settlement in Plymouth in 1620. The first armed encounters of the Revolutionary War occurred a century and a half later in Concord and Lexington. The deep and sheltered waters of the harbors bordering Newburyport, Gloucester, Salem, Boston, and New Bedford spawned thriving seaports, fisheries, and maritime commerce in Colonial times and into the nineteenth century. Today, these same harbors, along with the many smaller coves and inlets piercing the coast, are filled with motor yachts and sailboats. The Industrial Revolution got a head start in Massachusetts when Lowell and Holyoke, two of the first planned industrial cities in the country, evolved before the Civil War. In later years, between the end of the Civil War and the turn of the century, hundreds of mills were built along the swift-flowing Merrimack, Blackstone, Quaboag, and numerous other rivers, employing thousands of immigrants from Europe and Quebec.

Today, hundreds of smaller towns and villages in Massachusetts make up some of the state's most appealing and architecturally fascinating hallmarks. As you bike through a town, try to notice each building along the green. First you'll see the graceful white church, usually built before 1850, often on a little rise, standing proudly above the rest of the

2

town. Next look for the town hall, probably a handsome, white-pillared, Colonial-style building or an ornate wooden or stone Victorian one. Near the town hall you'll frequently find the library, a gracious brick or stone building dating from the turn of the century or the two decades before it. The small-town library is almost always recognizable, generally built to appear dignified yet inviting, with wide steps, a portico framing the front door, and often a dome or rounded roof.

Another building worth noticing is the schoolhouse. In the smaller towns, the schools are typically handsome old wooden or brick buildings, sometimes with graceful bell towers or cupolas. In some towns, such as Fairhaven, the high school is an architectural showpiece.

Mill towns at first may look depressing, but there is always some architectural beauty to be found. The mills themselves are often fascinating old Victorian structures, forbidding but ornamented with cornices and clock towers. Next to the mill is usually a small millpond with a little dam or falls. Many mill towns have orderly rows of identical two- or three-story wooden houses, built for the workers during the late 1800s. Unfortunately fire, neglect, and vandalism claim several mills each year, but a growing consciousness has arisen about preserving and maintaining these unique and impressive buildings. Many old mills have been recycled into apartments, condominiums, or offices.

Geographically, eastern Massachusetts is divided into six fairly distinct areas, and this book covers all of them except Cape Cod. Boston and its close suburbs, lying within the Route 128 semicircle and extending along the coast as far as Lynn to the northeast and Quincy to the southeast, is the most densely populated part of the state. Immediately north of Boston is a cluster of cities that are as densely populated as Boston itself—Cambridge, Somerville, Everett, Chelsea, Medford, Malden, Revere, and Winthrop. Beyond this urban cluster and Boston itself, along with Lynn and Quincy, the area consists primarily of affluent communities with gracious older homes and estates and a surprising amount of protected, lake-dotted woodland—including the Lynn Woods, Middlesex Fells, and Blue Hills reservations.

I've defined the North Shore as the land between the coast slanting northeastward from Lynn and the west bank of the Merrimack River

Town Hall, Swansea

where it enters New Hampshire. The North Shore has the most extensive concentration of old wealth in the state, expressed in its mansions, estates surrounded by acres of gently rolling meadows, and hundreds of tidy horse farms with simple white fences bordering large fields. The coastline is the nicest in the state, with mansions and estates lining most of the stretch between Swampscott and Ipswich. North of Cape Ann are extensive salt marshes and Crane Beach, one of the finest in the state. Salem, Marblehead, Gloucester, and Newburyport are historic communities where you'll find narrow streets lined with old wooden homes and broad avenues boasting the impressive Federal-style mansions of early merchants and sea captains. The wide Merrimack River, which at the turn of the century was the textile center of the country, enters the state from Nashua, New Hampshire, and flows through the three early mill cities of Lowell, Lawrence, and Haverhill, evenly spaced about 10 miles apart. East of Haverhill the river flows through an idyllic, undeveloped landscape of gentle green hills.

I've defined the South Shore as the shoulder of coast extending southeastward from Weymouth to Kingston Bay just north of Plymouth, inland to the northeast corner of Rhode Island, and bordered on the south by Route 44 between Providence and Plymouth. The South Shore is more built up and suburban than the North Shore. The coast is a varied mixture of estates and fine homes in Duxbury and Cohasset; summer beach colonies with rows of cottages and more modest homes in Marshfield, Scituate, and Hull; and vast salt marshes along the mouth of the North River between Marshfield and Scituate. Inland from Kingston Bay is a large cluster of lakes and ponds, and here you start to see the cranberry bogs that are a distinguishing feature of the southeastern part of the state. At the western edge of the region is the jewelry capital of the United States, along the axis from Attleboro to Pawtucket and Providence, Rhode Island.

Southeastern Massachusetts includes everything south of the South Shore, excluding Cape Cod. This region has unique characteristics— sandy soil, scrub pine, cranberry bogs, generally flat and often swampy terrain, and cedar-shingled houses with peaked roofs. In general this

5

area provides the easiest bicycling in the state. The historical center of the region is, of course, Plymouth, with its collection of landmarks and sites related to the Pilgrim settlement. The southern coast is delightful, with unspoiled beaches and a string of elegant small towns that at one time were shipbuilding communities and are now yachting and sailing centers. In the middle of the southern coast is New Bedford, the nation's prime whaling port during the mid-1800s and today the home of the East Coast's largest fishing fleet.

The western suburbs compose the broad belt of Massachusetts between the North Shore and the South Shore east of Worcester and Fitchburg. I've divided them into halves separated roughly by I–495. East of this highway, the predominant landscape is graciously suburban and punctuated by a large number of towns, most of them enjoyable. Many of the western suburbs are affluent, with prosperous farms and spacious homes on large wooded lots. Bicycling in this area is a pleasure, with gently rolling terrain that does not become hilly until you get west of Framingham. The best-known historic sites in this region are Battle Green in Lexington, the Old North Bridge in Concord, and the Wayside Inn in Sudbury. Not far from Route 128 are the two truly rural and unspoiled towns closest to Boston, Carlisle and Dover. West of Concord is the prime apple-growing region of the state, with dozens of orchards stretching along the hillsides in Stow, Bolton, Harvard, and Boxboro.

West of I–495 the landscape becomes genuinely more rural and hillier. Biking in the farther western suburbs is more challenging, but the lovely countryside makes the cycling worthwhile. Most of the small towns are elegant, unspoiled jewels. The Wachusett Reservoir, with its massive dam at the northern end in Clinton, is the second largest lake in the state. The southern half of the region is drained by the Blackstone River, running southeastward from Worcester to Woonsocket, Rhode Island. Fascinating old mill towns right out of the Industrial Revolution lie along the banks of the river and its tributaries. In this area is Purgatory Chasm, a deep cleft in the earth formed by some glacial cataclysm. The Blackstone Valley is currently being developed by the state into a linear historical park.

Massachusetts is fortunate to benefit from an active heritage of preserving the land and historic sites that began in the nineteenth century, before preservation was even considered in many other parts of the country. The state park system, run by the Department of Environmental Management, is admirable. A unique feature of the state park system is the renovation of old mills and factories, along with their adjacent waterways, into interpretive museums and visitor centers called Heritage State Parks. The names of two organizations, the Trustees of Reservations (TOR) and the Society for the Preservation of New England Antiquities (SPNEA), appear frequently in our descriptions of the rides. The first body is dedicated to acquiring and maintaining scenic areas, and it does the job admirably. TOR reservations are never shabby or shopworn, as so many public areas are; instead, they are impeccably clean and well landscaped. Some of the finest natural areas in the state, such as Crane Beach in Ipswich and World's End in Hingham, are TOR properties. The second body aims to acquire, preserve, and open to the public historic homes and mansions. Like TOR, it does a superb job. SPNEA properties are, however, open during limited hours, usually afternoons in the summer. Largely a volunteer and member-supported organization, it simply does not have the funds to keep longer hours. In addition to these two bodies, dozens of other local historical societies and conservationist groups, including the Massachusetts Audubon Society, maintain historic houses and areas of greenspace.

One final geographic feature you'll encounter across the state is the drumlin, a small, sharp hill left behind by the glaciers. Most drumlins are elliptical, like a football sliced lengthwise along the middle. They are usually less than a mile long and less than 200 feet high and lie along a northwest-southeast or north-south axis, the direction of glacial flow. The biggest concentration of drumlins lies within 10 miles of Boston. Most of those near the ocean, such as Orient Heights in East Boston or World's End in Hingham, offer outstanding views. Other clusters of drumlins are scattered across the state. In rural areas such as West Newbury, Groton, and Lunenburg, they transform the land into a rippling sea of rolling hills with broad pastures and orchards sweeping up and over them, providing some of the most inspiring and scenic bicycling in the state.

About the Rides

Ideally, a bicycle ride should be a safe, scenic, relaxing, and enjoyable experience that brings you into intimate contact with the landscape. In striving to make this goal possible, I've routed the rides along paved secondary and rural roads, avoiding main highways, cities, and dirt roads as much as I could. I've also tried to make the routes as safe as possible. Routes containing hazards, such as very bumpy roads or dead stops at the bottom of steep hills, have been avoided whenever reasonable alternate routes were available. Any dangerous spots remaining on a recommended route have been clearly indicated in the directions by a **CAUTION** warning. I've included scenic spots such as dams, falls, ponds, mill villages, ocean views, and open vistas on the rides whenever possible.

Nearly all the rides have two options—a shorter one averaging about 15 miles and a longer one that is usually between 25 and 30 miles long. All the longer rides are extensions of the shorter ones, with both options starting off at the same place. A few rides have no shorter option, and several have three alternatives. All the rides make a loop or figure-eight rather than backtracking along the same route. For each ride, I include both a map and directions.

If you've never ridden any distance, the thought of riding 15 or, heaven forbid, 30 miles may sound intimidating or even impossible. I want to emphasize, however, that anyone in normal health can ride 30 miles and enjoy it if he or she gets mildly into shape first. You can accomplish this painlessly by riding at a leisurely pace for an hour several times a week for about three weeks. At a moderate pace, you'll ride about 10 miles per hour. If you think of the rides by the hour rather than the mile, the numbers are much less frightening.

To emphasize how easy bicycle riding is, most bike clubs have a 100-mile ride, called a Century, each fall. Dozens of ordinary people try their first Century without ever having done much biking and finish it, and enjoy it! Sure, they're tired at the end, but they've accomplished the

8

feat and loved it. (If you'd like to try one, the biggest and flattest Century in the Northeast is held in southeastern Massachusetts on the Sunday after Labor Day, starting in Tiverton, Rhode Island—ask at any good bike shop for details.)

If you count short stops but not long ones, a 15-mile ride should take about two hours at a leisurely speed, a 20- to 25-mile ride about three hours, and a 30-mile ride about four hours. If you ride at a brisk pace, subtract an hour from these estimates.

A few of the rides in this book have short (half a mile or less) sections of dirt road, or go a short distance along roads that are one-way in the wrong direction. This was occasionally necessary when there was no simple alternate route or to avoid making the directions needlessly complicated. If you come to a dirt road, get the feel of it first. If it's hard-packed, you can ride it without difficulty, but if it's soft, you should walk instead because it's easy to skid and fall unless you're on a mountain bike. If you encounter a one-way road in the opposite direction, *always* get off your bike and walk. It's illegal and also very dangerous to ride against traffic because motorists simply aren't expecting you, especially if they are pulling out of a driveway or side street.

For every ride I've recommended a starting point, but you can start anywhere else along the route if it's more convenient. This is sometimes the best choice, especially if you live in Boston but don't have a car and would like to try the rides within biking distance of the city.

I have intentionally not listed the hours and fees of historic sites because they are subject to so much change, often from one year to the next. If it's a place you've heard of, it's probably open from 10 A.M. to 5 P.M., seven days a week. Unfortunately many of the less frequently visited spots have limited hours—often only weekday afternoons during the summer, perhaps one afternoon during the weekend. A few places of historic or architectural interest, such as the Rocky Hill Meetinghouse in Amesbury, are open only by appointment. The reason is a matter of funding and staffing. Most historic sites are maintained by voluntary contributions and effort, and it's simply impossible to keep them staffed more than a few hours a day or a few months a year. If you really want to visit a site, call beforehand and find out the hours.

There are no larger cities on the rides because most cities just aren't very pleasant to bike through. Do you really want to ride along congested streets lined with businesses and tenements, just to see a few points of interest? Also, once you get to the points of interest, there is usually no safe place to keep your bike. The best way to explore a city is on foot, so that you can look at the architecture of each building and visit places without having to worry about traffic or having your bike stolen. If you really want to explore a city—and Lowell, Lawrence, Fall River, New Bedford, and, of course, Boston are worth exploring—visit it by car or public transportation and leave your bike at home.

About the Maps

The maps are reasonably accurate, but they are not necessarily strictly to scale. Congested areas may be enlarged in relation to the rest of the map for the sake of legibility. All the maps contain these conventions:

1. Route numbers are circled.
2. Small arrows alongside the route indicate direction of travel.
3. The longer ride is marked by a heavy line. The shorter ride is marked by a dotted line where the route differs from that of the longer ride.
4. I've tried to show the angle of forks and intersections as accurately as possible.
5. Names of towns are in capital letters.

The maps show the main connecting roads, but I have shown them for reference only and not as recommended cycling routes. I must emphasize that I have not inspected most of the connecting roads and cannot vouch for their condition. Some of these roads are heavily traveled, very hilly, in poor condition, or unpaved.

Enjoying the Rides

You'll enjoy biking more if you add a few basic accessories to your bike and bring a few items with you.

1. **Handlebar bag with transparent map pocket on top.** It's always helpful to have some carrying capacity on your bike. Most handlebar bags are large enough to hold tools, a lunch, or even a light jacket. If you have a map or directions in your map pocket (or taped to the top of the bag), it's much easier to follow the route. You simply glance down to your handlebar bag instead of fishing the map or directions out of your pocket and stopping to read them safely. You may also wish to get a small saddlebag that fits under your seat, or a metal rack that fits above the rear wheel, to carry whatever doesn't fit in the handlebar bag.

Always carry things on your bike, not on your back. A knapsack raises your center of gravity and makes you more unstable; it also digs painfully into your shoulders if you have more than a couple of pounds in it. It may do for a quick trip to the grocery or campus but never for an enjoyable ride where you'll be on the bike for more than a few minutes.

2. **Water bottle and/or hydration pack.** It's vital to carry water with you—if you don't drink enough water, you will dehydrate. Bring two or three water bottles and keep them filled. Put only water in your water bottles—it quenches thirst better than any other liquid.

An excellent alternative or addition to water bottles is a hydration pack worn like a backpack. You drink through a tube conveniently positioned in front of you, eliminating the need to reach down to remove the bottle from your bike. Most hydration packs have the capacity of two or three bottles. It is important to allow the inner reservoir to dry when not in use to prevent mold and mildew; you can buy a flexible frame that will hold it open for this purpose.

3. **Basic tools.** Always carry a few basic tools with you when you go out for a ride, just in case you get a flat or a loose derailleur cable. Tire irons, a 6-inch adjustable wrench, a small pair of pliers, a small standard screwdriver, and a small Phillips-head screwdriver are all you need to take care of virtually all roadside emergencies. A rag and a tube of hand cleaner are useful if you have to touch your chain. If your bike has any Allen nuts (nuts with a small hexagonal socket on top), carry metric Allen wrenches to fit them. Most bike shops sell a handy one-piece kit with several Allen wrenches, along with standard and Phillips-head screwdrivers.

4. **Pump and spare tube.** If you get a flat, you're immobilized unless you can pump up a new tube or patch the old one. Installing a new tube is less painful than trying to patch the old one on the road. Do the patching at home. Pump up the tire until it's hard, and you're on your way. Carry a spare tube in your handlebar bag, or wind it around the seat post, but make sure it doesn't rub against the rear tire.

If you bike a lot and don't use a mountain bike, you'll get flats—it's a fact of life. Most flats are on the rear wheel because that's where most of your weight is. You should, therefore, practice taking the rear wheel off and putting it back on the bike, and taking the tire off and putting it on the rim, until you can do it confidently. It's much easier to practice at home than to fumble at it by the roadside.

5. **Dog repellent.** When you ride in rural areas, you're going to encounter dogs, no two ways about it. Even if you don't have to use it, you'll have peace of mind knowing you have something like ammonia or commercial dog spray to repel an attacking dog if you have to. More on this later.

6. **Bicycle computer.** A bicycle computer provides a much more reliable way of following a route than depending on street signs or landmarks. Street signs are often nonexistent in rural areas or are rotated 90 degrees by mischievous kids. Landmarks like "turn right at green house" or "turn left at Ted's Market" lose effectiveness when the green house is repainted red or Ted's Market goes out of business. Most computers indicate not only distance but also speed, elapsed time, and cadence (pedal revolutions per minute). The solar-powered models last a long time before the batteries need replacement.

7. **Bike lock.** This is a necessity if you're going to leave your bike unattended. The best locks are the rigid, boltcutter-proof ones such as Kryptonite and Citadel. The next best choice is a strong chain or cable that can't be quickly severed by a normal-sized boltcutter or hacksaw. A cheap, flimsy chain can be cut in a few seconds and is not much better than no lock at all.

In urban or heavily touristed areas, always lock both wheels as well as the frame to a solid object and take your accessories with you when you leave the bicycle. Many a cyclist ignoring this simple precaution has returned to the vehicle only to find one or both wheels gone, along with the pump, water bottle, and carrying bags.

8. **Rearview mirror.** Available at any bike shop, this marvelous safety device lets you check the situation behind you without turning your head. Once you start using a mirror, you'll feel defenseless without it. Most mirrors are designed to fit on either a bike helmet or the handlebars. Some fit directly onto the temple piece of eyeglasses.

9. **Bike helmet.** Accidents happen, and a helmet will protect your head if you fall or crash. Bike helmets are light and comfortable, and most cyclists use them.

10. **Food.** Always bring some food with you when you go for a ride. It's surprising how quickly you get hungry when you're biking. Some of the rides in this book go through remote areas with no food along the way, and that country store you were counting on may be closed on weekends or out of business. Fruit is nourishing and includes a lot of water. A couple of candy bars, some pastry, or an ice cream cone will provide a burst of energy for the last 10 miles if you're getting tired. (Don't eat candy or sweets before then—the energy burst lasts only about an hour, and then your blood-sugar level drops to below where it was before and you'll be really weak.)

11. **Bicycling gloves.** Gloves designed for biking, with padded palms and no fingers, will cushion your hands and protect them if you fall. For maximum comfort, use handlebar padding also.

12. **Kickstand.** Using a kickstand is the most convenient way to stand your bike upright without leaning it against a wall or other object. Keep in mind that a strong wind may knock your bike over and that in hot weather, a kickstand may sink far enough into asphalt to topple your bike.

13. **Bike rack.** It is easier to use a bike rack than to wrestle your bike into and out of your car or trunk. Racks that attach to the back of the car are most convenient—do you really want to hoist your bike over your head onto the roof? If you use a rack that fits onto the back of the car, make sure that the bike is at least a foot off the ground and that the

bicycle tire is well above the tailpipe. Hot exhaust blows out tires!

14. **Light.** Bring a bicycle light and reflective legbands with you in case you are caught in the dark. Ankle lights are lightweight and bob up and down as you pedal, giving additional visibility.

15. **Fanny pack.** Since many cycling shorts and jerseys don't have pockets, a small fanny pack is useful for carrying your keys, a wallet, and loose change.

16. **Toilet paper.**

17. **Roll of electrical tape.** You never know when you'll need it.

If you are not concerned with riding fast, the most practical bicycle for recreational riding is either a mountain bike or a hybrid between a mountain bike and a sport bike. Most people find them more comfortable than sport bikes because the riding position is more upright. The gearing is almost always lower than it is on sport bikes, which makes climbing hills much easier. (If you buy a mountain bike, be sure to get one with 18 or 21 speeds.) Mountain bikes usually have thumb-operated shift levers, so you don't have to move your hands when shifting gears. The fatter, thicker tires are very resistant to punctures. Mountain bikes are very stable—you're less likely to skid or fall if you should go off the road into soft dirt or if you hit an obstacle like a sand patch, pothole, sewer grate, or bad bump. Mountain bikes are rugged and resistant to damage; for example, a pothole will often dent the rim of a sport bike but will not usually hurt a mountain bike. The only disadvantage of mountain bikes is that they are a little slower than other bicycles because of the wider tires and less streamlined riding position.

If most of your riding is on pavement, you don't need standard mountain bike tires, which are about 2 inches wide with a deep, knobby tread. Use narrower tires (often called city tires or cross-training tires), which are 1⅜ or 1½ inches wide with a fairly smooth tread.

Take advantage of your gearing when you ride. It's surprising how many people with 21-speed bikes use only two or three of their gears. It takes less effort to spin your legs quickly in the low or middle gears than to grind along in your higher ones. For leisurely biking, a rate of about 80 revolutions per minute is comfortable. If you find yourself grinding along at fewer than 75 RPMs, shift into a lower gear. Time your RPMs periodically on a watch with a second hand or your bicycle computer—keeping your cadence up is the best habit you can acquire for efficient cycling. You'll be less tired at the end of a ride, and will avoid strain on your knees, if you use the right gears.

If you have a 10- or 12-speed bike, you'll find it much easier to climb hills if you get a freewheel (the rear cluster of gears) that goes up to 34 teeth instead of the standard 28 teeth. You may also have to buy a new rear derailleur to accommodate the larger shifts, but the expense will be more than worthwhile in terms of ease of pedaling. For the ultimate in hill-climbing ease, you need a bicycle with 18 or more speeds. The smaller the inner front chainwheel, the lower the low gear. I recommend a small chainwheel with 24 or 26 teeth.

When approaching a hill, always shift into low gear *before* the hill, not after you start climbing it. If it's a steep or long hill, get into your lowest gear right away and go slowly to reduce the effort. Don't be afraid to walk up a really tough hill; it's not a contest, and you're out to enjoy yourself.

Here are a few more hints to add to your cycling enjoyment: Adjust your seat to the proper height and make sure that it is level. Test for proper seat height by pedaling with your heels. Your leg should barely straighten out (with no bend) at the bottom of the downstroke. If your leg is bent, the seat is too low. If you rock from side to side as you pedal, the seat is too high.

Pedal with the balls of your feet, not your arches or heels, over the spindles. Toe clips are ideal for keeping your feet in the proper position on the pedals; they also give you added leverage when going uphill. The straps should be *loose* (or the spring tension on clipless pedals should be low) so that you can take your feet off the pedals effortlessly. In proper pedaling position, your leg should be slightly bent at the bottom of the downstroke.

Eat before you get hungry, drink before you get thirsty, and rest before you get tired. Two good guidelines are to drink one bottle of water per hour, and to take a five- or ten-minute break every hour. (Longer stops are more likely to make you feel stiff.) To keep your pants out of your chain, tuck them inside your socks. Wear pants that are as seamless as possible. Jeans or cut-offs are the worst offenders; their thick seams are uncomfortable. For maximum comfort, wear padded cycling shorts with no underwear, and cycling tights that fit over the shorts when the temperature is below 60 or 65 degrees. Use a firm, good-quality seat. A soft, mushy seat may feel inviting, but as soon as you sit on it, the padding compresses under your weight so that you're really sitting on a harsh metal shell.

If you have to use the bathroom, most fast-food restaurants have easily accessible rest rooms. If a restaurant is of the "Please wait to be seated" variety or has facilities "for customers only," either walk in briskly or order a snack. Most gas stations and libraries have public rest rooms; most convenience stores and country stores do not, but they will sometimes accommodate you if you ask urgently. Many cyclists discreetly get out of sight onto a footpath or one-lane dirt road that curves into the woods.

Using the Maps and Directions

Unfortunately a book format does not lend itself to quick and easy consultation while you're on your bike. The rides will go more smoothly if you don't have to dismount at each intersection to consult the map or directions provided in this book. You can solve this problem by making a photocopy of the directions and carrying it in your map pocket or taping it on top of your handlebar bag, and dismounting occasionally to turn the sheet over or to switch sheets. Most people find it easier to follow the directions than the map.

In the directions, I have indicated the name of a road if there was a visible street sign at the time I researched the route; I designated the road as "unmarked" if the street sign was absent or not clearly visible. (Many street signs are visible from only one direction or are obscured by tree branches or utility poles.) Street signs have a short life span—a couple of years on the average—and are often nonexistent in rural areas. Any sign with a double entendre, such as Cherry, will be adorning some teenager's room within a week. Very frequently, the name of a road changes without warning at a town line or a crossroads or other intersection.

Using a bicycle computer is virtually essential to enjoying the rides. The directions indicate the distance to the next turn or major intersection. Because so many of the roads are unmarked, you'll have to keep track accurately of the distance from one turn to the next. It is helpful to keep in mind that a tenth of a mile is 176 yards, or nearly twice the length of a football field.

In the written directions, it is obviously not practical to mention every intersection. I have not mentioned most crossroads or traffic lights if the route goes straight, nor have I mentioned forks where one branch is clearly the main road. Always stay on the main road unless directed otherwise.

In addition to distances and a description of the next intersection, the directions also mention points of interest and situations that require caution. Any hazardous spot—for example, an unusually busy intersection or a bumpy section of road—has been clearly indicated by a **CAUTION** warning. It's a good idea to read over the entire tour before taking it to familiarize yourself with the terrain, points of interest, and places requiring caution.

In the directions, certain words occur frequently, so let me define them to avoid any confusion.

To "bear" means to turn diagonally, somewhere between a 45-degree angle and going straight ahead. In these illustrations, you bear from road A onto road B.

To "merge" means to come into a road diagonally, or even head-on, if a side road comes into a main road. In the examples, road A merges into road B.

A "sharp" turn is any turn sharper than 90 degrees; in other words, a hairpin turn or something approaching it. In the examples, it is a sharp turn from road A onto road B.

Safety

It is an unfortunate fact that thousands of bicycle accidents occur each year, with many fatalities. Almost all cycling accidents, however, are needless and preventable. Most accidents involve children under sixteen and are caused by foolhardy riding and failure to exercise common sense. The chances of having an accident or serious injury can be greatly reduced greatly by having your bike in good mechanical condition, using two pieces of safety equipment (a rearview mirror and a helmet), being aware of the most common biking hazards, and not riding at night unless prepared for it.

Before going out for a ride, be sure your bike is mechanically sound. Its condition is especially worthy of attention if you bought the bike at a discount store, where it was probably assembled by a high school kid with no training. Above all, be sure that the wheels are secure and the brakes work. If your wheels are fastened with quick-release levers, be certain that they are clamped properly. If you're not sure how to do this, ask someone at a bike shop to show you; your safety depends on it.

Be certain that your shoelaces are firmly tied, or use footwear with

Velcro closures. A loose shoelace can wrap around the pedal axle or get caught in the chain, trapping you on the bicycle.

Invest in a rearview mirror and a bicycle helmet, both available at any bike shop. Most mirrors attach to either your helmet or your handlebars and work as well as a car mirror when properly adjusted. When you come to an obstacle such as a pothole or a patch of broken glass, a glance in the mirror lets you know whether it's safe to swing out into the road to avoid it. On narrow or winding roads, you can always be aware of the traffic behind you and plan accordingly. Best of all, a mirror eliminates the need to peek back over your shoulder—an action that is not only awkward but also potentially dangerous because riders sometimes unconsciously veer toward the middle of the road while peeking.

A bicycle helmet is the cyclist's cheapest form of life insurance. A helmet not only protects your head if you land on it in a fall but also protects against the sun and the rain. All responsible cyclists wear helmets, so you shouldn't feel afraid of looking odd if you use one. Helmets are light and comfortable; once you get used to one, you'll never even know you have it on. Helmets are legally required for children in Massachusetts and adjacent states.

While on the road, use the same old common sense that you use while driving a car. Stop signs and traffic lights are there for a reason—obey them. At intersections, give cars the benefit of the doubt rather than trying to dash out in front of them or beat them through the light. Remember, they're bigger, heavier, and faster than you are. And you're out to enjoy yourself and get some exercise, not to be king of the road.

Several situations are inconsequential to the motorist but potentially hazardous for the bicyclist. When biking, try to keep aware of these:

1. **Road surface.** Not all roads in Massachusetts are silk-smooth. Often the bicyclist must contend with bumps, ruts, cracks, potholes, and fish-scale sections of road that have been patched and repatched numerous times. When the road becomes rough, the only prudent course of action is to slow down and keep alert, especially going downhill. Riding into a deep pothole or wheel-swallowing crack can cause a

nasty spill. On bumps, you can relieve some of the shock by getting up off the seat.

2. **Sand patches.** Patches of sand often build up at intersections, sharp curves, the bottoms of hills, and sudden dips in the road. Sand is very unstable if you're turning, so slow way down, stop pedaling, and keep in a straight line until you're beyond the sandy spot.

3. **Storm-sewer grates.** Federal regulations have outlawed thousands of hazardous substances and products but unfortunately have not yet outlawed the storm sewer with grates parallel to the roadway. This is a very serious hazard because a cyclist catching the wheel in a slot will instantly fall, probably in a somersault over the handlebars. Storm sewers are relatively rare in rural areas but always a very real hazard.

4. **Dogs.** Unfortunately man's best friend is the cyclist's worst enemy. When riding in the country you will encounter dogs, pure and simple. Even though many communities have leash laws, they are usually not enforced unless a dog seriously injures someone or annoys its owner's neighbors enough that they complain—a rare situation because the neighbors probably all have dogs too.

The best defense against a vicious dog is to carry a commercial dog spray called Halt, which comes in an aerosol can and is available at most bike shops. Repellent is effective only if you can grab it instantly when you need it—*don't* put it in your handlebar pack, a deep pocket, or any place else where you'll have to fish around for it. For Halt to work you have to squirt it directly into the dog's eyes, but if the dog is close enough to really threaten you, it's easily done.

The main danger from dogs is not being bitten but rather bumping into them or instinctively veering toward the center of the road into traffic when the dog comes after you. Fortunately almost all dogs have a sense of territory and will not chase you more than a tenth of a mile. If you're going along at a brisk pace and you're in front of the dog when it starts to chase you, you can probably outrun it and stay ahead until you reach the animal's territorial limit. If you're going at a leisurely pace, however, or heading uphill, or the dog is in the road in front of you, the only safe thing to do is dismount and walk slowly forward, keeping the bike between you and the dog, until you leave its territory. If the dog is truly menacing, or there's more than one, repellent can be comforting to have.

If you decide to stay on the bike when a dog chases you, always get into a low gear and spin your legs as quickly as possible. It's hard for a dog to bite a fast-rotating target. Many cyclists swing their pump at the animal, but this increases the danger of losing control of your bike. Often, yelling "Stay!" or "No!" in an authoritative voice will make a dog back off.

A word of caution about using commercial dog spray: It can be legally argued that dog spray comes under the Massachusetts firearms law, which carries a mandatory one-year jail sentence for carrying an unlicensed firearm. Such a case would probably not hold up in court, but because of the potential hazard, a zealous police officer might give you a hassle if he or she noticed it on your bike. The law states in Section 10 of Chapter 269, "Whoever . . . carries . . . a firearm . . . as defined in Section 121 of Chapter 140 . . . shall be punished by imprisonment. . . ." When you go to the definition in Section 121 of Chapter 140, it says, "Firearm shall mean a pistol, revolver or other weapon of any description loaded or unloaded, from which a shot or bullet can be discharged." A court would have to decide whether dog spray fits this definition.

5. **Undivided, shoulderless four-lane highways.** This is the most dangerous type of road for biking. If traffic is very light there is no problem, but in moderate or heavy traffic, the road becomes a death trap unless you ride assertively. The only safe way to travel on such a road is to stay in or near the center of the right lane, rather than at the edge, forcing traffic coming up behind you to pass you in the left lane. If you hug the right-hand edge, some motorists will not get out of the right lane, brushing past you by inches or even forcing you off the road. Some drivers mentally register a bicycle as being only as wide as its tire, an unsettling image when the lane is not much wider than a car.

Several rides in this book contain short stretches along highways. If traffic is heavy enough to occupy both lanes most of the time, the only truly safe thing to do is walk your bike along the side of the road.

6. **Railroad tracks.** Tracks that cross the road at an oblique angle are a severe hazard because you can easily catch your wheel in the slot between the rails and fall. NEVER ride diagonally across tracks—either walk your bike across or, if no traffic is in sight, cross the tracks at right angles by swerving into the road. When riding across tracks, slow down and get up off the seat to minimize the shock of the bump.

7. **Oiled and sanded roads.** Many communities occasionally spread a film of oil or tar over the roads to seal cracks and then spread sand over the road to absorb the oil. The combination is treacherous for biking. Be very careful, especially going downhill. If the sand is deep or if the tar or oil is still sticky, you should walk.

8. **Car doors opening into your path.** This is a severe hazard in urban areas and in the center of towns. To be safe, any time you ride past a line of parked cars, stay 4 or 5 feet away from them. If traffic won't permit this, proceed very slowly and notice whether the driver's seat of each car is occupied. A car pulling to the side of the road in front of you is an obvious candidate for trouble.

9. **Low sun.** If you're riding directly into a low sun, traffic behind you may not see you, especially through a smeared or dirty windshield. Here your rearview mirror becomes a lifesaver because the only safe way to proceed is to glance constantly in the mirror and remain aware of conditions behind you. If you're riding directly away from a low sun, traffic coming toward you may not see you and could make a left turn into your path. If the sun is on your right or left, drivers on your side may not see you, and a car could pull out from a side road into your path. To be safe, give any traffic that may be blinded by the sun the benefit of the doubt, and dismount if necessary. Because most of the roads you'll be on are winding and wooded, you won't run into blinding sun frequently, but you should be aware of the problem.

10. **Kids on bikes.** Children riding their bikes in circles in the middle of the road and shooting in and out of driveways are a hazard: The risk of collision is always there because they aren't watching where they're going. Any time you see kids playing in the street, especially if they're on bikes, be prepared for anything and call out "Beep-beep" or

"Watch out" as you approach. If you have a loud bell or horn, use it.

11. **Wet leaves.** Wet leaves are very slippery. Avoid turning on them.

12. **Metal-grate bridges.** When wet, the metal grating becomes very slippery, and you may be in danger of falling and injuring yourself on the sharp edges. If the road is wet, or early in the morning when there may be condensation on the bridge, please walk across.

A few additional safety reminders: If bicycling in a group, ride single file and at least 20 feet apart. Use hand signals when turning—to signal a right turn, stick out your right arm. If you stop to rest or examine your bike, get both your bicycle and yourself *completely* off the road. Sleek black bicycle clothing is stylish, but bright colors are more visible and safer.

Finally, use common courtesy toward motorists and pedestrians. Hostility toward bicyclists has received national media attention; it is caused by the 2 percent of discourteous cyclists (mainly messengers and groups hogging the road) who give the other 98 percent—responsible riders—a bad image. Please do not be part of the 2 percent!

Bicycles and Public Transportation

Thanks to the efforts of the Massachusetts Bicycle Coalition, bicycles are allowed on some of the routes of the Massachusetts Bay Transit Authority (the T) on weekends and off-peak hours. You must obtain a bicycle permit first from the commuter rail pass outlet at Mailboxes Etc. in the Transportation Building at 8 Park Plaza in Boston between 8:30 A.M. and 5:00 P.M. on weekdays. Permits are also available at some other commuter rail pass outlets; for more information call the MBTA (617–222–3200) or visit its Web site (www.mbta.com/ticketbooth). The permit costs $5.00 and is good for three years. Bikes are allowed only on the three in-town lines using subway cars—the Red, Blue, and Orange Lines—and on commuter rail trains (the Purple Line). Bikes are not allowed on trolleys (the Green Line) or MBTA buses.

It must be emphasized that this program was implemented with some reluctance by MBTA officials, and that it may be curtailed at any time. The Massachusetts Bicycle Coalition urges cyclists to use the program, so that the MBTA will see that there is continued interest in it. The more cyclists take advantage of the program, the more likely it will be continued or expanded in the future.

The only other public transportation practical for bicycles are the ferries between Boston Harbor and East Boston, Hingham, Hull, Provincetown, and Gloucester. Bikes are allowed on Amtrak trains and most inter-city buses only if boxed.

Cyclists who depend on public transportation may wish to consider a folding bicycle that fits into a small bag. Several brands, which are sturdy yet easily assembled and disassembled, are available at better bike shops. Folding bikes are suitable for most of the rides in this book. It may take a little while to get used to the steering and handling because of the small wheels.

Bikeways

Bikeways, or bicycle paths, are few and far between in eastern Massachusetts, although many are being planned. The Minuteman Bikeway between the Alewife T station in Cambridge and Bedford, completed in 1993, is a welcome addition; it is incorporated into ride number 4. (Two other rides in this book, numbers 63 and 64, utilize the bikeway along the Cape Cod Canal.) In the Boston area, bikeways run along both sides of the Charles River in the Back Bay and in Cambridge. In good weather, they are jammed with pedestrians and joggers. The Southwest Corridor Bikeway (also called the Pierre Lallement Bikeway) runs 4 miles from the Forest Hills T station in Jamaica Plain to Back Bay Station, paralleling the T Red Line tracks and the Amtrak line. It runs through marginal neighborhoods and crosses some busy streets. Another bikeway follows an abandoned railroad line for about a mile from the Alewife T station to Davis Square in Somerville.

Bikeways are a mixed blessing. If well designed and well maintained, like the Cape Cod Rail Trail or the East Bay Bicycle Path in Rhode Island, they are a pleasure. If poorly designed or maintained, they are much more dangerous than the roads that they're supposed to avoid. Many bikeways are too narrow or have curves that are too sharp, and many have unsafe road crossings. Unless maintenance is vigilant, a bikeway will rapidly fill up with leaves, glass, and debris, and the surface will deteriorate. In good weather, all bikeways in populated areas are crowded with pedestrians, joggers, in-line skaters, skateboarders, children, dogs, and other noncyclists.

The Massachusetts Bicycle Coalition is actively striving to improve and increase bikeways. If you'd like to join in its efforts, contact it at 44 Bromfield Street, Suite 207, Boston, MA 02108 (phone 617–542–2453).

Feedback

I'd be very grateful for any comments, criticisms, or suggestions about the rides in this book. Road conditions change, and a new snack bar or point of interest may open up along one of the routes. An intersection may be changed by road construction or improvement, or a traffic light may be installed. I'd like to keep the book updated by incorporating changes as they occur or modifying a route if necessary in the interest of scenery or safety. Many of the changes in each new edition are in response to riders' suggestions. Please feel free to contact me through The Globe Pequot Press, P.O. Box 480, Guilford, CT 06437 with any revision you think helpful.

Chapter 1:
The Immediate Suburbs of Boston

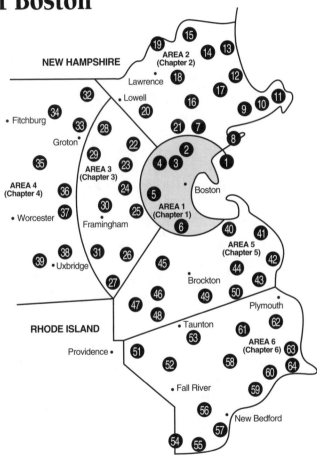

1 Nahant

Number of miles:	7
Terrain:	Rolling, with several short, steep hills.
Food:	Grocery and snack bar near center of town.
Start:	Nahant Beach parking lot, on the east side of the causeway from Lynn to Nahant. There is a modest parking fee on beach days. Get here early on those days; the huge lot fills up by 10 o'clock. Do not park in Nahant itself; you'll get a ticket. If you wish, you can park in Lynn just north of the rotary at the beginning of the causeway and bike along the beach on the bike path or through the beach parking lot. This adds 3 miles to the ride. On beach days, the bike path will be clogged with pedestrians.

This is a short ride that makes up in coastal scenery what it lacks in distance. It's easy to spend half a day biking these 7 miles if you take time to poke around the rocky ledges and remains of old forts along the shore, especially at the eastern tip of the island.

Nahant is an island 2 miles off the coast of Lynn and Revere, about 2 miles long and a half mile wide, connected to Lynn by a causeway. It contains some of the most pleasant and scenic bicycling close to Boston. Nahant is a wealthy community with fine homes and a number of man-

DIRECTIONS

FOR

THE RIDE

1. From the Nahant end of the parking lot, head along the main road, following the ocean on your right. Go 0.5 mile to Castle Road, which bears right.

2. Bear right for 0.7 mile to small crossroads shortly after school on left (Gardner Road). You will now do a small counterclockwise loop and return to this point after 0.6 mile.

3. Right up a little hill for 0.6 mile to this same intersection (Colby Way on left), making four 90-degree left turns. **CAUTION:** The first and fourth turns come up at bottom of short hills.

At the third turn is Fort Buckman, a park on a rocky outcropping with fine ocean views. It used to be a military installation originally built during the Spanish-American War. When you leave the park, you'll go up a short, steep hill. As you complete the loop, notice the square stone tower built into a house at the top of the hill on your left.

4. When you complete the loop, turn right for 0.25 mile to Flash Road on right, just past the school.

5. Right for 0.3 mile to fork (main road bears right on Spring Road).

6. Bear right for 0.2 mile to Emerald Road, which bears right.

7. Bear right for 0.2 mile to end (merge left on Willow Road, unmarked, at ocean).

8. Bear left for 0.7 mile to Vernon Street on right, at small round traffic island. You'll pass the town wharf on your right after 0.4 mile.

9. Right for 0.2 mile to end (Swallow Cave Road, unmarked).

10. Right for 0.1 mile to end, in front of a mansion. You'll pass two old lookout towers on your left. A path on the left side of the gate leads 100 yards to a small cave hollowed out by the sea. At high tide, the ocean spills into the cave.

11. Make a U-turn and go 0.7 mile to Pleasant Street, which turns right between the library and town hall.

After 0.2 mile, you'll pass the Northeastern University Marine Science Center on your right. This area encompasses East Point, the magnificent rockbound far tip of Nahant. Fascinating old bunkers are built

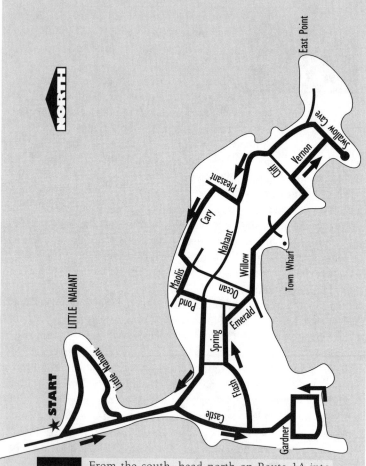

NORTH

START

LITTLE NAHANT

Little Nahant

Maolis

Pond

Spring

Flash

Castle

Gardner

Emerald

Ocean

Nahant

Cary

Willow

Pleasant

Town Wharf

Cliff

Vernon

Swallow Cave

East Point

HOW TO GET THERE

From the south, head north on Route 1A into Lynn and stay straight on main road to rotary. Bear right at rotary onto the causeway to Nahant. The parking lot is to the left of the causeway.

From the north, head south on Route 1 to Route 60. Go east on Route 60 for 2 miles to Route 1A, at second rotary. Continue with directions from the south, heading north on Route 1A into Lynn.

into the rocky ledges. A road leads to the top of the bunkers, providing superb views.

12. Right for 0.1 mile to Cary Street, your second left (dead end if you go straight).

13. Left for 0.4 mile to small crossroads (Maolis Road, unmarked), just after you turn 90 degrees inland. The road on the right is very narrow.

14. Right for less than 0.2 mile to first left (Pond Street, unmarked).

15. Left for 0.2 mile to crossroads and stop sign (Nahant Road, unmarked).

16. Right for 0.9 mile to Little Nahant Road on right. (It goes up a steep hill.) You will now go around Little Nahant, a small island connected to the causeway just north of Nahant itself.

17. Right for 0.2 mile to end, at top of steep hill (Simmons Road on left).

18. Turn right (still Little Nahant Road) and immediately curve sharply left on main road. Go 0.7 mile to end, at yield sign. The entrance to the beach parking lot is on your right when you come to the end.

---

sions lining its rocky, convoluted coastline. For most of the ride you will be within sight of the ocean, and as you head along the southern shore you'll see the Boston skyline, 10 miles away, rising up across the water. Traffic on Nahant is refreshingly light because it is an island with a small population (only 4,000) and no public parking.

For a longer trip, the Nahant ride can easily be added to ride number 8, Lynn–Swampscott–Marblehead, for a total of 30 miles.

The Saugus Ironworks Ride:
Melrose–Stoneham–Wakefield–Saugus

Number of miles:	18 (11 with shortcut omitting Stoneham and Wakefield)
Terrain:	Gently rolling with several short, sharp hills.
Food:	Groceries and restaurants in the towns.
Start:	Square One Mall, at Route 1 and Essex Street in Saugus, on the west side of Route 1. Take the Essex Street exit toward Melrose. The exit is just north of Route 99 and about 4 miles south of Route 128 (I–95). Park at the Essex Street entrance to the mall.
Facilities:	Rest rooms at Saugus Ironworks.
Caution:	The ride goes through four older town centers and some busy intersections. Riders should have some experience with cycling in traffic.

On this ride you explore four pleasant middle-class communities about 10 miles directly north of Boston. The region is far enough from the city to be suburban rather than urban, with stretches of greenery, gracious residential neighborhoods, and roads that are not clogged with traffic (except for parts of Saugus near Route 1). All four towns have attractive, well-defined centers with handsome churches, city halls, and other public buildings. The historical highlight of the ride is the Saugus Ironworks, one of the earliest industrial enterprises in America; it dates from around 1650.

The ride starts from the outskirts of Saugus, which is best known for its 4-mile-long commercial strip on Route 1, the busiest in Massachusetts. (Don't worry—you won't bike on it.) After less than a mile, you'll enter the pleasant residential community of Melrose, where a cluster of fine old buildings—the town hall, two handsome churches with a school between them, and the graceful stone Soldiers and Sailors Memorial Hall, used as an auditorium—grace the main street. Adjoining the downtown area is delightful Ell Pond, with a park spreading along its northern shore. From here, the route leads a short way across the Stoneham town line, where you'll pass through a portion of the Middlesex Fells Reservation, a large expanse of wooded hills and ponds. You'll go along Spot Pond, which is completely surrounded by forest except for the Stone Zoo. From here you head into the center of town, with a compact business block and two distinctive white churches.

From Stoneham, the route climbs past gracious old houses and descends briskly into Wakefield, the most affluent of the four communities and one of the most visually pleasing suburbs inside the Route 128 semicircle. The center of town, a New England classic, could almost be from a rural town 20 miles farther from Boston. The large triangular green, at the southern end of Lake Quannapowitt, is framed by stately Colonial-style homes, a classic white church, and a handsome stone one. Across from the green lies a beautifully landscaped park stretching along the lakeshore, complete with a graceful old bandstand in the middle.

From Wakefield you'll head into Saugus, where the marvelous Victorian town hall will greet you as you pull into the center of town. Just outside of town is the Saugus Ironworks, a splendid example of historical reconstruction that is part of the National Park system. With meticulous attention to detail, the furnace, forge, massive waterwheels, and the dam across the Saugus River have been restored to working order. And to top all this off, it's free. From the Ironworks it's about 2 miles to the end of the ride.

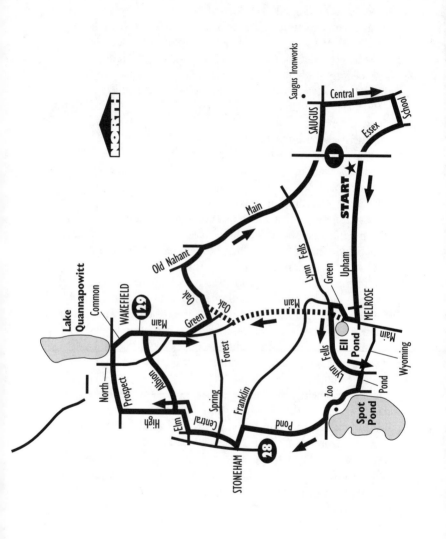

DIRECTIONS

FOR

THE RIDE

1. Right (west) on Essex Street for 2 miles to second traffic light (Main Street), in the center of Melrose. Notice the fine stone church on your right at the intersection.

2. Right for 0.4 mile to fork where Green Street (unmarked) bears right, immediately before third traffic light. You'll pass Ell Pond on your left. Here the short ride goes straight.

3. Bear right and just ahead turn left at traffic light (Lynn Fells Parkway, unmarked). Go 1.4 miles to fourth traffic light (Pond Street on right), not counting the blinking lights near the beginning. A sign may point right to MDC Zoo and Route 28.

4. Right for 0.3 mile to stop sign at top of hill.

5. Bear right for 0.6 mile to Pond Street, which bears right. You'll follow Spot Pond on your left and pass the Stone Zoo.

6. Bear right for 1 mile to end.

7. Left for 0.3 mile to end, in the center of Stoneham.

8. Turn sharply right on Central Street (unmarked), passing fire station on right. (Don't turn 90 degrees right on Route 28). Go 0.5 mile to third traffic light (Elm Street).

9. Right for 0.2 mile to third left (High Street).

10. Left for 1 mile to second crossroads and stop sign (Prospect Street). You'll climb and then descend steeply.

11. Right for 0.9 mile to traffic light at bottom of hill (North Avenue). As you're coming down the hill, a little red schoolhouse built in 1847 is on your left.

12. Straight for 0.3 mile to Common Street, which bears right at the Wakefield town green. You'll see Lake Quannapowitt on your left.

13. Bear right for 1.1 miles to Green Street, which bears left uphill. **CAUTION:** Busy road. Watch for cars backing up near the beginning. Then you'll cross bad diagonal railroad tracks.

At the beginning you'll pass the magnificent First Baptist Church on the right and go through downtown Wakefield. Then you'll pass Crystal Lake on your right.

14. Bear left for 0.5 mile to Oak Avenue on left, just before stop sign.

15. Left for 0.9 mile to end, at yield sign (Old Nahant Road). **CAUTION:** The end is at bottom of steep hill.

16. Right for 0.25 mile to end (Main Street, unmarked).

17. Right for 2.9 miles to rotary with a monument in the center of Saugus (Central Street, unmarked). **CAUTION:** Watch for traffic entering and exiting Route 1 after 2 miles. The Victorian town hall is on the far side of the rotary.

18. Left for 0.2 mile to the Saugus Ironworks on right.

19. Backtrack to the rotary in the center of town. Continue straight for 0.8 mile to School Street on right, midway up short hill.

20. Right for 0.4 mile to end (Essex Street, unmarked).

21. Right for 0.5 mile to fork where one road goes straight and the other bears left.

22. Bear left at fork. **CAUTION** here—much of the traffic coming up behind you will be going straight to get onto Route 1 North. Go almost 0.4 mile to mall entrance on right. **CAUTION:** Just past the overpass above Route 1, watch for traffic entering and leaving the highway.

Directions for shorter ride

1. Follow directions 1 and 2 for the long ride.

2. Straight for 1.5 miles to Oak Street on right, at traffic light. It's shortly after an attractive brick school on the right.

3. Turn right and just ahead curve left on main road. Go 0.1 mile to fork just after stop sign (Oak Street bears right).

4. Bear right for 0.9 mile to end, at yield sign (Old Nahant Road). **CAUTION:** The end is at bottom of steep hill.

5. Follow directions for the long ride from number 16 to the end.

3 Woburn–Winchester–Arlington–Belmont

Number of miles:	19 (13 without Arlington–Belmont extension)
Terrain:	The short ride is gently rolling. The long ride is rolling with several steep hills, one a real monster almost 0.4 mile long.
Food:	Groceries and restaurants in the towns.
Start:	Parking lot at the corner of Winn and Wyman Streets in Burlington, at the Woburn town line, across from church (don't park at the church itself). The start is 0.5 mile south of Route 128 (take exit 34, Winn Street). If you live in or near Boston and don't have a car, you can start from the center of Arlington or Belmont.

Just northwest of Cambridge, the older, well-to-do suburbs stretching out to Route 128 provide surprisingly pleasant biking. The area is suburban in the gracious sense of the word, with well-spaced older homes on well-landscaped lots and tree-lined streets. A series of rolling hills across Winchester, Arlington, and Belmont add effort to biking but also heighten the attractiveness of the area. Adding variety to the landscape are Horn Pond in Woburn and the long, slender Mystic Lakes 2 miles south. The Minuteman Bikeway, the longest bicycle trail in the state outside Cape Cod, passes through the region but is not on the route. The

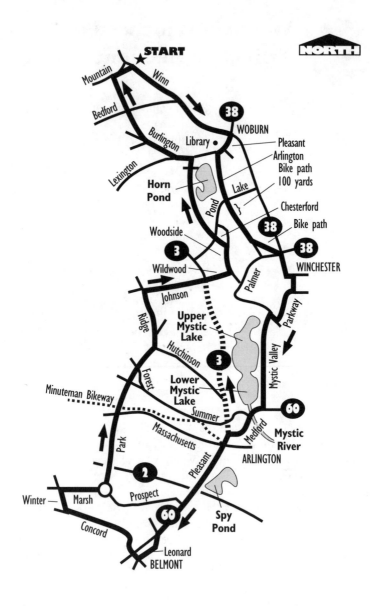

1. Right (south) on Winn Street for 1.2 miles to stop sign in the center of Woburn (Pleasant Street, unmarked, on right). It's one-way in the wrong direction if you go straight.

2. Right for 0.2 mile to Arlington Road, which bears left at traffic light. You'll pass the library on your right.

3. Bear left (don't turn 90 degrees left on Warren Avenue) for 0.9 mile to crossroads and stop sign at the end of Horn Pond.

4. Straight for 0.1 mile to a dead end, and then straight onto a narrow bicycle path (the Horn Pond Bikeway). **CAUTION:** Watch for glass and bumps. Follow the path 100 yards to end and then go straight on another paved road.

5. Follow the paved road 0.3 mile to Horn Pond Brook Road, which bears left (sign points to BIKEWAY).

6. Bear left for 100 yards to a dead end, and then go straight onto another bike path for 0.3 mile to end. **CAUTION:** Low branches. You'll ride along Horn Pond Brook on your left. Wedge Pond, a delightful little duck pond, is in front of you when you reach the end.

7. Jog left and immediately right at traffic light (Main Street). Go 0.25 mile to end (Church Street). At the end, notice the graceful white church 100 yards to your right.

8. Left under railroad bridge and immediately bear right (still Main Street). **CAUTION** here—cross traffic does not have to stop. This is downtown Winchester. Go 0.1 mile to traffic light (Mystic Valley Parkway, unmarked).

    Immediately before the light on your left is another tiny duck pond with the water cascading over curving stone steps. It's worth crossing the street to see this delightful spot.

9. Right for 0.6 mile to end.

10. Right for less than 0.2 mile to first left (still Mystic Valley Parkway).

11. Left for 1.8 miles to a small rotary (Route 60, High Street). You'll ride along the Mystic Lakes.

12. Right and just ahead straight at another rotary. Go 0.5 mile to end,

at traffic light (Mystic Street). Here the short ride turns right.

13. Left (**CAUTION** here) for 1.7 miles to fifth traffic light (Clifton Street on right, Leonard Street on left). At the beginning you'll pass the Minuteman Bikeway on your right immediately before you cross Massachussetts Avenue in the center of Arlington.

14. Left for 0.25 mile to traffic island where the main road bears left under railroad bridge. You'll go through downtown Belmont.

15. Go straight (don't bear left) and then immediately turn right at end (Concord Avenue, unmarked). Go 1.3 miles to Winter Street, which bears right.

You'll pass the handsome brick town hall on your right at the beginning. Then you cross Route 60 and climb very steeply for almost 0.4 mile.

16. Bear right for 0.2 mile to crossroads and blinking light (Marsh Street).

17. Right for 0.9 mile to rotary (Park Avenue bears left).

18. Bear left for 1.2 miles to traffic light at bottom of steep hill (Massachusetts Avenue). **CAUTION:** This intersection comes up suddenly while you're going downhill.

At the top of the hill is a big water tower. If you go to the back of the tower and head a couple of blocks downhill on Eastern Avenue, which runs perpendicular to the route, you'll come to a playground with a splendid view of Boston.

19. Straight for 0.6 mile to stop sign (merge left on Forest Street, unmarked), just after traffic light.

To see the Old Schwamb Mill, take your first right on Lowell Street for 0.2 mile, and turn left on Mill Lane.

20. Bear left and immediately bear right uphill (still Forest Street). Go 0.4 mile to fork at top of hill where the main road (Ridge Street) bears left.

21. Bear left and stay on main road for 0.8 mile to crossroads and stop sign (Johnson Road). Don't bear right on Lockeland Road after 0.25 mile.

22. Right for 1 mile to traffic light (Route 3, Cambridge Street).

23. Straight for 0.4 mile to where the main road curves 90 degrees right and Woodside Road turns left.

24. Left (**CAUTION** here) for 0.2 mile to Chesterford Road, which bears left. You'll pass Winter Pond.

25. Bear left for 0.2 mile to end, at stop sign.

26. At end, go straight onto a blocked-off lane that runs along the west shore of Horn Pond (you'll see the pond on your right after a short distance). After 0.7 mile you'll come to a parking lot. At the far end of the lot, curve right, following the pond, for 0.4 mile to the end of the blocked-off section (Water Street on left). **CAUTION:** Watch for glass, joggers, and pedestrians.

27. Straight for 0.2 mile to end (Pleasant Street, unmarked).

28. Left for less than 0.2 mile to fork (Burlington Street bears right).

29. Bear right for 0.4 mile to three-way fork (main road bears right).

30. Bear right (still Burlington Street) for 0.7 mile to end (Mountain Road).

31. Right for 0.1 mile to Wyman Street (unmarked) on right. It's immediately after Manor Avenue on right.

32. Right for less than 0.2 mile to parking lot on left.

Directions for shorter ride

1. Follow directions for the 19-mile ride through number 12.

2. Right for 2.6 miles to Wildwood Street, at traffic light. Mystic Street becomes Cambridge Street; this road is also Route 3.

3. Right for 0.4 mile to where the main road curves 90 degrees right and Woodside Road turns left.

4. Follow directions for the long ride from number 24 to the end.

bikeway is on ride 4.

The ride starts from the town line of the pleasant, fairly affluent community of Woburn. After a mile, you'll go through the compact downtown area and then pass the pride of the town, the magnificent

Gothic-style stone library designed by H. H. Richardson and built in 1878. It's one of the finest in the state, and it's worth going inside to see its high vaulted ceilings and wooden alcoves. Just outside the town, you'll bike along Horn Pond. The former Middlesex Canal passed next to it, and during the canal's heyday in the early 1800s, boatloads of Bostonians would visit the pond for a day's outing. From here it's a short ride to Winchester, another pleasant community, this one with two delightful duck ponds adjoining the center of town. Just outside Winchester is a relaxing ride along the shore of the Mystic Lakes, two ponds separated by a narrow neck of land. The Mystic River flows as a small stream from the southern end of the lakes, dramatically increasing in size until it enters Boston Harbor.

The ride now turns north, paralleling the opposite shore of the Mystic Lakes in Arlington and then Winchester again. Here you'll pass through gracious older residential neighborhoods and then back into Woburn, where you'll bike along the other side of Horn Pond through a large lakefront park. The last 2 miles run through a surprisingly undeveloped area, where you'll pass several nurseries and greenhouses.

The long ride heads farther south into Belmont, wealthiest of the communities on the ride. The downtown area contains smart shops in attractive brick buildings, and an impressive, turreted town hall. Belmont has a fair amount of greenspace and open fields in the western edge of the town, including the Rock Meadow Reservation, the Habitat Institute for the Environment (a wildlife sanctuary with nature trails), and an Audubon sanctuary. Any one of these spots is a good place to relax after the steep climb out of town. You'll then cross back into Arlington, where you'll climb more gradually to the highest point in the area, a 375-foot hill crowned by a stately concrete water tower. Two blocks off the route there's a superb view of Boston from a playground sloping along the hillside.

After a fast downhill plunge, you can detour 0.2 mile off the route to see the Old Schwamb Mill, a wooden building that was a mill during the 1800s and is now an arts and crafts center. From here you'll climb into the wealthy, wooded western edge of Winchester and rejoin the short ride about a mile before you come to Horn Pond.

The Minuteman Bikeway:
Arlington–Lexington–Bedford–
Burlington–Woburn–Winchester

Number of miles:	23
Terrain:	Gently rolling.
Food:	Groceries and restaurants just off the route in Lexington and Bedford. Neighborhood grocery in Woburn.
Start:	Center of Arlington, at Massachusetts Avenue and Mystic Street (Route 60), a mile east of Route 2. The municipal parking lots next to the starting point are free on weekends.
Caution:	The Minuteman Bikeway is very heavily used on weekends in good weather by both cyclists and noncyclists. Keep alert for walkers, joggers, in-line skaters (who outnumber bicyclists about 3 to 2), children, and dogs. When passing, call out "Passing on your left" or "Coming through" in a clear voice. The trail also crosses some busy roads. Keep your pace moderate. I suggest getting an early start so that you can enjoy the bikeway before it becomes busy.

This ride explores the same general area as ride 3 but immediately west of it. The route follows the Minuteman Bikeway, the longest bicycle trail in the state outside Cape Cod, for most of its length—an 8.6-mile

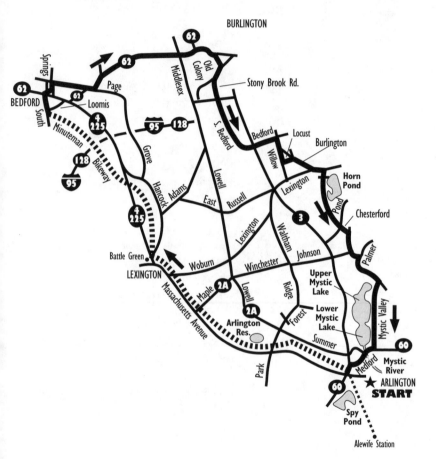

BURLINGTON

62

Springs

62
Page

62
BEDFORD

South

Loomis

62

4
225

Minuteman

128
95

Bikeway

4
225

95   128

Grove

Adams

Hancock

East

Old Colony

Middlesex

S. Bedford

Lowell

Russell

Stony Brook Rd.

Bedford   Locust

Willow

Burlington

Horn
Pond

Lexington

Pond

Chesterford

3

Lexington

Waltham

Johnson

Palmer

Battle Green

Woburn

Winchester

Upper
Mystic
Lake

LEXINGTON

Maple   2A

Lowell

Ridge

Lower
Mystic
Lake

Mystic Valley

60

Massachusetts Avenue

2A

Forest

Arlington
Res.

Summer

Medford   Mystic
River

Park

★ ARLINGTON
START

60

Spy
Pond

Alewife Station

1. Head northwest on the Minuteman Bikeway, paralleling Massachusetts Avenue on your left, for 8.6 miles to end, in Bedford.

After 1.5 miles, the trail passes within 100 yards of the Old Schwamb Mill and Shaker workshop center. If you'd like to visit them, watch for a street paralleling the bikeway on the left (Frazer Road). It's just after an athletic field on the right. Get on Frazer Road (it's safest to walk off the bikeway). Turn right as you leave the bikeway and immediately curve left away from it. The mill and workshop center are just ahead.

Continuing along the trail, after 0.6 mile you'll see a ballfield on the right. A footpath leads from the far side of the field 50 yards to the Arlington Reservoir, a small secluded pond straddling the Arlington-Lexington town line. The trail skirts downtown Lexington 2.6 miles farther on, on your left. Battle Green, where the first shots of the Revolutionary War were fired, is at the western end of the downtown area. You'll cross above Route 128 about 2 miles past downtown Lexington; from here it's another 2 miles to the end of the bikeway.

2. At the end of the bike trail, turn 90 degrees right uphill on South Road. (Don't turn sharply right on Loomis Street.) Go 0.4 mile to traffic light (Route 62), in the center of Bedford. Notice the impressive white church on your left at the intersection.

3. Go straight and just ahead bear right at fork on Springs Road. Go less than 0.2 mile to end (merge left at stop sign).

4. Bear left for 0.25 mile to crossroads and stop sign (Pine Hill Road on left, Page Road on right).

5. Right for 0.7 mile to stop sign (merge head-on onto Route 62).

6. Go straight and stay on Route 62 for 2 miles to traffic light after large athletic field on left (Middlesex Turnpike). Route 62 bears left and then bears right near the beginning.

7. Go straight. After 0.6 mile Route 62 turns left, but continue straight. Stay on main road for almost 0.9 mile to Old Colony Road, which turns right up a short, steep hill.

Notice the distinctive modern church on your right just past the point where Route 62 turns left.

8. Right for 0.3 mile to end (Lexington Street, unmarked).

9. Right for almost 0.6 mile to Stony Brook Road on left. The main road curves sharply right at the intersection

10. Left for 2 miles to third traffic light (Willow Street). You'll pass an old-fashioned little grocery on the left just before the intersection.

11. Right for 0.3 mile to Locust Street on left, just after school on right.

12. Turn left and stay on main road for 0.6 mile to end, at T-intersection. **CAUTION:** Bad sewer grate after almost 0.4 mile.

13. Left for less than 0.2 mile to Woburn Parkway on right.

14. Right for 0.2 mile to end (Water Street on right).

15. Straight onto a blocked-off lane that follows the shore of Horn Pond on your left. Go 0.4 mile to parking lot on left.

16. Turn left into lot. At the far end continue straight, following the pond on your left. Go 0.3 mile to fork at far end of pond. **CAUTION:** Watch for pedestrians.

17. Bear right uphill, passing electric power station on left. Go 0.3 mile to end of blocked-off road.

18. Straight onto Chesterford Road for 0.2 mile to stop sign (merge left).

19. Bear right for 0.5 mile to crossroads at second stop sign (Palmer Street on left, Fletcher Street on right). You'll pass Winter Pond at the beginning.

20. Right for 0.6 mile to Mystic Valley Parkway on right, just before the road goes under a railroad bridge.

21. Right for 1.8 miles to a small rotary (Route 60, High Street). You'll ride along the Mystic Lakes on your right.

22. Right and just ahead straight at another rotary. Go 0.5 mile to end, at traffic light (Mystic Street). Route 60 turns left here.

23. Left (**CAUTION** here) for 0.1 mile to traffic light (Massachusetts Avenue) in the center of Arlington.

If you wish, you can follow the southeastern section of the Minuteman Bikeway 1.3 miles to the Alewife T station and backtrack to Arlington Center. You'll pass Spy Pond, which is surrounded by houses and apartments. To get on this section of the bikeway, cross Massachusetts Avenue diagonally (it's safest to walk), follow it 100 yards to the first right (Swan Place), turn right, and turn immediately left onto the bikeway.

---

stretch between Arlington Center and Bedford. The trail, which was completed in 1993, follows a former Boston and Maine railroad line. Because of this, the scenery along the bikeway is what one would expect to see from a train. The trail is isolated from the communities through which it passes as it slips behind homes, factories, and warehouses. The bikeway passes in back of the handsome storefronts and public buildings in the centers of Arlington and Lexington; to see them, you have to get off the trail onto Massachusetts Avenue. The bikeway is well designed and wide enough to be safe, but it is heavily used, and caution is necessary (see **CAUTION** notice in the introductory box at beginning of this ride description).

The ride begins by following the trail from Arlington to Bedford. After 1.5 miles you'll come within 100 yards of the Old Schwamb Mill, a wooden building that has been producing high-quality picture frames since 1864. It also serves as an arts and crafts center. Workshops in crafting Shaker furniture are held across the street. About 3 miles ahead you'll skirt downtown Lexington and pass near Battle Green, where the first skirmish of the American Revolution took place in 1775. Facing the green is the Buckman Tavern, where the Minute Men assembled for battle. In Bedford, the northwestern terminus of the trail, you'll head 0.5 mile into the center of town. Bedford is a pleasant residential community with an unusually large and elegant white church.

From Bedford you'll follow quiet secondary roads to Burlington and then Woburn, both attractive residential towns. In Woburn you'll ride along Horn Pond through a large lakeside park on a road blocked off to cars. Just beyond Horn Pond the route enters the affluent town of Winchester, where you'll enjoy a relaxing ride along the shore of the Mystic Lakes, two ponds separated by a narrow neck of land. From the southern end of the Mystic Lakes, it's less than a mile to the starting point.

Newton–Brookline

Number of miles:	19 (14 without Brookline extension)
Terrain:	Gently rolling, with several hills.
Food:	Numerous groceries and restaurants.
Start:	Riverside MBTA terminal on Grove Street, Newton, just east of Route 128. There is a modest parking fee.

This ride takes you exploring in two affluent suburbs immediately west of Boston filled with large, gracious homes from the nineteenth and early twentieth centuries. You'll start from the western edge of Newton at the Riverside T terminal, a convenient spot for taking public transportation into Boston. Newton is a classic "streetcar suburb" that evolved with public rail transit during the second half of the nineteenth century. This sparked the construction of residential areas, generally aimed at a well-to-do market, beyond the confines of Boston itself yet easily accessible to the city for daily commuting. Newton is pleasant to bicycle through, with tree-lined, curving streets and spacious older wooden or brick homes surrounded by attractively landscaped yards. The first part of the route follows broad, gracefully curving Commonwealth Avenue, which has a grassy island in the middle for most of its length.

The long ride heads past the handsome, Gothic-style buildings of Boston College and then along the Chestnut Hill Reservoir. Just ahead you'll enter Brookline, which geographically should be part of Boston because it is surrounded by the city along three-quarters of its perimeter. The southern half of Brookline is even more elegant than Newton, with a broad belt of mansions and estates just south of Route 9. You'll cycle through this idyllic area where it's hard to believe that you're only

DIRECTIONS
FOR
THE RIDE

1. Left on Grove Street for 0.4 mile to traffic island at top of hill (main road curves right).
2. Curve right and stay on main road for almost 0.5 mile to traffic light (Auburn Street on right).
3. Right for 0.3 mile to traffic light (Commonwealth Avenue, unmarked).

4. Right for 3.6 miles to Hammond Street, which bears right at traffic light at top of hill. Here the short ride bears right.

You'll pass the impressive Newton City Hall on your right after 2 miles. The long, steady hill leading up to Hammond Street is the infamous "Heartbreak Hill" on the Boston Marathon route.

5. Straight for 0.7 mile to traffic light at bottom of hill (Thomas More Road, unmarked, on right).
6. Right for almost 0.5 mile to crossroads and stop sign (Beacon Street).

You'll pass Boston College on your right and then the Chestnut Hill Reservoir on your left. When you get to Beacon Street, notice the handsome granite pumping station in front of you.

7. Left for 0.3 mile to Reservoir Road (unmarked), which bears right at traffic island.

This affluent area, called Chestnut Hill, is near the point where Newton, Brookline, and the Brighton section of Boston meet. The ornate building on your right just beyond the intersection is another pumping station.

8. Bear right and immediately curve left (still Reservoir Road). Just ahead is a small railroad bridge blocked off to cars. Walk across on the sidewalk and continue less than 0.2 mile to fork immediately after stop sign (Crafts Road bears left). You are now in Brookline.
9. Bear left for 0.2 mile to another fork, at stop sign (Eliot Street bears right, Dean Road bears left.
10. Bear left for 0.3 mile to traffic light (Chestnut Hill Avenue).
11. Straight for 0.3 mile to third crossroads and stop sign (Clinton Road).

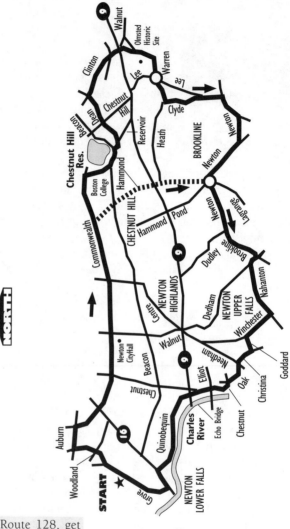

NORTH

HOW TO GET THERE

From Route 128, get off at Grove Street (exit 22). Bear right at end of ramp and go 0.2 mile to terminal on left.

12. Right for 0.5 mile to stop sign (merge left on Buckminster Road).

13. Bear left for 0.1 mile to fork, at traffic island.

14. Bear right and just ahead cross Route 9 at traffic light. Go 100 yards to fork at grassy traffic island (Walnut Street bears both left and right).

As soon as you cross Route 9, a footpath bears right up a short hill to the picturesque Brookline Reservoir, which is circled by a walkway.

15. Bear right and just ahead go straight at stop sign onto Warren Street. Go 0.7 mile to wooded rotary. You'll pass the Frederick Law Olmsted National Historic Site on your right after 0.1 mile.

16. Take the second road off the rotary (still Warren Street). Don't get on Lee Street (unmarked), a divided parkway. Go 0.2 mile to Clyde Street on left.

17. Left for 0.6 mile to end (merge right onto divided parkway). You'll pass the entrance to The Country Club (the oldest golf club in the country, founded in 1882), on your right.

18. Bear right (still Clyde Street) for 0.3 mile to end (Newton Street).

19. Right for 0.25 mile to fork (Newton Street bears right).

20. Bear right for 0.9 mile to rotary.

21. Take the third road off the rotary onto divided parkway (still Newton Street). **CAUTION:** The rotary is busy; it's safer to walk your bike around if traffic is heavy. Go 1.5 miles to traffic light (Dedham Street, unmarked). Newton Street becomes Brookline Street at the Newton city line.

22. Turn right and just ahead bear left at traffic light onto Nahanton Street. Go 0.6 mile to Winchester Street on right.

23. Right for 0.7 mile to Goddard Street on left, just after Wallace Street on left.

24. Left for 0.2 mile to end (Christina Street).

25. Right for 0.7 mile to second traffic light (Chestnut Street).

26. Left for 0.4 mile to Ellis Street on left, just after traffic light. This area is called Newton Upper Falls.

27. Left for 2 miles to traffic light (Route 16).

You'll go under Echo Bridge at the beginning. To verify the accuracy of the name, walk to the bank of the Charles River on your left directly beneath the bridge and holler. A walkway on top of the bridge provides a fine view of the river and a dam just upstream. Beyond the bridge Ellis Street becomes Quinobequin Road, a beautiful winding road paralleling the river on your left.

28. Left (**CAUTION** here) for 0.2 mile to Grove Street on right. This area is called Newton Lower Falls.

29. Turn right and immediately go straight (don't bear right on Moulton Street). Stay on main road for 0.8 mile to terminal on left.

Directions for shorter ride

1. Follow directions for the long ride through number 4.

2. Bear right for 2.1 miles to rotary. **CAUTION** crossing Route 9 at second traffic light—the intersection is very busy.

You'll pass a graceful stone church on your right shortly before Route 9. This affluent area, called Chestnut Hill, is near the point where Newton, Brookline, and the Brighton section of Boston meet.

3. Take the second road off the rotary onto divided parkway (Newton Street). **CAUTION:** The rotary is busy; it's safer to walk your bike around if traffic is heavy. Go 1.5 miles to traffic light (Dedham Street, unmarked). Newton Street becomes Brookline Street at the Newton city line.

4. Follow directions for the long ride from number 22 to the end.

---

5 miles from downtown Boston. You'll pass the Frederick Law Olmsted National Historic Site, a rambling old building that was for many years the home and office of the country's foremost landscape architect of the nineteenth century. Olmsted is most famous for designing Central Park in New York City. He also designed an elaborate, linear park system for Boston, including Franklin Park, Jamaica Pond, the Muddy River between Brookline and Jamaica Plain, and the Back Bay Fens. Some of his original plans are on display at the site, which is open from Friday through Sunday.

The Blue Hills Ride:
Milton–West Quincy

Number of miles:	18 (11 with shortcut)
Terrain:	Rolling, with one long, tough hill and several short ones.
Food:	Restaurant in West Quincy. Howard Johnson's near end.
Start:	Trailside Museum, Route 138, Milton, 1 mile north of Route 128. It's just after the ski area.

Directly south of Boston is an area that's a pleasant surprise. Instead of dreary suburbs or industrial barrens, there are old mansions and gracious estates, a long, stately parkway with a broad, grassy island down the middle, and the elegant town center of Milton. Surrounding all this is the wonderful Blue Hills Reservation, the largest protected expanse of greenspace in the metropolitan area, yet very close to Boston. Five miles long, the reservation contains one of the most prominent natural features in the Boston area, the range of rugged wooded hills rising to a height of 630 feet at its western end on top of Great Blue Hill. Foot trails hop from hill to hill, providing some superb views; horseback riders and cross-country skiers can enjoy 65 miles of bridle paths. Also on the grounds are a natural history museum, an Audubon Society education center, and two ponds.

The ride starts at the Trailside Museum, a natural history museum run by the Massachusetts Audubon Society, at the foot of Great Blue Hill. It contains both live and stuffed animals and birds native to Massachusetts. Large animals are exhibited outdoors. From behind the museum, a trail leads half a mile to the summit, where an observation

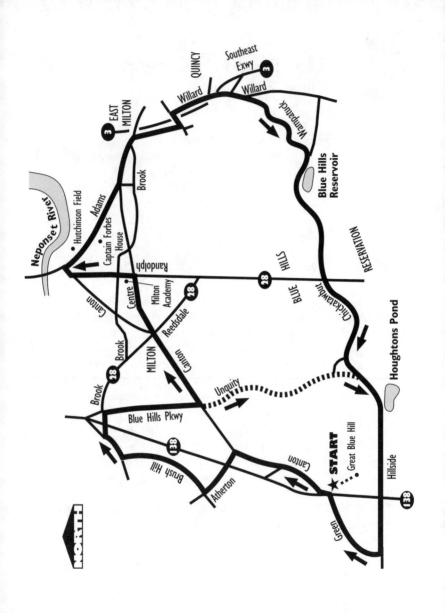

DIRECTIONS

FOR

THE RIDE

1. Right (north) on Route 138 for 0.2 mile to Canton Avenue (unmarked), which bears right (sign may say TO HYDE PARK).

2. Bear right and stay on main road for 1.3 miles to Atherton Street on left. It's 0.5 mile past Dollar Lane on left. There's a graceful stone gatehouse on the right just past Dollar Lane.

3. Turn left and just ahead cross Route 138 at traffic light. Go 0.4 mile to crossroads and stop sign (Brush Hill Road).

4. Right for 1.2 miles to stop sign (merge right onto divided parkway).

5. Bear right for 0.2 mile to Brook Road (unmarked), which bears slightly right.

6. Bear right and just ahead cross Route 138 at traffic light. Go 0.1 mile to stop sign and a divided parkway (Blue Hills Parkway, unmarked).

7. Right for 1.2 miles to stop sign where the divided road ends (Canton Avenue, unmarked). Here the short ride goes straight.

8. Left for 1 mile to traffic light at five-way intersection (Reedsdale Road, Route 28). The Milton town green is on your left just before the light, and the handsome brick library is on your right at the intersection.

9. Straight for 0.5 mile to traffic light (Randolph Avenue). You'll pass Milton Academy just before the light.

10. Left for 0.8 mile to end (Adams Street, unmarked). You'll pass a fine stone church on your right toward the end. Get in a low gear at end.

11. Right for 1.5 miles to traffic light immediately before the bridge over I–93. (Sign says TO I–93 SOUTH.)

You'll pass Hutchinson Field on your left and the Robert Bennett Forbes House on your right after 0.2 mile. Then you'll pass Aquinas College, a two-year Catholic women's school, on your right.

12. Bear right, paralleling I–93 on left, for 0.6 mile to crossroads (Robertson Street; a sign may say to EAST MILTON, WEST QUINCY).

13. Left and just ahead right at traffic light (Willard Street). Stay on

main road for 0.6 mile to fork just after you go under I–93. (Riccuti Drive bears right).

14. Bear left (**CAUTION** here) for 0.2 mile to fork where the ramp onto I–93 bears left and Willard Street bears right.

15. Bear right and just ahead bear right again, following sign that may say TO MILTON, CANTON, BLUE HILLS. Go 1.3 miles to stop sign (merge right). Most of this stretch is uphill.

16. Bear right for 1.6 miles to traffic light (Route 28). You'll pass the Blue Hills Reservoir on your left. Half a mile ahead is a small parking area on the right with a fine view of Boston. From here it's all downhill to Route 28.

17. Straight for 1.3 miles to fork where the main road bears slightly left.

18. Bear left for 0.2 mile to stop sign (merge left).

19. Bear left for 1.5 miles to traffic light (Route 138). You'll pass Houghtons Pond on your left at the far end of a large parking lot after 0.5 mile.

20. Straight for 0.7 mile to Green Street (unmarked), a small crossroads just beyond the Blue Hills Office Park on left.

21. Right for 1.2 miles to end (Route 138).

22. Turn right, and the museum is just ahead on your left.

Directions for shorter ride

1. Follow directions for the long ride through number 7.

2. Straight onto Unquity Road (unmarked) for 3.8 miles to traffic light (Route 138). You'll pass Houghtons Pond on your left at the far end of a large parking lot after about 2.5 miles.

3. Follow the directions for the long ride from number 20 to the end.

---

tower affords one of the best views to be found of Boston and vicinity. You'll head past estates and rolling hillsides to the center of Milton, a New England jewel with a large green framed by the town hall and two classic white churches. Shortly after the green, you'll pass the elegant brick buildings of Milton Academy, one of the state's top preparatory schools.

A mile ahead you'll parallel the Neponset River estuary along a hillside with magnificent views. Sloping down the hill to the water's edge is Hutchinson Field, a lush, grassy meadow with a vista of the river and the Boston skyline. The field is one of the properties of the Trustees of Reservations, whose main office is next door. Across the street is the imposing Captain Robert Bennett Forbes House, which contains exhibits of the China trade (in which Forbes made his fortune). Just ahead you'll enter the Blue Hills Reservation and traverse its entire length on smooth roads winding through the woods, passing Houghtons Pond, which has a beach. At the end you'll go by more estates along a tiny lane just over the Canton town line.

Chapter 2:
The North Shore

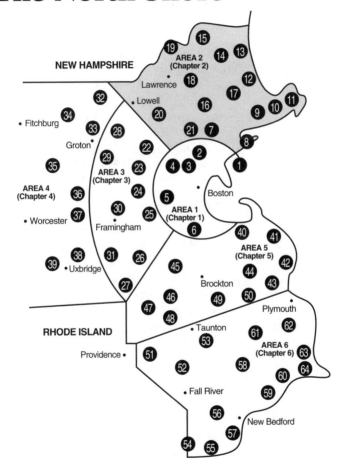

Lynnfield–North Reading

Number of miles:	23 (14 without North Reading loop)
Terrain:	Gently rolling.
Food:	Several groceries and restaurants. 99 Restaurant 0.6 mile from start.
Start:	Currier Plaza, a small shopping center at Salem and Summer streets in Lynnfield. It's just south of Route 128 and 0.5 mile west of Route 1.

This is a tour of affluent residential areas north of Boston, passing through the elegant town center of Lynnfield and the traditional New England town of North Reading. The landscape is midway between rural and suburban and very pleasant for biking. If you're looking for a fairly easy and relaxing ride, this is a good choice.

The ride starts from the southern part of Lynnfield, the wealthier of the two communities on the ride. Soon you'll pass Pillings Pond and arrive at the town center. The large, triangular green is graced by a stately white church and a meetinghouse built in 1714.

From Lynnfield you'll proceed on lightly traveled side roads to the charming town center of North Reading. The large green, complete with bandstand, slopes uphill to a white church with a clock tower built in 1829. Just past the green is the town hall, a striking Victorian building. The return trip follows pleasant secondary roads through a different section of Lynnfield. You'll ride along the opposite shore of Pillings Pond on a road not much wider than a bicycle path.

The short ride omits the western loop by heading north on Haverhill Street to the center of North Reading.

1. Right on Salem Street for 0.8 mile to traffic light (Walnut Street, unmarked). The 99 Restaurant on your left shortly before the light, is a good spot to eat after the ride.

2. Right for 0.7 mile to Thomas Road on right. It goes up a short hill.

3. Right for 0.4 mile to end (Summer Street, unmarked).

4. Turn left and stay on main road for 1.5 miles to end (Main Street, unmarked) in the center of Lynnfield. You'll pass Pillings Pond on your right. The town green is on your left at the end.

5. Left for 0.4 mile to Chestnut Street on right.

6. Right for 1.7 miles to end (Lowell Street). After 0.4 mile, notice the old house on the left with a steep-pitched roof and small, diamond-paned windows.

At the end, the ride turns left, but you can shorten the distance to 11 miles by turning right for 1 mile to crossroads and stop sign (Main Street) and resuming with direction number 23.

7. Turn left and stay on main road for 1.4 miles to crossroads and stop sign (Haverhill Street). Here the short ride turns right.

8. Left for 1.1 miles to Franklin Street on right, at traffic island.

9. Right for 0.25 mile to small crossroads (Pearl Street). It's just after Partridge Road on right.

10. Right for 0.4 mile to Route 28, at stop sign.

11. Cross Route 28 onto Mill Street, bearing right as you go through the intersection. **CAUTION:** Route 28 is very busy. Stay on main road for 0.5 mile to end.

12. Left for 0.25 mile to fork (Concord Street bears left).

13. Bear slightly right (still Park Street). Stay on main road for 1.6 miles to Woburn Street (unmarked) on right, immediately before bridge over I–93.

14. Right for 0.7 mile to crossroads and stop sign (Route 62, Salem Street).

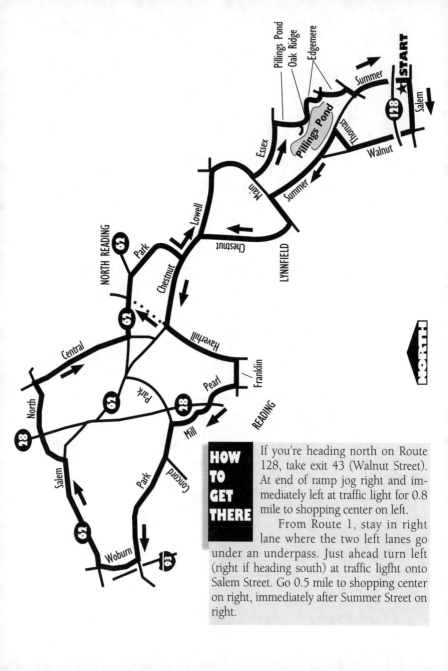

Pillings Pond
Oak Ridge
Edgemere

START

Summer

Salem

128

Thomas

Essex

Pillings Pond

Walnut

Main

Summer

LYNNFIELD

Lowell

Chestnut

NORTH READING

61

Park

Chestnut

Central

Haverhill

61

Franklin

Pearl

READING

North

28

61

Park

28

Mill

Salem

Park

Concord

61

Woburn

93

NORTH

HOW TO GET THERE

If you're heading north on Route 128, take exit 43 (Walnut Street). At end of ramp jog right and immediately left at traffic light for 0.8 mile to shopping center on left.

From Route 1, stay in right lane where the two left lanes go under an underpass. Just ahead turn left (right if heading south) at traffic ligfht onto Salem Street. Go 0.5 mile to shopping center on right, immediately after Summer Street on right.

15. Right for 1.4 miles to North Street on left, opposite ball field on right.

16. Left for 0.4 mile to traffic light (Route 28).

17. Straight for 0.7 mile to crossroads and blinking light (Central Street, unmarked), midway down short hill.

18. Right for 1.3 miles to crossroads and stop sign (Route 62).

19. Left for 0.9 mile to fork where Park Street bears right at gas station. You'll go through the center of North Reading shortly before the fork, passing the green and former town hall (now a library), built in 1875, on your left.

20. Bear right for 1 mile to end.

21. Turn left up a short hill. Stay on main road for 1.4 miles to crossroads and stop sign (Main Street). Don't turn right on Chestnut Street after 0.4 mile.

22. Right for 0.8 mile to Essex Street on left. It's just after a grocery with gasoline pumps on the left.

23. Left for 0.9 mile to Pillings Pond Road on right, after high school.

24. Right for 0.6 mile to fork where Oak Ridge Terrace, a narrow lane, bears left.

25. Bear left for 0.3 mile to Edgemere Road (unmarked) on right. It's a narrow lane that comes up while you're climbing a short hill. If you come to Birch Road on the left, you've gone 100 feet too far.

   You'll follow Pillings Pond on your right.

26. Turn right, still following pond, for 0.5 mile to end (Wildewood Drive on left).

27. Right for 0.4 mile to end.

28. Right and just ahead left at crossroads and stop sign (Summer Street, unmarked). Go less than 0.5 mile to entrance to shopping center on right, immediately before end.

Directions for shorter ride

1. Follow directions for the long ride through number 7.

2. Right for 0.6 mile to crossroads and stop sign (Route 62) in the cen-

ter of North Reading. You'll pass an attractive stone church on your right.

3. Right for 0.3 mile to fork where Park Street bears right at gas station. You'll pass the green and former town hall (now a library), built in 1875, on your left.

4. Follow directions for the long ride from number 20 to the end.

8 Lynn–Swampscott–Marblehead

Number of miles:	20
Terrain:	Gently rolling.
Food:	Numerous stores and restaurants on the route.
Start:	Lynn Shore Drive in Lynn, just north of the causeway to Nahant.

This is a tour of the nicest coastline close to Boston if you don't count Nahant. (You can do the Nahant ride too—from the starting point go along either the bike path or the Nahant Beach parking lot on the east side of the causeway to Nahant, following the ocean on your left. Added distance is 10 miles.) The area is similar to Cape Ann but only half the distance from Boston, with beautiful stretches of shoreline graced by elegant mansions and estates, some rocky headlands, and the maze of narrow streets lined with restored antique homes in the center of Marblehead. The town lies along a peninsula jutting northeastward into the Atlantic. Just east of it is Marblehead Neck, a bowling-pin-shaped island 1 mile long and a half-mile wide, rimmed with elegant homes and connected to the mainland by a causeway. Between the two are the deep, sheltered waters of Marblehead Harbor, one of the yachting and sailing capitals of New England. The view of Marblehead across the harbor from the Neck, sloping up a low hillside crowned by Abbott Hall, the proud Victorian town hall that dominates the town, is inspiring.

You start the ride by heading up the Lynn shoreline, the best face of this otherwise drab industrial city, with a well-landscaped strip of parkland along the ocean on your right and gracious older homes and apartment buildings on your left. You then continue up the coast through Swampscott, an affluent community with attractive older homes, many

65

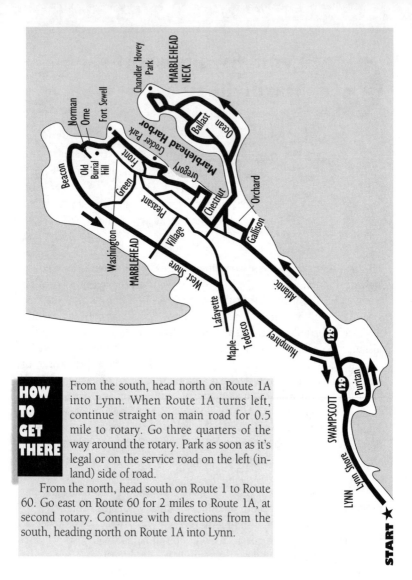

HOW TO GET THERE

From the south, head north on Route 1A into Lynn. When Route 1A turns left, continue straight on main road for 0.5 mile to rotary. Go three quarters of the way around the rotary. Park as soon as it's legal or on the service road on the left (inland) side of road.

From the north, head south on Route 1 to Route 60. Go east on Route 60 for 2 miles to Route 1A, at second rotary. Continue with directions from the south, heading north on Route 1A into Lynn.

DIRECTIONS
FOR
THE RIDE

1. Head north on Lynn Shore Drive, following the ocean on your right. Go 1.6 miles to Puritan Road, which bears right at traffic light along the ocean. After 1.1 miles you'll pass the Swampscott town green on your left, with the town hall a block inland.

2. Bear right and stay on main road for 1.2 miles to end (Atlantic Avenue, Route 129). Several dead-end lanes on the right lead to the rocky coastline past elegant homes and estates.

3. Turn right and immediately go straight (don't bear left on Humphrey Street). Go 2 miles to Gallison Avenue on right, just after Vassar Avenue on right.

4. Right and just ahead left on Orchard Street. Go 0.3 mile to second crossroads and stop sign.

5. Right for less than 0.2 mile to yield sign (merge right).

6. Bear right for 0.6 mile to fork at far end of causeway to Marblehead Neck (Harbor Avenue bears left, Ocean Avenue bears right).

7. Bear right for 1.7 miles to Chandler Hovey Park, at the dead end at the northern tip of Marblehead Neck. After 1.3 miles, opposite house number 376, a paved footpath on the right leads 100 yards to Castle Rock, which provides a stunning view of the rugged, Mainelike coastline.

8. Leaving the park, turn right on Kimball Street for 0.2 mile to end.

9. Turn right and just ahead bear right at fork, at little traffic circle (Harbor Avenue, unmarked, bears right). Go 0.25 mile to crossroads just beyond the crest of a little hill (Ballast Lane).

10. Right for 0.5 mile to stop sign (merge right). You'll go along Marblehead Harbor on your right. The brick building with the tall clock tower on the far side of the harbor is Abbott Hall, the town hall.

11. Bear right for 0.8 mile to traffic light (Atlantic Avenue). You'll cross the causeway in the opposite direction.

12. Right for 0.3 mile to Chestnut Street on right, just after church on left.

13. Right for less than 0.4 mile to Gregory Street (unmarked) on right, just after you turn left away from the harbor.

14. Right for 0.4 mile to stop sign where a small road turns right downhill.

15. Right and immediately right again on Water Street. Go 0.6 mile to Fort Sewell, at end. At the beginning you'll pass Crocker Park, a rocky outcropping with a magnificent view of Marblehead Harbor, on your right. Then you'll follow the harbor closely.

16. Backtrack from Fort Sewell and just ahead make a forced right turn (it's one-way in the wrong direction if you go straight). Go 0.1 mile to where the main road turns left and a smaller road, Orne Street (unmarked), bears right. A sign may point left TO LYNN, BOSTON.

17. Bear right and stay on main road for 0.4 mile to end (Norman Street on left, Beacon Street on right). After 0.25 mile the Old Burial Hill is on your left. It was founded in 1638 and is a great place to compare old gravestones. Across the road is still another waterfront park, Fountain Park.

18. Right for 2.6 miles to second traffic light (merge right on Lafayette Street, unmarked). You'll pass Dolliber Cove on your right at the beginning.

19. Bear right for 0.25 mile to Maple Street, which turns sharply left at traffic island.

20. Sharp left for 0.2 mile to traffic light.

21. Bear right on Humphrey Street. (Don't turn 90 degrees right on Tedesco Street.) Go 1.5 miles to yield sign (merge right on Route 129).

22. Bear right for 2.5 miles back to start, following the ocean on your left.

---

quite elegant, lining the shore and the hillsides rising from it.

From Swampscott it's a short ride into Marblehead. First you'll go around the Neck. At its northern tip is Chandler Hovey Park, a beautiful spot with a nearly 360-degree view of the sea and a tall old lighthouse. Then you'll go around Marblehead itself, where you're much better off on a bike than in a car as you weave along its narrow streets without worrying about finding a parking place. You'll pass two delightful waterfront parks, Chandler Park and Fort Sewell. The latter commands a small peninsula and contains the remains of a Revolutionary fort. Just north of town is Old Burial Hill, one of the state's outstanding historic cemeteries, with many slate headstones, dating back to the 1700s and even earlier, stretching up the terraced hillside.

Estates and Estuaries:
Hamilton–Ipswich–Essex–Manchester–Beverly–Wenham

Number of miles:	27 (16 without Hamilton–Ipswich–Essex–Manchester extension)
Terrain:	Gently rolling, with several moderate hills.
Food:	Grocery and restaurants in Essex. The local specialty here is clams. Grocery and restaurants in Manchester. Convenience store in Beverly.
Start:	Hamilton-Wenham commuter rail parking lot, Route 1A and Walnut Road, Hamilton, at the Wenham town line. It's 3 miles north of Route 128, next to the Hamilton Shopping Center. The entrance is on Walnut Road. There is a modest parking fee on weekdays.

The region northeast of Beverly is the North Shore at some of its finest: a magnificent landscape of rocky coastline with mansions perched above it; the broad, gently rolling fields of gentleman farms and old-moneyed estates; and gracious horse farms partitioned by white wooden fences. The town centers are classic New England gems. A fine network of smooth, little-traveled secondary roads weaving across the landscape provides bicycling at its best.

The ride starts off by heading across Hamilton, passing through magnificent horse-farm and estate country. Hamilton is a gracious, well-to-do community where many of the residents are likely to feed the family horse in the morning. You'll pass Asbury Grove, a Methodist campground containing small, Gothic-style cottages and a central tabernacle. It is similar to Oak Bluffs in Martha's Vineyard but not as extensive or ornamented. Asbury Grove was founded in 1858.

Hamilton's best-known landmark is the Myopia Hunt Club, an extensive estate founded in 1875 that is the major center for polo in the state. Polo matches are held on Sunday afternoons at 3 o'clock and are fascinating to watch. If you'd like to go to them after the ride, the club is on Route 1A a half-mile north of the starting point.

From Hamilton you'll pass more horse farms as you follow country lanes through the southern part of Ipswich into Essex, another delightful town with a cluster of antiques shops and the fascinating Ipswich Shipbuilding Museum on the main street. If you like clams, you're in the right place—all the restaurants serve clams that were on the ocean floor only a few hours before. The best-known spot is Woodman's, on the right as you're heading down Route 133. The remainder of the town consists of vast salt marshes extending along the estuaries of the Essex and Castle Neck rivers, wooded hills, and some broad farms.

From Essex you'll enjoy a smooth ride to Manchester, a gracious seaside town with oceanfront estates belonging to Boston's bluebloods; fine old homes on the streets adjacent to the center of town; and beautiful Singing Beach, one of the North Shore's nicest. In the town center is the handsome town hall and a graceful white church dated 1809.

The ride heads southwest from Manchester into Beverly on Route 127, which parallels the ocean. The sea is visible in only a few spots because most of the shoreline is hidden by large parcels of private land. Like others across the state, Beverly is a two-sided community. The negative side, which you won't come anywhere near, is a congested, unattractive commercial area surrounded by factories and closely stacked houses. The positive side is the eastern half of the city and the northernmost section along the Wenham line, consisting primarily of woods, some gracious residential neighborhoods, and the magnificent Atlantic shore. The two easternmost communities of Prides Crossing and Beverly Farms have been havens for Boston's landed gentry since

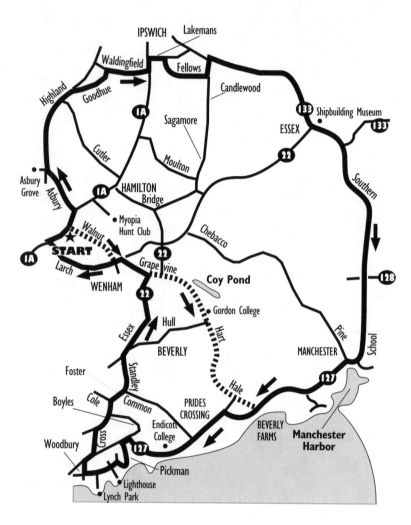

IPSWICH   Lakemans

Waldingfield   Fellows

Highland   Goodhue   Candlewood

1A

Sagamore   133   Shipbuilding Museum

ESSEX

Cutler   Moulton   22

Asbury
Grove

Asbury   1A   HAMILTON   Southern

Bridge

Myopia
Hunt Club   Chebacco

Walnut

START   128

1A   Larch   22   Grape Vine   Coy Pond

WENHAM   22   Gordon College

Hull   Hart

Essex   BEVERLY   Pine

Foster   MANCHESTER   School

Standley

Boyles   Cole   Common   Hale   127

Woodbury   Cross   PRIDES
CROSSING   BEVERLY
FARMS   Manchester
Harbor

Endicott
College

127

Pickman

Lighthouse
Lynch Park

DIRECTIONS
FOR
THE RIDE

1. Left out of parking lot and immediately right (north) on Route 1A. Go 0.2 mile to Asbury Street on left. *Note:* The 16-mile ride turns right out of parking lot onto Walnut Road.

2. Left for 1 mile to crossroads and stop sign (Highland Street). Here the ride turns right, but if you go straight you'll enter Asbury Grove. The center of the campground is 0.25 mile from Highland Street.

3. Right for 2.3 miles to Goodhue Street (unmarked), a smaller road that bears right.

4. Bear right for 0.5 mile to end (Waldingfield Road, unmarked).

5. Right for 0.8 mile to end (Route 1A).

6. Left for 0.2 mile to Lakemans Lane on right.

7. Right for 0.3 mile to Fellows Road on right.

8. Right for 1.2 miles to end (Candlewood Road, unmarked).

9. Left for 0.4 mile to end (Route 133).

10. Right for 3.6 miles to fork (Route 133 bears left, Southern Avenue bears right).

You'll go through the center of Essex after 3 miles. If you turn right on Route 22 for 0.2 mile, you'll come to the town hall, a distinctive Victorian building with a portly clock tower. The Essex Shipbuilding Museum is on your left immediately after Route 22. Woodman's, famous for fried clams, is on your right shortly before the fork.

11. Bear right for 4.1 miles to end (Route 127), in the center of Manchester. Notice the handsome stone church on your right as you start to come into the town.

12. Bear right for 0.7 mile to Harbor Street on left, immediately after the Old Corner Inn on left.

Here the ride goes straight, but for some ocean views turn left for 0.25 mile to end and then turn either right or left. If you turn right for 0.2 mile, you'll come to Black Cove, a beautiful rockbound inlet. If you turn left for 0.25 mile, you'll come to Tucks Point, a small peninsula at the mouth of Manchester Harbor with a yacht club and a little water-front park.

13. Straight (left if your coming from Harbor Street) for 4.2 miles to Pickman Road on left. It's the second left after Route 127 curves 90 degrees left beyond Endicott College. **CAUTION:** There are three diagonal railroad crossings with frequent train traffic. Walk your bike over them.

You'll pass a graceful wooden church on your right after the second railroad crossing, in the village of Prides Crossing (part of Beverly).

14. Left for 0.3 mile to Neptune Street on left.

15. Left for 0.5 mile to Woodbury Street, a crossroads just past the entrance to Lynch Park on left. The view from the tip of the peninsula at the far end of the park is impressive.

To look at the lighthouse, turn left at first crossroads on Bay View Avenue for 0.2 mile.

16. Right for 0.2 mile to end (merge right on Route 127).

17. Bear right for 0.1 mile to Cross Street (unmarked) on left, immediately after Corning Street on left.

18. Left for 0.3 mile to diagonal crossroads and stop sign (Cross Lane, unmarked, bears right).

19. Bear right for 0.7 mile to fork immediately after railroad tracks (Cole Street bears left, Foster Street bears right). **CAUTION:** Bumpy spots.

20. Bear right and stay on main road for 1.1 miles to end (Route 22, Essex Street). Foster Street becomes Standley Street.

21. Turn right and stay on Route 22 for 1.4 miles to T-intersection (Grapevine Road). Route 22 bears left at fork after less than 0.2 mile.

22. Left for 0.7 mile to end (Larch Row).

23. Left and just ahead straight at crossroads (don't curve left on main road). Go 1.6 miles to end (Route 1A, Main Street).

Here the ride turns right, but if you turn left for 0.3 mile you'll come to the lovely town center of Wenham. On the left is the Claflin-Richards House, built in 1664, and an adjoining museum of nineteenth-century dolls, toys, and games.

24. Right for 0.5 mile to shopping center on right, at Walnut Road. **CAUTION:** Dangerous diagonal railroad tracks at the intersection; please walk across.

Directions for shorter ride

1. Right on Walnut Road for 1.1 miles to crossroads and stop sign (Larch Row). There's a small church with distinctive Gothic-style architecture on the far right corner.

2. Left (**CAUTION** here) and just ahead right on Grapevine Road. Stay on main road for 4.4 miles to end (Route 127). You'll pass Gordon College on your left after about 2 miles. The lane along the lake behind the campus is delightful.

3. Right for 3 miles to Pickman Road on left. It's the second left after Route 127 curves 90 degrees left beyond Endicott College. **CAUTION:** There's a diagonal railroad crossing as you turn onto Route 127, and two more diagonal crossings farther on. Walk your bike over them.

You'll pass a graceful wooden church on your right after the second railroad crossing, in the village of Prides Crossing (part of Beverly).

4. Follow directions for the long ride from number 14 to the end.

---

the railroad was built in the 1800s. In the wedge of land between Route 127 and the ocean, dozens of mansions rise in isolated splendor at the end of quarter-mile-long driveways.

After riding through Prides Crossing, with its touristy country store at the railroad crossing, it's about a mile to Endicott College, one of the most spectacularly located in the state. Several of its buildings are elegant mansions perched directly on the rocky shoreline. A mile farther on, a handsome lighthouse built in 1871 (not open to the public) stands on a small peninsula. Just beyond it is Lynch Park, commanding a promontory jutting into the ocean. As city parks go, it is a pleasure—clean, well landscaped, and well maintained. The last few miles head inland along winding lanes.

The short ride bypasses Hamilton, Ipswich, Essex, and Manchester by heading directly to Beverly Farms and then Prides Crossing. You'll pass through a long slice of Wenham, going past horse farms and country estates, and then by Gordon College, beautifully situated on an unspoiled lake.

Manchester Harbor

Gateway to Cape Ann:
West Gloucester–Essex–
Manchester–Magnolia

Number of miles:	23
Terrain:	Gently rolling, with two short hills.
Food:	Groceries and restaurants in the towns. The regional favorite dish is clams, especially in Essex.
Start:	Junction of Routes 127 and 133 in Gloucester, just west of the small bridge over the Blynman Canal. Park on Route 127 on the ocean side of the road.

The area just west of Cape Ann has the glorious seascape scenery of the cape itself without the tourists and the traffic. Like Cape Ann, the region is characterized by gracious old towns; the rocky coastline with mansions and estates perched above it in baronial splendor; little sandy beaches tucked between craggy headlands; and lonely, unspoiled salt marshes along the northern shore.

The ride starts from West Gloucester, the less-urban portion of the city on the western side of the canal that separates Cape Ann from the mainland. You will head westward along the rural, unspoiled northern shore past woods, small farms, and salt marshes to Essex, another picturesque community. In the center of town just off the route, are several antiques shops, a museum of shipbuilding, snack bars serving clams dredged up from the ocean floor only a few hours before, and the mouth of the Essex River, filled with small fishing boats.

From Essex it's a smooth ride to Manchester, a stately seaside community with a graceful white church, built in 1809, dominating the center of town. Also in town are the Trask House, an elegant Federal-period

77

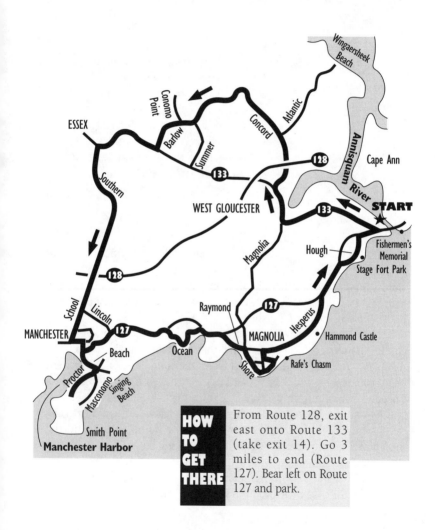

HOW TO GET THERE

From Route 128, exit east onto Route 133 (take exit 14). Go 3 miles to end (Route 127). Bear left on Route 127 and park.

DIRECTIONS

FOR

THE RIDE

1. Head west on Route 133 for 2.4 miles to Concord Street on right (sign may say TO WINGAERSHEEK MOTEL AND BEACH).

2. Right for 3.3 miles to fork where Summer Street bears left and Concord Street (unmarked) bears right across small bridge. **CAUTION:** Bumps, potholes, and sandy spots on the second half of this section.

After 1.2 miles Atlantic Street is on your right. This is a pleasant, narrow road that winds for 2 miles past salt marshes to Wingaersheek Beach.

3. Bear right for 0.4 mile to fork where Conomo Point Road (unmarked) bears right.

4. Bear left for 0.6 mile to end (Route 133).

5. Right for 1.3 miles to Southern Avenue on left. It's shortly after Grove Street, also on left.

You'll pass Farnham's on your right; this is a well-known restaurant specializing in clams. When you get to Southern Avenue, the ride turns left, but if you go straight for 0.5 mile, you'll come to the center of Essex, where you can browse through several antiques shops and visit the fascinating Essex Shipbuilding Museum.

6. Left for 4.1 miles to end (Route 127), in the center of Manchester. You'll pass a handsome stone church on your right as you start to come into the town.

7. Turn left on Route 127. Just ahead it jogs right and immediately left. At this point go straight across railroad tracks onto Beach Street for 0.4 mile to crossroads at top of hill (Masconomo Street). Just past the tracks on your right is a little park overlooking Manchester Harbor.

8. Turn right on Masconomo Street. Just ahead is a fork. Bike along each branch until the road becomes private, then backtrack to Beach Street. The right-hand branch leads 0.5 mile to a fine view of Manchester Harbor, and the left-hand branch winds 0.6 mile to Lobster Cove, a small inlet bound by rocky headlands.

9. Right for 0.2 mile to end, at Singing Beach.

10. Make a U-turn and go 0.7 mile back to Route 127 (Summer Street on right).

11. Right for 1.6 miles to Ocean Street on rightr, at bottom of short hill.

12. Right for 0.9 mile to end (Route 127 again). You'll go along two little coves—the first one is called White Beach, the second one Black Beach.

13. Right for 0.4 mile to Raymond Street (unmarked), which bears right (sign may say TO MAGNOLIA).

14. Bear right for 0.5 mile to crossroads with tall streetlight in the middle. This is Magnolia, which is part of Gloucester.

15. Turn 90 degrees right onto Shore Road, following the ocean on your right. Go 0.7 mile to end (merge right onto a wider road). You will turn sharply left here.

16. Sharp left and just ahead right at crossroads at top of hill (Lexington Avenue). Go less than 0.2 mile to end (Hesperus Avenue, unmarked). You'll go through the Magnolia business district.

17. Right for 1.8 miles to end (Route 127).

After almost 0.7 mile you'll see a small dirt parking lot and metal fence on your right. From here a path leads 0.25 mile to the ocean for the view of Rafe's Chasm. Then you'll pass Hammond Castle on your right 0.5 mile farther on.

18. Right for 0.7 mile to Hough Avenue on right. A sign may say VISITOR INFORMATION.

19. Right for 0.5 mile to stop sign (merge right on Route 127). You'll go through Stage Fort Park, a large oceanfront park.

20. Bear right for 0.2 mile to starting point. (If you continue straight on Route 127, the bridge over the Blynman Canal to Cape Ann is immediately ahead. Just beyond the bridge is the famous statue of the weathered fisherman at the helm of his boat.)

mansion, and an old cemetery filled with weathered slate gravestones dating to 1800 and before. Just south of town is Smith Point, a rockbound, steep-spined peninsula rimmed with mansions of Boston Brahmins and landed gentry. The northern shore of the neck offers fine views of boat-filled Manchester Harbor. As you leave Smith Point you visit Singing Beach, one of the North Shore's finest, a wide, graceful curve of smooth but squeaky (singing) sand with rocky headlands at each end and a succession of mansions gracing the water's edge.

From Manchester you'll follow the coast across the Gloucester town line into Magnolia, a gracious nineteenth-century resort community with a row of smart shops and a delightful lane hugging the shore of the small peninsula on which the village is located. Just up the road a short trail leads to the shore, where you'll get a view of Rafe's Chasm, a spectacular narrow defile in the cliffs rising from the sea about 75 feet deep. A little farther on is one of the North Shore's most distinctive landmarks, the Hammond Museum, often called the Hammond Castle. It is a medieval-style castle, complete with moat and drawbridge, spectacularly located on the oceanfront cliffs. It was built in 1928 by John Hays Hammond, inventor of systems to control the movement of vehicles from a distance by radio and an avid collector of medieval artifacts. Until legislation prohibited the practice, it was fashionable for the wealthy to plunder the European landscape for bits and pieces of old castles and palaces, which is exactly what Hammond did to construct his own. Inside is a fascinating collection of medieval furniture, tapestries, armor, and other relics. The centerpiece of the castle is a magnificent organ with more than 8,000 pipes, on which concerts are given during the summer. From behind the building you can see Normans Woe, the offshore rocks made famous by Longfellow's poem "The Wreck of the Hesperus."

From the Castle it's about 2 miles to the canal separating Cape Ann from the mainland, where the ride starts. Just before the canal is Stage Fort Park, a dramatic oceanfront expanse that's worth exploring.

Rockport Harbor with the peak-roofed building that is referred to as Motif Number One

Cape Ann:
Gloucester–Rockport

Number of miles:	27 (11 with East Gloucester area only, 20 with shortcut from Rockport)
Terrain:	Gently rolling, with a few short hills.
Food:	Numerous groceries and snack bars along the way.
Start:	Junction of Routes 127 and 133 in Gloucester, just west of the bridge over the Blynman Canal. Park on Route 127 on the ocean side of the road.
Caution:	On good weekend days, Cape Ann is crowded with people and traffic. It's not much of a hazard because it won't be moving much faster than you. The main hazards are car doors opening into your path, drivers pulling out in front of you without looking, and having your bike stolen. Don't leave your bike unlocked, and if you leave it, take your accessories with you (pump, handlebar bag, tools, and the rest).

You've probably been to Cape Ann. If you haven't, everything you've heard about it is true. It's one of the most popular places to visit in the state, and with good reason. Nowhere else on the coast do four distinct elements—a working fishing port; historic communities filled with graceful, well-maintained old buildings; a glorious coastline with

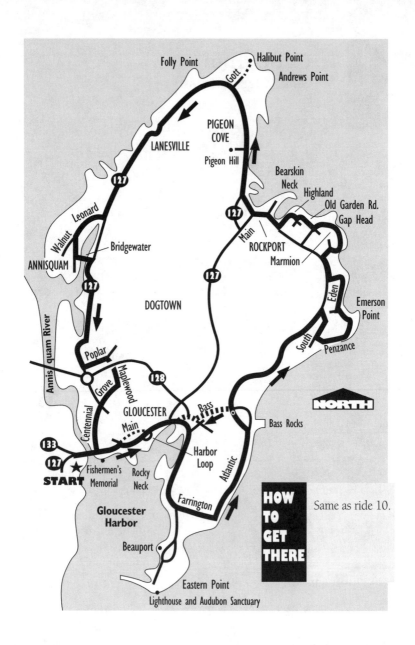

Folly Point

Halibut Point

Andrews Point

Gott

PIGEON COVE

LANESVILLE

Pigeon Hill

Bearskin Neck

Highland

Old Garden Rd.

127

Gap Head

Main

ROCKPORT

Walnut

Leonard

127

Bridgewater

ANNISQUAM

127

Marmion

127

DOGTOWN

Eden

Emerson Point

Annisquam River

South

Penzance

Poplar

Maplewood

128

Grove

GLOUCESTER

Bass

NORTH

Centennial

Main

Bass Rocks

Harbor Loop

Atlantic

133

Rocky Neck

127

★

Fishermen's Memorial

Farrington

START

Gloucester Harbor

Beauport

HOW TO GET THERE

Same as ride 10.

Eastern Point

Lighthouse and Audubon Sanctuary

DIRECTIONS
FOR
THE RIDE

1. Head east on Route 127 over the bridge. Stay on Route 127 for 0.6 mile to Harbor Loop on right. The Fishermen's Memorial statue is on your right just beyond the bridge.

2. Right for 0.25 mile to end (Route 127 again). This is a small loop closer to the harbor.

3. Right for 0.5 mile to fork at yield sign (Route 127 bears left).

4. Bear right and just ahead bear right uphill at traffic light on East Main Street. Stay on main road for 1.1 miles to Rocky Neck Avenue on right (sign may say TO ROCKY NECK ART COLONY). You'll follow the harbor on your right.

5. Right for 0.4 mile to end, and then backtrack to main road. The small Rocky Neck peninsula is the center of the Gloucester art colony.

6. Right for 0.5 mile to a smaller road that bears right along the water through a pair of stone pillars.

Here the ride bears left, but if you bear right and go 0.6 mile, the Beauport mansion is on your right. Just past the mansion, a private road continues 0.6 mile to the Eastern Point Audubon Sanctuary and the Coast Guard station just beyond it at the tip of the peninsula. People are allowed to use the road to get to the Audubon Sanctuary. **CAUTION:** Watch for speed bumps.

On summer weekends, a guard may be stationed at the beginning of the road leading to the Beauport mansion. If you are stopped, say that you are going to the Audubon Sanctuary and the guard will wave you through.

7. Bear left for 2.7 miles to crossroads and stop sign at bottom of hill (Bass Avenue). You'll pass a graceful stone church on your right at the beginning; then you'll enjoy a spectacular ride along the ocean. At Bass Avenue the 11-mile ride turns left.

8. Go straight and stay on main road for 2.8 miles to South Street, which turns sharply right at traffic island. It's at the top of a long, gradual hill.

9. Sharp right for 0.4 mile to Penzance Road on left, just before ocean.

10. Turn left and stay on main road for almost 0.9 mile to Eden Road on right. (Don't go straight on dead-end road after 0.6 mile.)

11. Right along ocean for 0.8 mile to end (Route 127A). **CAUTION:** The first half of Eden Road is very bumpy; slow down and enjoy the scenery.

12. Right for 0.3 mile to Marmion Way on right.

13. Turn right and stay on main road for 0.9 mile to small crossroads midway up a hill (Richards Avenue on left, Old Garden Road on right). You'll pass an old radio tower on your right.

14. Right for 0.4 mile to crossroads and stop sign (Highland Avenue).

15. Right for 0.3 mile to end (Route 127A). On your right is tiny Rockport Harbor. The small red wooden building on the opposite shore with the peaked roof is Motif Number One, one of the most frequently painted places in the country.

16. Turn right. After 0.2 mile the road widens into Dock Square and a narrow lane turns right onto Bearskin Neck. This is the heart of Rockport. On a nice day you'll have to walk your bike through the throngs of tourists swarming amid the clutter of craft shops, boutiques, and ice cream stands.

17. From Bearskin Neck, continue on the main road for 0.2 mile to fork where Main Street bears left and Beach Street bears right. Here the ride bears right, but you can cut it short to 20 miles by bearing left for 0.3 mile to stop sign and then going straight on Route 127 for about 3.5 miles back to Gloucester.

18. Bear right for 0.4 mile to stop sign (merge right onto Route 127).

19. Bear right for 1.8 miles to Gott Avenue (unmarked) on right. Route 127 curves left at the intersection, and a sign may point right TO STATE PARK.

After 0.6 mile you'll see Landmark Lane on your left. This road climbs a steep hill with a broad, grassy park at the top and a magnificent view of Rockport and the surrounding coastline. To visit Halibut Point, turn right on Gott Avenue and just ahead left on footpath for 0.4 mile to ocean.

20. Continue on Route 127 for 2.9 miles to Leonard Street on right, im-

mediately before church on right. (Sign may say TO ANNISQUAM VILLAGE.)

21. Right for 0.4 mile to fork (Walnut Street bears right uphill). You are now entering Annisquam.

22. Bear left downhill for 0.2 mile to Bridgewater Street (unmarked) on left, immediately after Rogers Lane on right.

23. Turn left on Bridgewater Street. You'll immediately come to a footbridge that crosses Lobster Cove. The ride crosses the bridge, but if you wish, you can make a small clockwise loop by turning right at the bridge, following the cove on your left. Go 0.3 mile to end (Leonard Street) and turn right for less than 0.2 mile to Bridgewater Street on right.

24. Cross the footbridge. At the far end of the bridge, continue 100 feet to end (merge right on Route 127).

25. Bear right for 2.4 miles to Poplar Street on left, at blinking light immediately before rotary.

26. Left for 0.4 mile to Maplewood Avenue on right. The main road bears left at the intersection.

If you're adventurous, you can visit Dogtown, the wooded, uninhabited interior of Cape Ann, which is dotted with cellar holes of eighteenth-century dwellings. To get there, turn left on Cherry Street just before Maplewood Avenue. Go 0.7 mile to a lane bearing right up a steep hill, and follow the lane until it becomes dirt. A mazework of paths weaves through the scrubby, rolling landscape. It's very easy to get lost.

27. Right for 0.2 mile to second crossroads (Grove Street), just before an old factory on left.

28. Turn right and stay on main road for 0.3 mile to end, following cemetery on left.

29. Jog left and immediately right on Centennial Avenue for 0.6 mile to end (Route 127). **CAUTION:** Bumpy railroad bridge at the beginning. You'll enjoy a fast descent near the end.

30. Right across bridge back to starting point.

Directions for shorter ride

1. Follow directions for the long ride through number 7.
2. Left for 0.5 mile to traffic light where Route 128 turns right.
3. Straight for 0.3 mile to fork at top of hill (Main Street, unmarked, bears right).
4. Bear right for 0.6 mile until you merge right on Route 127. **CAUTION:** Watch for traffic and pedestrians.

You'll go through downtown Gloucester. If you wish, you can turn right on Pleasant Street and then take your next left on Middle Street, which goes past the Victorian city hall and other old buildings.

5. Straight for 0.4 mile back to starting point, just beyond bridge.

---

dozens of picturesque coves, rocky headlands and curving beaches; and a major artists' colony and crafts center—blend into such a thoroughly appealing and satisfying composite. And the only way to fully experience it—to smell the sweet, freshly caught fish; to feel the power of surf crashing against rocks; to let the impression of each mansion and each little cove and beach imprint itself on your mind—is to tour it on a bicycle.

Much of Cape Ann's unique charm stems from its refreshingly unspoiled condition despite the annual onslaught of millions of visitors. Except for a couple of ugly motels on the East Gloucester shore and the cutesy-fake strip of shops on Bearskin Neck in Rockport, you will see none of the unsightly commercial development and ripoff tourist traps that mar so many other naturally beautiful areas across the country. No sleazy fast-food joints or shabby rows of beach cottages despoil the shore; instead you'll find gracious older homes, delightful old villages gracing the inlets and hillsides along the Cape's northern shore, and sometimes nothing manmade at all.

To fully enjoy the trip, pick a comfortable day, ideally not on a weekend, and take the whole day to find out what Cape Ann has to offer. Explore the historic old center of Gloucester, visit the forty-room

Lobsterman's cottage in Rockport

Beauport mansion, poke around the art galleries on Rocky Neck, walk out to tips of land like the breakwater at the end of Eastern Point or rockbound Halibut Point at the northern extremity of the cape. When you get back to Gloucester, step onto the old wharves and watch the day's catch being unloaded. Don't try to rush—Cape Ann is too special for that.

You'll circle the cape in a counterclockwise direction, heading first by the famous Fishermen's Memorial, a statue of the hardy fisherman gripping the helm of his boat. It was erected in 1923 during Gloucester's tricentennial. You'll go along the wharves and by fish-processing plants lining the inner harbor. The old center of town, just off the route a couple of blocks inland from the harbor, is worth a look. The graceful Victorian town hall, built in 1871, and the handsome library are New England classics. Also gracing downtown are several fine churches and elegant old homes.

You'll now head down to Eastern Point, the estate-lined peninsula forming the southern tip of Cape Ann. First you'll visit Rocky Neck, center of the artists' colony. A mile farther down is Beauport, one of the state's most impressive mansions. Its forty rooms overflow with antiques and decorative artwork from every period of American history. It was the home of Henry Davis Sleeper, a prominent interior designer and antique collector early in the century. Maintained by the Society for the Preservation of New England Antiquities, it is unfortunately not open on weekends except in September and October, and then only in the afternoon. It's open on weekdays all day from May through October.

At the southern end of Eastern Point is an Audubon sanctuary, a Coast Guard station, a graceful old lighthouse, and a half-mile-long breakwater extending nearly halfway across the entrance to Gloucester Harbor. You'll now head up the eastern shore of the Cape, hugging the ocean on one of the finest coastal roads in the state. As you proceed to Rockport you'll go inland just a bit, then hug the shore again on little lanes.

Rockport is visually a delight, with the tiny boat-clogged harbor, complete with Motif Number One, the red fishing shack that has long been a favorite subject for painters and photographers. Even the cutesy gift shops look properly old and weathered from the back. The gently curving beach, with the graceful churches and old white houses of the town stretching behind it, is delightful. A mile north of Rockport you can climb 200-foot-high Pigeon Hill for a magnificent view of the town. Just ahead is Halibut Point, the northern tip of Cape Ann, an impressive spot where the surf washes onto broad, flat rocks. It's maintained by our old friends, the Trustees of Reservations.

Beyond Halibut Point you'll cross the town line back into Gloucester and go through a string of unspoiled little villages—Lanesville, Bay View, Annisquam, and Riverdale. From here it's a short distance back to the starting point with the best descent of the ride.

Ipswich Ride

Number of miles:	21 (11 with Crane Beach section only, 11 with Great Neck section only)
Terrain:	Flat, with a tough climb to the Crane estate on Castle Hill and a couple of short, steep hills on Great Neck.
Food:	Stores and restaurants in the center of Ipswich. The local specialty is clams. Cider doughnuts, other homemade pastries, and fresh cider in the fall at Goodale Orchards.
Start:	Municipal parking lot behind the business block at Route 1A and Topsfield Road in downtown Ipswich. Entrance is on Hammatt Street, which is off Route 1A, 1 block north of Topsfield Road. Some parking spots are restricted. You can also park on Hammatt Street.

Ipswich ranks as one of the most beautiful towns in the state, both architecturally and geographically. If you're a historic-house enthusiast, you'll exult: The town has more pre-Revolutionary homes—some going back to the 1600s—than any other locale north of Williamsburg, Virginia. Beyond the center of town is an unspoiled mixture of wooded hills; broad, gently rolling horse farms and gracious country estates; vast salt marshes stretching to the horizon; the Great Neck peninsula rising

DIRECTIONS
FOR
THE RIDE

1. Right on Hammatt Street to end (Route 1A).
2. Right for 0.4 mile to where the main road curves sharply right.

After 0.1 mile you will cross the Ipswich River over the Choate Bridge, built in 1764. This graceful stone arch is one of the oldest bridges in the country. At the sharp curve the John Whipple House, a fine example of Colonial architecture, is on your right. Built in 1640, it has numerous period furnishings and an herb garden. Across the road is the Thomas Franklin Waters Memorial, a Federal-era mansion with articles from the China trade and a carriage collection. Both buildings are open to visitors.

At the intersection the long ride curves right, but to do only the Great Neck section (11 miles) go straight on Poplar Street (**CAUTION** here). Go 0.1 mile to first left (Turkey Shore Road) and resume with direction number 12.

3. Curve right and just ahead turn left on Argilla Road. Go 0.5 mile to Heartbreak Road on right.
4. Right for 0.7 mile to end (Route 133).
5. Left for 1.1 miles to Northgate Road on left (sign says TO CASTLE HILL, CRANE BEACH).
6. Left for 0.7 mile to end (Argilla Road again, unmarked).
7. Right for 2.4 miles to the entrance to Crane Beach. You'll pass Goodale Orchards on the right after 0.3 mile. The entrance fee for bicycles is reasonable and also grants admission to Castle Hill.
8. Leaving Crane Beach, backtrack 0.25 mile to the entrance to Castle Hill on right.

The climb to the top is unquestionably worth the effort. You'll be rewarded by the view of the mansion along the smooth lawn, called the Grand Allee, which undulates between two groves of trees in a rippling green ribbon for nearly 0.5 mile between the mansion and the cliff overlooking the ocean. From the edge of the cliff, a panorama of sea, marsh,

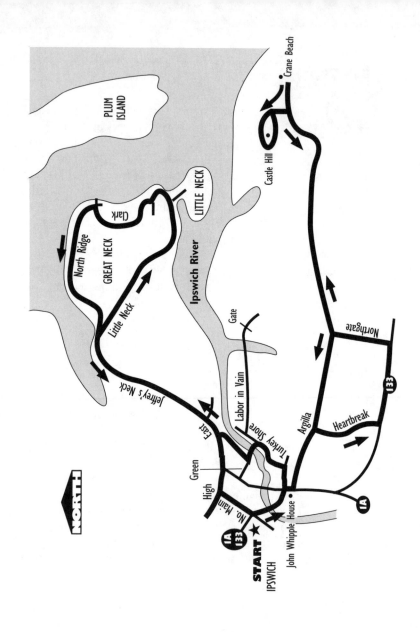

and dune spreads before you. At the far end of the lawn, a path on the right leads down to (accurately named) Steep Beach.

9. From Castle Hill, stay on the main road for 4 miles to end (Routes 1A and 133).

10. Right for 100 yards to Poplar Street on right. Here the long ride turns right, but to do only the Crane Beach section (11 miles), curve sharply left on main road for 0.5 mile to Hammatt Street on left, and left to parking lot just ahead on left.

11. Right for 0.1 mile to Turkey Shore Road on left.

12. Left for 0.25 mile to the first left (Green Street, unmarked), which crosses the Ipswich River.

Here the ride turns left, but if you wish, you can continue straight for 0.9 mile to a rustic, arched bridge over an inlet—it's a delightful spot. (Shortly after Green Street, the main road turns 90 degrees right at stop sign onto Labor in Vain Road.)

13. Left and just ahead right on Water Street at the far side of the bridge. Go 0.4 mile to the far end of the parking lot for the town wharf.

14. Jog left and then immediately right onto the main road. Stay on main road for 1.8 miles to fork (North Ridge Road bears left).

15. Bear right and stay on main road for 1.4 miles to fork where the right-hand branch goes over a causeway. (Don't go straight up steep hill after 0.5 mile.)

On the far side of the causeway is Little Neck, a drumlin with older summer homes. This area is private.

16. Bear left for 0.2 mile to fork where Bayview Road bears left and Clark Road bears right. The land across the bay is the southern tip of Plum Island.

17. Bear right for 0.8 mile to Colby Road (unmarked) on left, just after Skytop Road on left. The large concrete building on the top of the hill is an Air Force installation.

18. Left for 1 mile to yield sign (merge right just past bottom of hill).

19. Bear right for 2.1 miles to East Street on right, immediately after Spring Street on right. You'll pass the town wharf on the left shortly before the intersection.

20. Bear right for 0.5 mile to a cemetery on your right that rises in terraces up a steep hillside. East Street becomes High Street, the heart of Old Ipswich, with most of the houses predating 1800.

21. At the cemetery make a U-turn and backtrack 0.3 mile to North Main Street (unmarked) on right at small brick traffic island. It's the third right.

22. Right for 0.3 mile to crossroads and stop sign at bottom of hill (Routes 1A and 133).

Notice the varied old buildings lining both sides of the green. The modern church in the center of the green, clashing with all the architecture surrounding it, comes as a surprise. It was built to replace a classic New England church that burned to the ground in 1965 after being struck by lightning.

23. Right and just ahead left on Hammatt Street. Parking lot is just ahead on left.

---

steeply from the bay; and magnificent 4-mile-long Crane Beach, New England's finest beach north of Cape Cod.

The ride starts from the center of Ipswich, lying between two greens and surrounded by a marvelous variety of buildings, all painstakingly restored and maintained, that span every architectural style from early Colonial days to 1900. You'll head first to Crane Beach through an idyllic landscape of salt marshes, horse paddocks, and estates. The majestic Crane mansion, resembling a palace from the Italian Renaissance, crowns Castle Hill near the beach. The wide beach is unique in that it is almost completely unspoiled—no hot dog stands, no cottages, no anything except sand, dunes, and lots of people on a hot day. The beach and the Castle Hill estate are owned by the Trustees of Reservations.

From Crane Beach you'll return to the center of town and then head through an endless expanse of salt marshes to the Great Neck peninsula, just north of Crane Beach. Rising steeply from the bay as a succession of four round drumlins, the peninsula is bordered by salt marshes on the west, the broad Plum Island Sound on the north, the southern tip of Plum Island on the east, and Crane Beach on the south. The roads rimming the peninsula offer spectacular views of this unique seascape. From Great Neck you return through the salt marshes to Ipswich.

13 Newburyport–Newbury–Rowley

Number of miles:	22 (17 without western loop)
Terrain:	Gently rolling, with one hill.
Food:	Grocery and snack bar in Rowley.
Start:	Rupert A. Nock Middle School, on Low Street in Newburyport. It's between Johnson Street and Toppans Lane.

This ride takes you exploring among the broad salt marshes, prosperous farmland, and gracious estates just inland from the coast south of Newburyport. You'll pass imposing mansions built by sea captains and merchants in Newburyport and also Governor Dummer Academy, one of the oldest preparatory schools in the country. The area abounds with country roads that promise relaxed and delightful biking.

Situated at the mouth of the Merrimack River, Newburyport became a thriving shipbuilding community during the 1700s and then evolved as a commercial center. The most successful sea captains and merchants built elegant mansions along a 2-mile stretch of High Street, which you'll go along at the beginning of the ride.

The downtown and waterfront areas, lying just off the route between High Street and the river, have been restored and are worth exploring. Gracious brick buildings from the Federal era line State Street, the main downtown street. At the base of State Street, next to the river, is Market Square, where the old brick mercantile buildings have been recycled into a mini-mall of antiques shops, galleries, and craft shops. The result is tasteful rather than touristy. The library, built in 1771, is an especially fine building, as is the stately granite Custom House, built in 1835 and

1. Right on Low Street for 0.2 mile to traffic light (Hale Street on left, Toppans Lane on right).

2. Right for 0.4 mile to end (Route 113).

3. Right for 1.9 miles to traffic light immediately after Newbury town green on right (Rolfes Lane on left, Hanover Street on right).

As you're going along, notice the numerous mansions built by the sea captains and merchants. Cushing House, at 98 High Street, is open to the public. Just beyond Route 1 you'll pass the stately Bulfinch-designed courthouse and the old granite jail. A few blocks to your left are the downtown and waterfront. Also notice the fine yellow school on your left opposite the Newbury town green.

4. Right for less than 0.2 mile to fork (Green Street bears left).

5. Bear left for 0.9 mile to end (Hay Street, unmarked) at grassy traffic island.

6. Right for 0.8 mile to Newman Road (unmarked) on left, just after small bridge. **CAUTION:** Bumpy sections.

7. Left across salt marsh for 1.1 miles to crossroads (Route 1A). Just before Route 1A you'll come to Old Town Hill on the left, maintained by the Trustees of Reservations. The view from the top is the scenic highlight of the ride.

8. Right for 4.1 miles to traffic light in the center of Rowley (Hammond Street on left, Church Street on right). Here the short ride turns right. You'll cross the Parker River just after you start down Route 1A.

9. Straight for 0.2 mile to Summer Street (unmarked), which bears right at the town green. The graceful town hall is on your left at the intersection.

10. Bear right for 0.4 mile to end (Bradford Street).

11. Left for 0.2 mile to yield sign (merge right on Route 133).

12. Bear right for 1.1 miles to traffic light (Route 1).

13. Straight for 0.8 mile to Daniels Road on right (sign may say ROWLEY COUNTRY CLUB).

HOW TO GET THERE

If you're heading north on I–95, take the Scotland Road exit (exit 56). Turn right on Scotland Road for 3 miles to end (Low Street), and left for 0.2 mile to school on right. If you're heading south, exit east from I–95 onto Route 113 (take exit 57). Go 0.3 mile to Low Street (unmarked) on right, at traffic light. Turn right on Low Street and go 1.3 miles to school on left, just past traffic light.

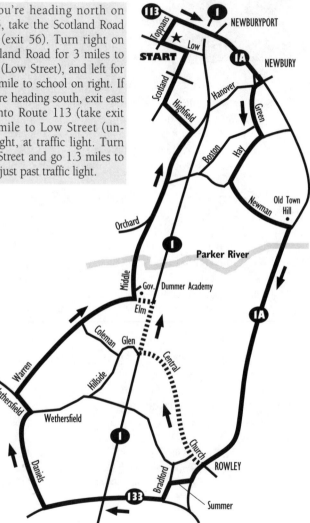

14. Right for 1.5 miles to Wethersfield Street on left at traffic island. It's shortly after Long Hill Road, which turns sharply left.

15. Left for 0.4 mile to second right, Warren Street.

16. Right for 0.9 mile to yield sign (merge right).

17. Bear right for 1.7 miles to crossroads (Old Road on right, Middle Road on left). The buildings of Governor Dummer Academy cluster around the intersection.

18. Turn left and stay on main road for 2.9 miles to Highfield Road on left. (Don't bear right on Boston Road, unmarked, after 2.1 miles). **CAUTION:** The first 0.5 mile of Middle Road is very bumpy and needs to be repaved.

19. Left for 0.7 mile to end (Scotland Road, unmarked).

20. Right for 1.1 miles to end (Low Street).

21. Left for 0.2 mile to school on right.

Directions for shorter ride

1. Follow directions for the long ride through number 8.

2. Turn right and just ahead merge right at stop sign on Central Street (unmarked). Go 2 miles to crossroads and stop sign (Route 1).

3. Right for 0.6 mile to Elm Street (unmarked) on left at blinking light (sign may say GOVERNOR DUMMER ACADEMY).

4. Left for 0.2 mile to crossroads (Middle Road on right), just beyond the footbridge. The buildings of the Governor Dummer Academy are on both sides of the road.

5. Follow directions for the long ride from number 18 to the end, turning right on Middle Road instead of left.

---

now a maritime museum. Adjoining the downtown are narrow streets lined with old wooden homes.

Just south of Newburyport is Newbury, a small town consisting mainly of salt marshes and farmland. In the village center are several historic homes from the 1600s and 1700s. Just outside town you'll pass

Old Town Hill, a small glacial drumlin rising 170 feet above the Parker River. Maintained by the Trustees of Reservations, it offers an outstanding view of the Parker River, Plum Island, and the broad estuary separating it from the mainland.

From Newbury you'll head along Route 1A past broad salt marshes and well-kept farms to Rowley, an attractive small town with several antiques shops and even an antiques flea market. As numbered routes go, Route 1A is one of the best in the state for bicycling—smooth, flat, not heavily traveled, and with a good shoulder. In Rowley you'll head inland, and after a few miles you'll go through the gracious campus of the Governor Dummer Academy, founded in 1763. The return to Newburyport leads along country lanes as you follow the Parker River a short distance, cross it, and proceed past stately old farmhouses and immaculate fields.

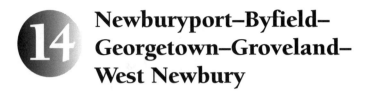

Newburyport–Byfield–Georgetown–Groveland–West Newbury

Number of miles:	28 (18 without Byfield–Georgetown–Groveland extension)
Terrain:	Rolling, with one tough hill. The long ride has an additional steep hill.
Food:	Grocery in Byfield. Grocery and snack bar in Georgetown. Grocery in West Newbury.
Facilities:	Rest rooms at Maudslay State Park.
Start:	Rupert A. Nock Middle School, on Low Street in Newburyport. It's between Johnson Street and Toppans Lane.

This is a tour of the delightfully rolling, prosperous farm country on the southern side of the Merrimack Valley along the river's lower reaches. The area has a succession of gently rounded hills with broad fields sweeping up and over them. Near the end you'll parallel the wide Merrimack River, curving between the hillsides with farms and estates on its banks, along a narrow rural lane. You will pass Maudslay State Park, one of the state's newest and most glorious. It was formerly the 476-acre estate of financial baron F. S. Moseley (Maudslay is the ancestral English spelling). The river is refreshingly undeveloped along its easternmost section between Haverhill and Newburyport. The long ride dips farther south into a more wooded area to the old town of Georgetown and then back north to the handsome village center of Groveland.

The ride starts from the elegant and historic small city of Newburyport, which became a prosperous shipbuilding and commercial center

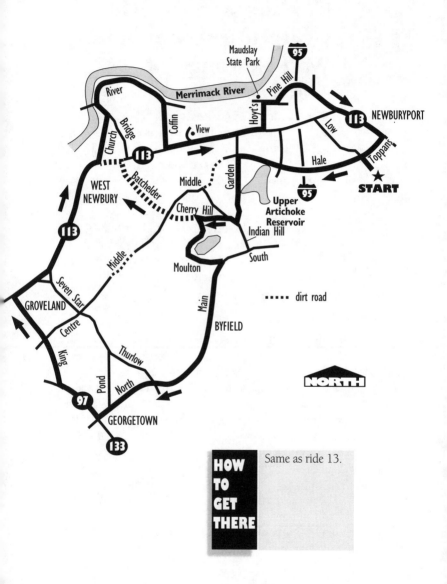

Maudslay
State Park

Merrimack River

River

Bridge

Coffin

View

Church

Pine Hill

Hoyt's

113 NEWBURYPORT

Low

113

Hale

Toppans

★
START

WEST
NEWBURY

Batchelder

Middle

Garden

Upper
Artichoke
Reservoir

113

Cherry Hill

Indian Hill

Middle

Moulton

South

Seven Star

GROVELAND

Centre

King

Thurlow

Pond

North

97

Main

BYFIELD

····· dirt road

GEORGETOWN

133

NORTH

HOW TO GET THERE

Same as ride 13.

DIRECTIONS
FOR
THE RIDE

1. Right on Low Street for 0.2 mile to traffic light (Toppans Lane on right, Hale Street on left).

2. Left for 1.8 miles to unmarked fork immediately after stop sign.

3. Bear right for 1.1 miles to crossroads and stop sign (Garden Street, unmarked). You'll pass the Upper Artichoke Reservoir on your left.

4. Left for 1.1 miles to end.

5. Turn right and just ahead turn left on Cherry Hill Street. Go 0.4 mile to Moulton Street on left. Here the short ride bears right.

6. Left for 1.6 miles to unmarked road on right immediately before large rock on right. It's shortly after Spring Hill Road on right.

7. Turn right and then immediately bear right at end (Main Street, unmarked). Go 4.7 miles to traffic light in the center of Georgetown (Route 97 goes straight and turns right). You'll pass through Byfield, which is part of West Newbury, after 1 mile.

8. Right for 1.1 miles to King Street, which bears right. You'll pass an antiques mall, formerly an old factory, on your right.

9. Bear right for 1.3 miles to crossroads and stop sign (Center Street).

10. Straight for 1.2 miles to end (Route 113), at a little green in the old village center of Groveland. You'll have a steep climb followed by a fast descent.

11. Turn right and stay on main road for 2.9 miles to Church Street on left, at top of hill just beyond traffic light. A sign may say TO ROUTE 110, MERRIMAC. Notice the two churches on your left at the intersection, one on each corner. This is West Newbury.

12. Left for 1 mile to stop sign (merge left on Bridge Street). You'll follow the Merrimack River on your left at the end.

13. Bear left and just ahead turn right on River Road up sharp hill (shift into low gear before the turn). Go 2.1 miles to fork. **CAUTION:** Bumpy sections.

14. Bear right for 0.9 mile to end (Route 113). **CAUTION:** Bumpy sec-

tions. Some of West Newbury's back roads need repaving.

15. Left for 2.2 miles to Hoyt's Lane or Gypsy Lane on left (the sign, visible from the opposite direction, says both names), just before top of hill.

There's a tough hill at the beginning. At the top, stop behind the John C. Page School o\n your left for a superb view of the valley.

16. Left for 0.6 mile to end. At the end, Maudslay State Park is in front of you. It's legal to ride on the network of dirt paths that wind through the park, but it's safer and more relaxing to walk.

17. Turn right (left if you're coming from the park). Stay on main road for 1.8 miles to end, at stop sign (merge head-on onto Route 113).

18. Straight (**CAUTION** here) for 0.9 mile to Toppans Lane on right. It's immediately before the red-brick high school on right and just after house number 249 on right.

19. Right for 0.4 mile to traffic light (Low Street).

20. Turn left, and school is just ahead on left.

Directions for shorter ride

1. Follow directions for the long ride through number 5.

2. Bear right for 2 miles to end (Route 113).

3. Left for 0.5 mile to Church Street on right, just before traffic light. A sign may say TO ROUTE 110, MERRIMAC.

You'll pass the dignified West Newbury town hall and then a graceful brick soldiers' and sailors' memorial hall, both on your left. When you get to Church Street, notice the two churches at the intersection, one at each corner.

4. Right for 1 mile to stop sign (merge left on Bridge Street). You'll follow the Merrimack River on your left at the end.

6. Follow directions for the long ride from number 13 to the end.

during Colonial times. In the first half of the 1800s, the most successful merchants and sea captains built mansions along High Street. The waterfront area and the graceful brick commercial buildings in the downtown section have been restored and are worth visiting after the ride.

Leaving Newburyport, you'll quickly get into open countryside, where large farms expand toward the horizon, and go along the undeveloped Upper Artichoke Reservoir. A quiet back road leads to West Newbury, a handsome town on a hilltop overlooking the river, with two fine churches facing each other at the summit. From here you'll descend to the riverbank and enjoy a delightful ride along its shore on a country lane. The return leg to Newburyport passes farms and estates. You'll go by a large school, formerly the Cardinal Cushing Academy, perched on a hilltop 200 feet above the river. The view from behind the building is outstanding. Maudslay State Park is just ahead.

The long ride heads farther south past the idyllic Moulton Street Reservoir to the small village of Byfield and then on to the handsome crossroads town of Georgetown. Several antiques stores, including a complex with 30 dealers in one building, are in or just outside the center of town. Beyond Georgetown you'll pass through the old center of Groveland, where a white church and stately wooden homes cluster around a small green. After a few miles you'll pick up the short ride in West Newbury.

The Millyard, Amesbury

Whittier Country:
Amesbury–Merrimac–Newton, New Hampshire–Plaistow, New Hampshire–Haverhill

Number of miles:	29 (18 without Newton–Plaistow–Haverhill extension)
Terrain:	Rolling, with several moderate hills.
Food:	Grocery and restaurant in Merrimac. Grocery in Newton, New Hampshire. Burger King 0.4 mile west of starting point on Route 110.
Start:	Cross Roads Plaza, a shopping center on Route 110 in Salisbury, just east of I–95 at the Amesbury town line. If you're heading north on I–495, take exit 55 (Route 110 East) and go one mile to shopping center on right, just past I–95.

This is a tour of the rolling countryside along the north bank of the Merrimack River at the northern tip of the state and extending several miles into New Hampshire. At the end of the ride you'll parallel the river, a broad ribbon winding between gentle green hills, farms, estates, and gracious old homes overlooking its waters. The region is rural and excellent for biking, with a wealth of lightly traveled country roads. Unlike the stretch west of Haverhill, the river is surprisingly undeveloped along its lower reaches, paralleled by very pleasant secondary roads.

The ride starts by going through the lovely old town of Amesbury, with an unusual mixture of old mills and gracious, well-kept residential

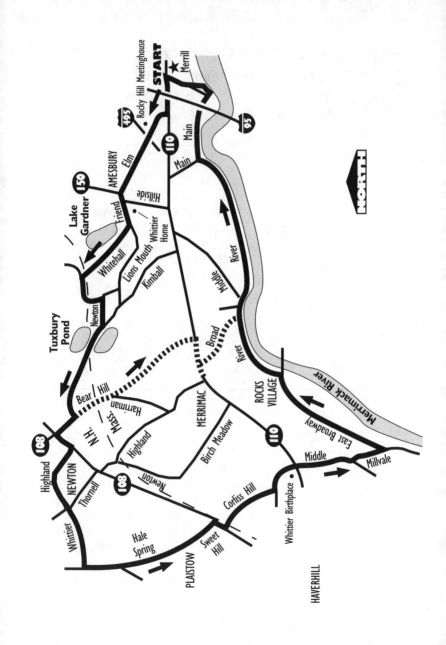

DIRECTIONS

FOR

THE RIDE

1. Right out of the west side of the parking lot, and just ahead turn left (west) at traffic light on Route 110. Go 0.4 mile to traffic light just after the I–95 interchange (Elm Street on right).

2. Right for 1.7miles to yield sign at small round traffic island in the center of Amesbury. After 0.4 mile, immediately before the I–495 overpass, the Rocky Hill Meetinghouse is on your right.

3. Left for 100 yards to Friend Street, which bears right. There's a small park called The Millyard behind the buildings on your right, with a stream tumbling over a dam and beneath a footbridge.

4. Bear right for 0.3 mile to Whitehall Road, which bears right. You'll pass the Whittier home on your left on the corner of Picard Street.

5. Bear right for 1.7 miles to stop sign where the main road turns right and a smaller road turns left. You'll pass Lake Gardner on the right, with Powwow Hill rising sharply behind it.

6. Left for 1.1 miles to Newton Road on right (it's easy to miss). It's 0.3 mile after the entrance to Tuxbury Pond Camping Area on the right.

7. Right for 0.7 mile to end (merge right; no stop sign). Just before the end, there's a fine dam and millpond on your right.

8. Bear right for 2.1 miles to end (Bear Hill Road on left). Here the short ride turns left. You'll follow Tuxbury Pond on your right near the beginning.

9. Right for 0.3 mile to crossroads and blinking light (Route 108 is straight ahead and also on left). There's a grocery just beyond the intersection.

10. Left for 0.6 mile to Highland Street on right, in Newton, New Hampshire.

11. Turn right and stay on main road for 1.8 miles to crossroads and stop sign (West Main Street). There's an attractive old church on your left at the intersection.

12. Straight for 1.8 miles to end.

13. Left for 0.8 mile to fork just beyond railroad bridge (Hale Spring Road bears slightly left).

14. Bear left at fork for 0.3 mile to crossroads and stop sign (Smith Corner Road).

15. Straight for 1.7 miles to end (Route 108).

16. Right for less than 0.2 mile to Corliss Hill Road on left. It's a narrow lane that goes up a steep hill.

17. Left for 1.1 miles to end.

18. Left for 0.4 mile to crossroads (Route 110). Just before the intersection, you'll pass the Whittier birthplace on the right. This old farmhouse is the locale for the poem "Snowbound."

19. Straight (**CAUTION** here—no stop sign) for 1.5 miles to fork (Millvale Road bears slightly left). You'll pass a Jewish cemetery on your left and then a fine old church, dated 1744, on your right.

20. Bear left for 0.7 mile to stop sign (merge right on East Broadway, unmarked). You will turn sharply left here.

21. Turn sharply left. **CAUTION:** Watch for sand. Stay on the main road for 2.7 miles to River Road (unmarked) on left, immediately before the bridge over the Merrimack. There's an old restored fire station on the far left corner. This is Rocks Village, which is part of Haverhill.

22. Left along river for 1.8 miles to fork where Middle Road goes straight and River Road (unmarked here) bears right.

23. Bear right for 3.5 miles to Main Street on right, at stop sign. It's 0.5 mile beyond a Victorian mill on the riverbank, built in 1877.

24. Right along river for 1.1 miles to stop sign just after you go under I–95 (merge right).

25. Bear right and then immediately turn left on Merrill Street (**CAUTION** here). Go 0.4 mile to end (merge right).

26. Bear right for .25 mile to shopping center on right.

Directions for shorter ride

1. Follow directions for the long ride through number 8.

2. Turn left and stay on main road for 3 miles to end (Route 110).

   After 0.7 mile, at the state line, you'll see a granite marker on your left dated 1890. There's a glorious view from the top of the ridge, with glimpses of the Merrimack in the distance.

3. Right for 0.5 mile to Broad Street (unmarked) on left, at bottom of hill (sign says TO I–95).

The Landing School, a one-room schoolhouse built in 1857, is on your right at the intersection. Here the ride turns left, but if you continue straight for 0.1 mile, you'll come to the center of Merrimac. There's a grocery here and a good restaurant if you turn right in the center of town.

4. Left for 1 mile to end.

5. Left along river for 0.1 mile to fork where Middle Road goes straight and River Road (unmarked) bears right.

6. Follow directions for the long ride from number 23 to the end.

---

areas. The handsome nineteenth-century commercial area clusters around a central square. Amesbury is most famous as the longtime home of poet John Greenleaf Whittier, author of "Snowbound" and "Barefoot Boy." You'll bike past his house, which contains his original furnishings and is open to the public. Just outside town is another historic landmark, the Rocky Hill Meetinghouse, a graceful yet simple wooden structure built in 1785. It is maintained by the Society for the Preservation of New England Antiquities and is open by appointment.

Leaving Amesbury, you'll crisscross the Massachusetts–New Hampshire border as you head on to Merrimac, passing between two ponds and then climbing onto an open ridge with a glorious view of the valley. Merrimac is another pleasant town with an ornate brick Victorian town hall, complete with clock tower. From here you'll parallel the river for 5 miles back to Amesbury in a beautiful, relaxing ride.

The long ride heads farther west to the pretty little town of Newton, New Hampshire, typical of the many graceful small communities dotting the southernmost section of that state. A classic white church and old town hall, just off the route, grace the center of town. Beyond Newton you'll wind through forested hills, small farms, and over a ridge with a fine view of the valley. You'll go by Whittier's birthplace in Haverhill and finally arrive at the Merrimack River. For the rest of the ride you'll parallel the river. At first the road is inland just a bit, rolling up and down past gracious estates and gentleman farms, with views of the river from the crest of the hills. After a while the road converges with the riverbank and follows it all the way back to Amesbury, passing through the attractive waterfront villages of Rocks Village and Merrimacport.

16

Middleton–
North Andover–Boxford–
Topsfield

Number of miles:	26 (18 without Middleton–North Andover extension)
Terrain:	Gently rolling, with a couple of short hills.
Road surface:	0.6 mile of dirt road in Middleton on the longer ride.
Food:	Grocery and restaurant in Middleton. Country store in Boxford. Grocery and restaurant in Topsfield.
Start:	Masconomet Regional High School, Endicott Road in Boxford, just east of I–95. Take exit 51. Park at the tennis courts on the east side of the school.

This is a tour of the gently rolling, wooded, and well-to-do communities on the northern edge of the Boston metropolitan area, midway between the city and New Hampshire. The region is rural rather than suburban, with development limited to large, expensive homes on spacious wooded lots. The town centers of Boxford and Topsfield are New England classics.

At the beginning of the ride, you'll bike through Middleton, a relatively undeveloped town consisting primarily of forest and small farms, many with horse paddocks. You'll head along lovely Middleton Pond, completely surrounded by pine groves, and then go through the Harold Parker State Forest, which is located in the southern part of North Andover. You'll bike past two forest-rimmed ponds and then a pleasant mixture of small farms and attractive newer homes set back from the

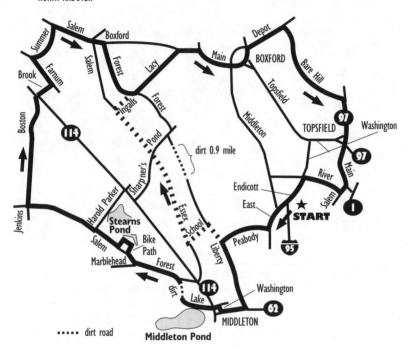

NORTH ANDOVER

Summer
Salem
Boxford
Depot
BOXFORD
Bare Hill
Salem
Forest
Lacy
Main
Brook
Farnum
Topsfield
Middleton
TOPSFIELD
Washington
Boston
114
Forest
Ingalls
Sharpner's Pond
dirt 0.9 mile
97
97
Main
Salem
River
Endicott
East
START
Harold Parker
Stearns Pond
Bike Path
Essex
School
Peabody
95
1
Jenkins
Salem
Marblehead
Forest
Liberty
dirt
Lake
114
Washington
62
MIDDLETON
Middleton Pond

····· dirt road

DIRECTIONS

FOR

THE RIDE

1. Left on Endicott Road for 1.1 miles to Peabody Street on right. You'll cross the Ipswich River shortly before the intersection.

2. Right for 1.2 miles to end (Liberty Street). Here the short ride turns right.

3. Left for 1.3 miles to end (Route 62).

4. Right for less than 0.7 mile to Washington Street on right, just before traffic light.

5. Right and just ahead left at end (Central Street). Go 0.1 mile to traffic light (Route 114) in the center of Middleton. Notice the attractive brick library, built in 1890, on the far left corner.

6. Straight for 1.1 miles to end (Old Forest Street on right). The last 0.6 mile is dirt.

7. Left for 0.2 mile to crossroads at bottom of hill (**CAUTION** here).

8. Left for 1.3 miles to Salem Street (unmarked) on right, just after the North Reading town line (sign may say STATE FOREST).

9. Right for 0.2 mile to a bicycle path on your right. It comes up while you're going down a small hill. The path is blocked off to cars.

10. Right for 0.5 mile to end. The path makes a little loop past Sudden Pond and comes back out on the main road.

11. Right for 1.8 miles to crossroads and stop sign (Jenkins Road). You'll pass the Berry Pond Recreation Area, which has a small beach, on your left toward the end.

12. Right for 1.6 miles to end (merge left on Route 114).

13. Bear left (**CAUTION:** here) and just ahead turn right on Brook Street. Go 0.3 mile to end (Farnum Street, unmarked).

14. Left for 0.6 mile to Summer Street (unmarked), which turns sharply right at yield sign.

15. Sharp right for 1.1 miles to end (Salem Street).

16. Right for 0.8 mile to Forest Street on right, shortly after crossroads.

17. Right for 1.6 miles to fork (Lacy Street bears left).

18. Bear left for 1.7 miles to stop sign (merge right).

19. Bear right for 0.4 mile to end (merge right on Main Street, unmarked, at a little traffic island).

20. Bear right for 0.9 mile to crossroads and stop sign (Middleton Road).

21. Straight for less than 0.4 mile to fork.

22. Bear left for 0.25 mile to crossroads and stop sign (Middleton Road on left, Depot Road on right). This is the center of Boxford. There's a country store on your left just before the intersection.

23. Right for 1.2 miles to Bare Hill Road on right.

24. Right for 2.4 miles to end (Haverhill Road, Route 97).

25. Right for 0.8 mile to the Topsfield town green. When you get to the green, the Parson Capen House is to your left just around the corner.

26. Go straight on Main Street (unmarked); don't bear left on Route 97. Go 0.9 mile to Salem Road on right, just before Route 1.

27. Right and just ahead right again on River Road (unmarked), a narrow lane. Go 1.3 miles to crossroads and stop sign. This is a magnificent ride along the Ipswich River and then past broad fields and estates.

28. Left for 0.5 mile to school on left.

Directions for shorter ride

1. Follow directions 1 and 2 for the long ride.

2. Right for 0.4 mile to School Street on left.

3. Left for 0.8 mile to end (Essex Street).

4. Right for 1.9 miles to crossroads and stop sign (Sharpner's Pond Road).

5. Straight for 1.2 miles to Ingalls Street on right at traffic island with a rock.

6. Right for 0.4 mile to end (Forest Street).

7. Right for 0.2 mile to fork (Lacy Street bears left).

8. Follow directions for the long ride from number 18 to the end.

winding roads on large wooded lots. From North Andover you'll cross into Boxford, a gracious rural community that is one of the North Shore's most affluent suburbs and a paradise for bicycling. The town center is delightful, with a proud old church, a country store, and appealing, rambling wooden homes.

At the end of the ride, you'll pedal through Topsfield, another gracious, moneyed community where biking is a pleasure. The large green, with a stately white church and a marvelous Victorian town hall built in 1873, is one of the finest in the state. Just off the green is the Parson Capen House, built in 1681 and open to visitors. Just outside town you'll go along the Ipswich River and then through majestic estates with broad fields sloping down to the riverbank.

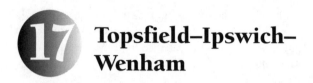

17 Topsfield–Ipswich–Wenham

Number of miles:	24 (12 without Ipswich extension)
Terrain:	Gently rolling.
Food:	Groceries and snack bars in the towns. The local specialty in Ipswich is clams.
Start:	Topsfield Village, a shopping center on Main Street in Topsfield, just south of the green.

This is a tour exploring three elegant old North Shore communities connected by delightful secondary roads winding past horse farms, country estates, and ponds and along the Ipswich River. You start from Topsfield, a handsome town with one of the finest traditional New England centers in the state. The large green is framed by an exceptionally fine classic white church and a marvelous Victorian town hall built in 1873. Adjoining the green is the Parson Capen House, built in 1681 and open to visitors. Topsfield is best known for its two giant annual fairs, the American Crafts Exposition in July and the Topsfield Fair in October. The latter is one of the country's oldest agricultural fairs, running since 1818. Surrounding the town are gentleman farms and estates spreading up rolling hills and the marshes of the Ipswich River, along which is the state's largest Audubon sanctuary.

From Topsfield you'll head through gently rolling farmland to Ipswich, a jewel of a town both geographically and architecturally. It boasts more pre-Revolutionary houses, some going back to the 1600s, than any other place in America north of Colonial Williamsburg. With the continuing efforts of a preservation-conscious citizenry, these buildings have been painstakingly restored and maintained. The center of town lies between a north green and a south green and contains a wonderful mixture of buildings of every architectural style from the early Colonial period to the turn of the century. Many of these houses are open to visitors; if you're a historic-house enthusiast, you can spend the entire day in town. If you want to see just one house, the one to visit is the John Whipple House, built in 1640. It has an herb garden and period furnishings.

The Ipswich River courses through town and passes under the graceful stone-arched Choate Bridge, built in 1764 and one of the oldest original bridges in the country. East of town are vast expanses of salt marsh, the steep-ridged Great Neck Peninsula, and magnificent Crane Beach and Castle Hill, all of which you can explore on the Ipswich ride.

A couple of miles out of town is the entrance to Turner Hill, a grand mansion built in 1903 that is now used for private functions. For many years it was the LaSalette Shrine and Seminary. Unfortunately the area is marked with "No trespassing" signs. Beyond Turner Hill you'll parallel the Ipswich River and wind through carefully maintained horse farms and estates to Wenham, another gracious and moneyed town with a stately white church and old town hall. Shortly before Wenham you'll pass Asbury Grove, a Methodist campground containing small Gothic-style cottages and a central tabernacle. It is similar to Oak Bluffs in Martha's Vineyard but not as extensive or ornamented. Asbury Grove was founded in 1858.

Next to the Wenham town hall is the Claflin-Richards House, built in 1664. It adjoins the Wenham Historical Association and Museum, which maintains a fascinating display of dolls, toys, and games from the 1800s. It's open in the afternoon every day except Saturday. From Wenham it's a short ride back to Topsfield, passing Wenham Lake and rolling, open hillsides.

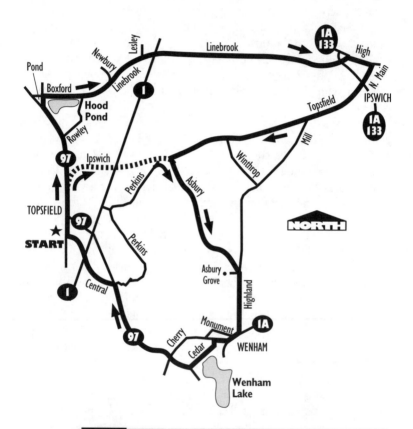

Pond

Boxford

Hood Pond

Newbury

Lesley

Linebrook

Linebrook

I

Linebrook

IA 133

High

N. Main

IPSWICH

IA 133

Topsfield

Rowley

97

Ipswich

Perkins

Winthrop

Mill

Asbury

NORTH

TOPSFIELD

97

★
START

Perkins

I

Central

Asbury
Grove

Highland

97

Cherry

Cedar

Monument

IA

WENHAM

Wenham Lake

HOW TO GET THERE

Take I–95 to the Topsfield Road exit (exit 52). Turn right on Topsfield Road for 1.4 miles (1.6 if you're coming from the north) to High Street Extension, which bears right just before white church. Bear right and just ahead turn right at the crossroads and stop sign. Shopping center is just ahead on right.

DIRECTIONS
FOR
THE RIDE

1. Left (north) on Main Street and just ahead straight on Route 97 at the green. Go 0.4 mile to fork (Route 97 bears left, Ipswich Road bears right). Here the short ride bears right.

The Parson Capen House is immediately north of the green on Howlett Street, the side street on your right running parallel to Route 97. It's a small building with a steeply pitched roof.

2. Bear left for 1.7 miles to Pond Street, a narrow lane that bears right at bottom of hill. It's 0.8 mile beyond Rowley Road, which also bears right.

3. Bear right for less than 0.2 mile to end (Boxford Road).

4. Right for 2.6 miles to traffic light (Route 1), staying on main road. Two smaller roads bear left, but curve right on the main road at both intersections.

You'll ride along Hood Pond on your right at the beginning. Boxford Road becomes Linebrook Road.

5. Go straight and stay on main road for 3.9 miles to diagonal crossroads and stop sign (Route 1A).

6. Straight (**CAUTION** here), passing behind gas station on left. Just ahead turn right at end on High Street (unmarked). Go 0.4 mile to third right (North Main Street, unmarked) at small brick traffic island.

As soon as you turn onto High Street, notice the cemetery on your left rising in terraces up the steep hillside. High Street is the heart of old Ipswich, and most of the houses on the street date to the 1700s.

7. Right for 0.3 mile to crossroads and stop sign at bottom of hill (Routes 1A and 133).

You'll go along Meeting House Green. The modern church in the center, clashing with the early buildings surrounding it, was built to replace the splendid traditional church that burned to the ground in 1965 after it was struck by lightning. It's surprising that this preservation-minded and history-conscious town did not rebuild the church to resemble the old one.

8. Go straight (**CAUTION**—busy intersection) and stay on main road for 4.4 miles to Asbury Street on left (sign says BRADLEY PALMER STATE PARK

after you turn left). **CAUTION:** Bad diagonal railroad tracks after 0.2 mile.

After 3 miles you'll follow the Ipswich River on your left and then pass a dam.

9. Left for 2.7 miles to stop sign (merge right on Highland Street, unmarked). This is a pleasant stretch past horse farms and estates.

10. Bear right for 1.4 miles to crossroads and stop sign (Route 1A, Main Street) in the center of Wenham. At the beginning you'll pass Asbury Grove on the right. The center of the campground is set back a quarter-mile from the road.

11. Right for 0.1 mile to second right (Cherry Street, unmarked). You'll pass the town hall and the doll museum on your left.

12. Right for 0.2 mile to Cedar Street on left.

13. Left for 0.9 mile to end (Route 97). You'll pass Wenham Lake on your left.

14. Right for 3.1 miles to diagonal crossroads where Perkins Row turns sharply right and Central Street bears left.

15. Bear left for 0.4 mile to crossroads and stop sign (Route 1). The Topsfield Fairgrounds are to your left on Route 1.

16. Straight for 0.5 mile to end (Main Street, unmarked).

17. Right for 100 yards to shopping center on left.

Directions for shorter ride

1. Follow direction number 1 for the long ride.

2. Bear right for 0.8 mile to traffic light (Route 1).

3. Straight for 1.2 miles to Asbury Street on right (sign says TO BRADLEY PALMER STATE PARK).

4. Right for 2.7 miles to stop sign (merge right on Highland Street, unmarked). This is a pleasant stretch past horse farms and estates.

5. Follow directions for the long ride from number 10 to the end.

Pedaler's Paradise:
North Andover–Boxford

Number of miles:	32 (16 without Boxford extension)
Terrain:	Delightfully rolling, with lots of little ups and downs. There's one hill on the long ride.
Food:	Country store in South Groveland. Country store in Boxford. Country store and ice cream shop in West Boxford.
Start:	Salem Street, Andover, just east of Route 28, adjacent to Phillips Academy. It's 1 mile south of the center of town.

If someone asked you to describe the ideal bike ride, with the limitation that it be in the eastern half of Massachusetts, you'd probably end up describing a ride like this one. Just southeast of Lawrence, on the wealthy, woodsy fringe of Boston suburbia, is a bicyclist's paradise of untraveled and well-paved country lanes, gentleman farms, lakeside runs with manicured estates sloping down to the shore, and a couple of graceful, unspoiled New England town centers with stately old homes and picket fences. You might also have mentioned pedaling along the oceanfront with crashing surf but sorry—you can't have everything.

The ride starts next to Phillips Academy, the classic New England preparatory school. Its large, impressive campus equals that of any college for elegance. You'll quickly cross the town line into North Andover, a double-faced town. The section closest to Lawrence (which you won't see on the ride) is a congested area of housing developments and industrial parks; everything else is a beautiful mixture of estates, woods, and

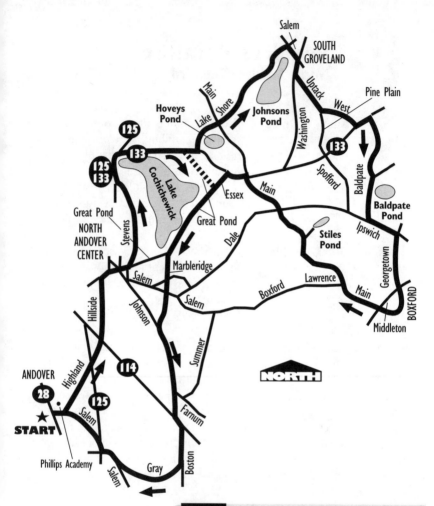

HOW TO GET THERE

If you're heading north on I–93, exit north onto Route 125 for 2.3 miles, and then exit north onto Route 28. Go about 3 miles to Salem Street on right, at traffic light. There's a tall brick tower at the intersection.

DIRECTIONS
FOR
THE RIDE

1. Head east on Salem Street (away from Route 28) and just ahead turn left at crossroads on Highland Road. Go 1.3 miles to diagonal crossroads and stop sign (Route 125).

2. Straight onto Hillside Road, a dead-end road. **CAUTION** crossing Route 125. Go less than 0.2 mile to the dead end. The end of Route 114 is in front of you on the far side of a small grassy field.

3. Walk about 100 feet across the field. Go straight (**CAUTION** crossing Route 114) for 1.3 miles to stop sign (merge right).

Stevens-Coolidge Place, an early nineteenth-century house with lovely gardens open to the public, is on the far side of the intersection. It's maintained by the Trustees of Reservations.

4. Bear right and just ahead bear right again at fork, passing a large green on your left. Go 0.2 mile to stop sign, at a five-way intersection.

There's a magnificent church on the far left corner. This is the lovely village of North Andover Center.

5. Go straight and just ahead bear left at fork on Stevens Street. Go 0.4 mile to fork (Pleasant Street bears left).

6. Bear right (still Stevens Street) for 1.1 miles to second stop sign (merge right on Routes 125 and 133). You'll pass Stevens Pond on your right at the beginning.

7. Bear right for 0.6 mile to where Route 125 goes straight and Route 133 (Great Pond Road) bears right. **CAUTION:** The last 0.2 mile is an undivided 4-lane road. Ride toward the middle of the right lane, so that traffic coming up behind you will pass you in the next lane to your left.

8. Bear right along Lake Cochichewick. Go 1.4 miles to diagonal crossroads where Bradford Street turns left and Great Pond Road bears right. Here the short ride bears right.

9. Straight for 0.3 mile to Lake Shore Road (unmarked) on left at a traffic island immediately after crest of hill.

10. Left (**CAUTION** here) for 2.9 miles to second crossroads and stop sign (Salem Street, unmarked). **CAUTION:** Bumps and potholes on the last

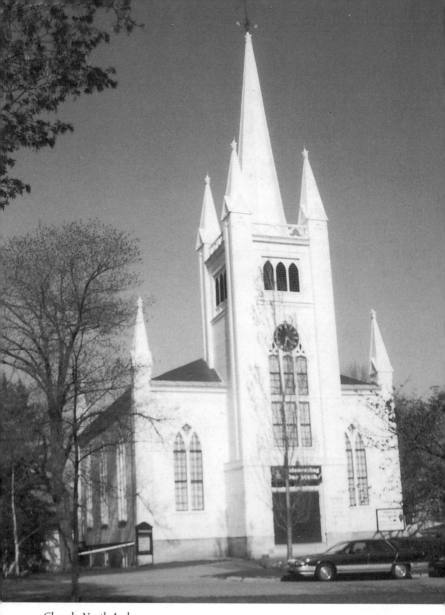

Church, North Andover

mile. You'll pass Hovey's Pond on your right near the beginning and go along Johnsons Pond toward the end.

11. Right for 0.3 mile to crossroads (Washington Street), in South Groveland.

12. Right for 0.3 mile to Uptack Road, a smaller road that bears left.

13. Bear left for 1.3 miles to fork (Pine Plain Road bears right, West Street bears left). You'll climb a tough hill, the worst one on the ride.

14. Bear left for 1 mile to end (Route 133).

15. Left for 0.4 mile to Baldpate Road on right.

16. Right for 1.4 miles to end, at small traffic island (Nelson Street on left). Shortly before the end, at top of hill, you'll see a rambling Victorian mansion on the right. This is Baldpate, a private psychiatric hospital.

17. Right (still Baldpate Road, unmarked) for 1 mile to end (Ipswich Road, unmarked). You'll pass Baldpate Pond on the left.

18. Left for 0.8 mile to crossroads (Georgetown Road). It's just after a small pond on right.

19. Bear right for 1.7 miles to yield sign (merge right). Just before the intersection you'll go through the center of Boxford and pass a country store on the right.

20. Bear right and stay on main road for 4.1 miles to crossroads and stop sign (Ipswich Road). Don't bear left on Lawrence Road after 0.9 mile.

   After 3.2 miles Stiles Pond Road is on your right. If you turn here and follow the paved road for 200 yards, you'll come to the Boxford town beach on your left.

21. Straight for 1 mile to another crossroads and stop sign (Route 133, Washington Street). This is the village of West Boxford.

22. Left for 0.4 mile to Essex Street on left, at traffic island. There is a good ice cream spot on the right at the beginning.

23. Left for 0.4 mile to stop sign at bottom of hill (merge left on Great Pond Road, unmarked).

24. Bear left for 1.6 miles to unmarked fork at traffic islands. (Great Pond Road bears right, Marbleridge Road bears slightly left.) You'll catch glimpses of Lake Cochichewick on your right.

25. Bear slightly left for 0.4 mile to crossroads and stop sign. (Main road bears right.)

26. Go straight (don't bear right) for 0.7 miles to end, going straight at two crossroads.

27. Left for 1 mile to fork where Farnum Street bears left and Johnson Street (unmarked) bears right.

28. Bear right for 0.6 mile to end (Route 114).

29. Left for 0.3 mile to Boston Street, which bears right uphill.

30. Bear right for 0.5 mile to fork (Gray Street bears right).

31. Bear right for 1.1 miles to yield sign (merge right on Salem Street, unmarked).

32. Bear right for 0.4 mile to crossroads and stop sign (Route 125).

33. Right and just ahead left at blinking light (still Salem Street). Go 1 mile back to starting point. **CAUTION:** Bumpy spots.

Directions for shorter ride

1. Follow directions for the long ride through number 8.

2. Bear right for 2.6 miles to unmarked fork at traffic islands. (Great Pond Road bears right; Marbleridge Road bears slightly left.) You'll pass the Brooks School on your right near the beginning.

3. Follow directions for the long ride from number 25 to the end.

---

large, well-landscaped newer homes on good-sized wooded lots. The old center of town is a gem, with a stately old church and a green framed by gracious Colonial-style homes. The centerpiece of the town is Lake Cochichewick, a large, refreshingly unspoiled lake surrounded by estates and wooded hills. You'll parallel the shore and then bike past the Brooks School, another preparatory school with a magnificent campus of graceful white wooden buildings and broad fields sweeping down to the lakefront. The rest of the ride brings you through the better of the town's two faces back to Phillips Academy.

The long ride makes a long loop through Boxford, which is even nicer than North Andover. Boxford epitomizes the gracious, well-to-do suburb that is rural rather than suburban, like the setting for the movie *Ordinary People*. (Funny how those ordinary people didn't have ordinary incomes.) Silk-smooth roads curve past woodlots, horse farms with pastures crisscrossed by rustic white wooden fences, rambling old homes, and impressive new ones harmoniously integrated with the landscape on two- and three-acre forested lots. The center of town is another New England classic, with a fine old church, a country store, and stately old homes. After looping through Boxford you'll pick up the route of the short ride back in North Andover in time to bike along the estate-lined southern shore of Lake Cochichewick.

America's Stonehenge Ride:

Haverhill–Salem, New Hampshire–Hampstead, New Hampshire–Atkinson, New Hampshire

Number of miles:	27 (12 without America's Stonehenge extension)
Terrain:	Rolling, with one tough hill near the beginning.
Food:	None en route for the short ride. Grocery and snack bar in Hampstead. Country store in Atkinson.
Start:	Haverhill High School, at Monument Street and North Broadway. If you're heading north on I–495, take the Route 97–Broadway exit (exit 50). At the end of the exit ramp, go straight onto Monument Street for 0.4 mile to school on right. If you're heading south on I–495, get off at the same exit, turn left at end of ramp onto Route 97 South, cross over highway, and take your first left at traffic light on Monument Street. The school is 0.4 mile ahead on right.

Just northwest of Haverhill, extending several miles into New Hampshire, is a delightful area for bicycling with gentle wooded hills, several lakes, some open hillsides with fine views, and unspoiled small towns. The long ride is highlighted by a visit to America's Stonehenge, formerly called Mystery Hill, a complex of prehistoric stone ruins and monoliths of unknown origin. It is one of the major archaeological sites in the Northeast.

The ride starts on the outskirts of Haverhill, a congested nineteenth-century mill city sloping up the hills on both sides of the Merrimack River. You quickly get into rural countryside as you head into Salem, New Hampshire, and ride along the twisting shore of Arlington Mill Reservoir, lined with older summer cottages nestled among pine groves. In the last thirty years, Salem has become a bedroom suburb of Boston, only forty-five minutes away along I–93, which runs through the middle of the town. The ride explores the section farthest from the highway, still mostly undeveloped.

Shortly beyond the reservoir you'll come to America's Stonehenge. The complex consists of an elaborate pattern of walls, tomblike buildings, wells, drains, remains of buildings, and rocks carved with mysterious inscriptions. Radiocarbon dating has shown the site to be more than 2,000 years old, eliminating the possibility that Indians, colonists, or early European explorers could have constructed it. Around the perimeter of the site, various stones are placed to serve as a giant astronomical calendar, lining up with the North Star, the cycles of the moon, sunrise and sunset on the longest and shortest days of the year, and other celestial phenomena. Some of the inscriptions match those of ancient Celtic tribes, raising the possibility that Europeans may have visited North America even before the Vikings. The most distinctive artifact in the site is a massive grooved stone slab supported on legs, most likely to have been used for sacrifices. America's Stonehenge is privately owned and is the scene of continuing research.

From America's Stonehenge you'll head to Hampstead and Atkinson, two unspoiled little New England towns. At the village crossroads in Hampstead stand the handsome Victorian town hall and a classic white church. Atkinson boasts the Atkinson Academy, a graceful schoolhouse dated 1803. Leaving Atkinson, you'll enjoy a soaring downhill ride. The homestretch back to Haverhill leads along broad, open ridges with sweeping views of the valley.

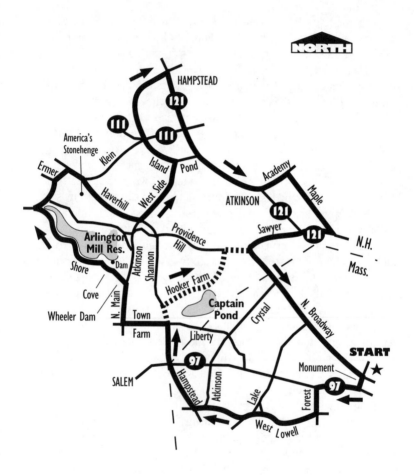

NORTH

HAMPSTEAD

111
121
111

America's
Stonehenge

Klein
Ermer
Haverhill
West Side
Island
Pond
Academy
Maple

ATKINSON

121
Sawyer
121

N.H.
Mass.

Arlington
Mill Res.

Providence
Hill

Atkinson
Shannon
Hooker Farm

Captain
Pond

Crystal

N. Broadway

Shore
Dam

Cove

Wheeler Dam

N. Main
Town
Farm
Liberty

97

START
★

Monument

97

SALEM

Hampstead
Atkinson
Lake
Forest

West Lowell

DIRECTIONS
FOR
THE RIDE

1. Turn left on Monument Street for 0.4 mile to traffic light (Route 97).

2. Right for 0.6 mile to Forest Street (unmarked) on left. There's a long, grassy traffic island at the intersection.

3. Left for 0.5 mile to crossroads and stop sign midway down short hill (West Lowell Avenue, unmarked).

4. Turn right and stay on main road for 1 mile to stop sign at top of hill (merge left). The last 0.6 mile is a steep climb. This is the toughest hill of the ride—don't get discouraged.

5. Bear left for 0.25 mile to another fork where Methuen Road bears left and a smaller road bears right.

6. Bear right for 1.2 miles to crossroads and stop sign (Hampstead Road, unmarked).

7. Right for 1.2 miles to traffic light (Route 97). You cross into Salem, New Hampshire, 100 yards before the light.

8. Straight for 0.6 mile to crossroads (Liberty Street on right, Town Farm Road on left). Here the short ride goes straight.

9. Turn left and stay on main road for 0.8 mile to crossroads and stop sign.

10. Right for 0.6 mile to Wheeler Dam Road on left. You'll pass a grocery on the right.

11. Left for 0.25 mile to fork (Cove Road bears left). Here the ride bears left, but if you bear right for 200 yards, you'll come to Wheeler Dam at the end of the Arlington Mill Reservoir. It's an impressive spot.

12. Bear left and just ahead bear left again at fork at top of hill (Shore Drive bears left). Go 2.6 miles to end, following the shore of the Arlington Mill Reservoir. **CAUTION:** This road is very curvy with potholes, bumps, and sandy spots; take it easy.

13. Right for 0.2 mile to fork (Millpond Road bears right). This is the village of North Salem, New Hampshire.

14. Bear left and stay on main road for 1 mile to end (Haverhill Road). Don't bear left on Ermer Road after 0.6 mile.

15. Right for 0.2 mile to fork where Klein Drive bears left and Haverhill Road bears slightly right.

16. Bear right for 1.3 miles to crossroads (Atkinson Road on right, West Side Road on left). Mystery Hill is on your right after 0.3 mile.

17. Turn left and stay on main road for 1.5 miles to end (Island Pond Road, unmarked).

Here the ride turns left, but you may cut 3.7 miles off the route (bypassing Hampstead) by turning right for 0.25 mile to end (Route 121). Turn right for 1.5 miles to Academy Avenue, which bears left at top of hill in Atkinson (country store on far left corner), and resume with direction 22.

18. Left for 0.8 mile to wide crossroads and stop sign (Route 111).

19. Straight for 1.6 miles to crossroads and blinking light (Main Street, Route 121) in the center of Hampstead. Here the ride turns right, but there's a grocery 50 yards to your left on Route 121. The graceful Victorian town hall is across the road from the grocery.

20. Right for 1.1 miles to Route 111, at traffic light.

21. Straight for 2.1 miles to Academy Avenue, which bears left at top of hill. There's a country store on the far left side of the intersection. This is the village of Atkinson.

22. Bear left for 0.5 mile to crossroads (Maple Avenue). You'll pass the graceful Atkinson Academy on your left.

23. Right for 1.5 miles to end (merge left on Route 121 at bottom of little hill). **CAUTION:** The end comes up suddenly. There's a splendid descent on this stretch—enjoy it! You will turn sharply right at the end.

24. Sharp right for 0.5 mile to Sawyer Avenue, which bears left downhill.

25. Bear left for 1.1 miles to North Broadway on left. (North Broadway also goes straight at the intersection.)

26. Left for 3.5 miles to crossroads and blinking light (Monument Street). **CAUTION:** Potholes and cracks on the first half of this section.

27. Turn left, and the school is just ahead on right.

Directions for shorter ride

1. Follow directions for the long ride through number 8.

2. Straight for almost 0.4 mile to Hooker Farm Road on right.

3. Right for 1.8 miles to end (Providence Hill Road on left). You'll pass Captain Pond on your right.

4. Right for 0.3 mile to North Broadway on right.

5. Right for 3.5 miles to crossroads and blinking light (Monument Street).

6. Turn left, and the school is just ahead on right.

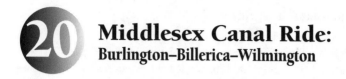

20 Middlesex Canal Ride:
Burlington–Billerica–Wilmington

Number of miles:	24 (15 without Billerica extension)
Terrain:	Rolling, with several short hills and one tough one.
Food:	Groceries and snack bars in the towns.
Start:	Vinebrook Plaza, a small shopping center on Middlesex Turnpike in Burlington, just north of Burlington Mall. There's a Tower Records at the entrance. It's 0.6 mile north of Route 128. Take exit 32B.

On this ride you'll explore three pleasant middle-class communities midway between Boston and Lowell. The region is primarily suburban, interspersed with some wooded stretches and a few small farms. Biking in this area is pleasant if you stay on the secondary roads. This ride features fascinating traces of the Middlesex Canal, which was completed in 1803 to connect Boston with the Merrimack River in Lowell. The canal was the first in the country and sparked the growth of Lowell as an early industrial center. A massive feat of civil engineering for its time, the canal had twenty locks, eight aqueducts, and forty-eight bridges. Today only traces remain, most notably the Shawsheen River Aqueduct, which you'll see on the longer ride. The canal suffered an early death with the completion of the Boston and Lowell Railroad in 1835. It took all day for the small-capacity, horse-drawn towboats to travel the length of the waterway, but the railroad could carry a much larger payload from Lowell to Boston in an hour. By 1850 the canal was virtually unused.

The ride starts by heading north along the ramrod-straight Middlesex Turnpike, sprouting with new, boldly architectured high-technology firms. After crossing Nutting Lake you'll come to the center of Billerica, which is surprisingly attractive for a populous bedroom suburb. The large, well-landscaped green, with a monument in the middle, is framed by a traditional white New England church and an ornate brick Victorian library. A couple of miles ahead is North Billerica, an old mill village with a row of identical houses, two grim but ornate Victorian mills, and a fine dam spanning the Concord River. Here the Middlesex Canal crossed the river at water level. To enable the horsemen pulling towboats to get across the river, the engineers built a floating bridge that could be opened to let traffic on the river itself pass through.

From here you'll parallel the remains of the Middlesex Canal, which is noticeable only as a slight depression running in a straight line across the land. When you cross the Shawsheen River into Wilmington, the three stone abutments of the aqueduct, one on each bank of the river and one in the middle, remain intact. The canal was built across the top of the river, fitting into the U-shaped slot visible in the center abutment. If the canal had been built at ground level, its waters would have been diverted by the river. The only solution was to build an aqueduct above the river, but this severely limited the size of the boats that the canal could accommodate.

From the aqueduct, the return trip to Burlington leads through some surprisingly rural stretches. You'll pass two wooden schoolhouses from the 1800s and a monument to the Baldwin apple, which was first grown nearby.

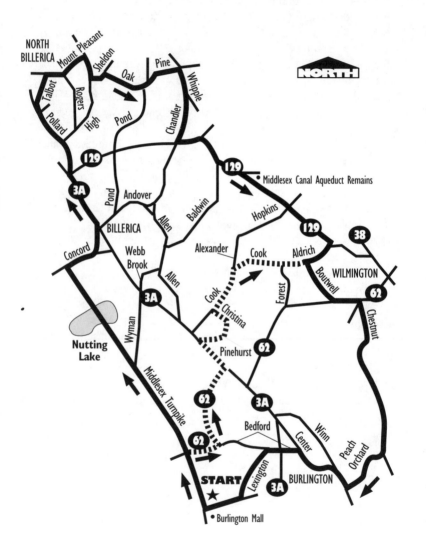

DIRECTIONS
FOR
THE RIDE

1. Right (north) on Middlesex Turnpike for 1.2 miles to Route 62 (unmarked) at second traffic light. Here the short ride turns right.

2. Straight for 4.2 miles to end, at traffic light (Concord Road). You'll cross Nutting Lake 1 mile before the end.

3. Right for 1 mile to end (Route 3A, Boston Road). Don't go straight on Charnstaffe Lane, a smaller road, after 0.7 mile.

You'll go alongside the Billerica town green on your left at the end. Notice the fine white church and Victorian library on the far side of the green.

4. Left for 1 mile to traffic light where Route 129 turns 90 degrees right and Pollard Street (unmarked) bears slightly right.

5. Bear right for 1.2 miles to a three-way fork immediately after stop sign. You'll cross the Concord River just before the fork.

6. Take the middle road, passing church on left, for 0.3 mile to fork at a grassy, triangular traffic island. It's just after a large oval green. This is North Billerica, also called Talbot Mills.

7. Bear right for 0.4 mile to another fork (Rogers Street bears right, Mount Pleasant Street bears left). You'll cross the Concord River again just before the fork. The dam on your right is impressive.

8. Bear left under railroad bridge for 0.4 mile to end, at stop sign.

9. Right for 0.2 mile to Sheldon Street on left, at traffic island.

10. Left for 0.3 mile to your second right, Oak Street.

11. Turn right and stay on main road for 1 mile to fork where Pond Street bears left and Pine Street bears right. You'll see Long Pond on your left just before the fork.

12. Bear right for 0.3 mile to crossroads and stop sign (Whipple Road).

13. Right for 0.4 mile to fork just after stop sign (Chandler Street, unmarked, bears slightly right).

14. Bear right for 1.1 miles to crossroads and stop sign (Route 129, Salem Road).

15. Turn left and stay on Route 129 for 2.3 miles to traffic light (Lake

Street on left, Hopkins Street on right). Route 129 bears right and then bears left at forks.

The remains of the Shawsheen River aqueduct of the Middlesex Canal are on your left after 1.5 miles.

16. Straight for 0.8 mile to Aldrich Road (unmarked) on right. There is a little red schoolhouse, built in 1875, on your left at the intersection.

17. Right for 0.5 mile to Boutwell Street on left, just after Mozart Avenue on left.

18. Left for 0.8 mile to stop sign (merge left on Route 62).

19. Bear left for 0.4 mile to Chestnut Street on right at traffic light.

20. Turn 90 degrees right (don't turn sharply right on Marion Street) for 2.7 miles to Peach Orchard Road, which turns right up a steep hill. The main road curves left at the intersection.

You'll pass another little red schoolhouse, built in 1894, on the left after 0.7 mile. The Baldwin apple monument, dated 1895, is on your right 0.1 mile after the schoolhouse.

21. Right for 0.9 mile to end (Winn Street, unmarked).

22. Right for 0.2 mile to fork (Center Street bears left uphill).

23. Bear left for 0.6 mile to Bedford Street, which bears left immediately before the Burlington green. There's a tough hill at the beginning of this stretch.

24. Bear left for less than 0.2 mile to traffic light (Route 3A, Cambridge Street).

25. Go straight (**CAUTION** here) and just ahead bear left on Lexington Street. Go 1.7 miles to end, opposite Burlington Mall.

26. Right for less than 0.2 mile to Meadow Road on right at traffic light.

27. Right and immediately left into Vinebrook Plaza.

Directions for shorter ride

1. Right (north) on Middlesex Turnpike for 1.2 miles to Route 62 (unmarked), at second traffic light.

2. Right for 0.6 mile to where Route 62 (Francis Wyman Road) turns left.

3. Left for 1.5 miles to end (Route 3A, Cambridge Street). There's a tough hill at the end.

4. Left for 0.6 mile to Pinehurst Avenue on right at second traffic light.

5. Right for 1.1 miles to end (Cook Street, unmarked). At the beginning you'll go through an older residential area typical of much of Billerica.

6. Right for 0.7 mile to fork (Alexander Road bears left, Cook Street bears right). **CAUTION:** Bumpy spots.

7. Bear right for 1 mile to Boutwell Street on right, shortly after Forest Street on right.

8. Right for 0.8 mile to stop sign (merge left on Route 62).

9. Follow directions for the long ride from number 19 to the end.

Reading–Wilmington–North Reading–Lynnfield–Wakefield

Number of miles:	26 (16 without Wilmington–North Reading extension)
Terrain:	Gently rolling, with a couple of moderate hills.
Food:	Groceries and snack bars in the towns.
Start:	Lord Wakefield Hotel or the adjacent Lakeside Office Park, North Avenue, Wakefield, just south of Route 128. Take exit 39.

This ride loops through a cluster of attractive middle-class to affluent communities midway between Boston and Lawrence. The region is semisuburban and semirural, with large expanses of greenspace in the northern sections of the ride as you head through the Harold Parker State Forest. The town centers are New England classics, with well-tended greens framed by old churches and town halls, unspoiled even though there may be residential and commercial development close by.

At the beginning of the ride, you'll pass through the graceful town center of Reading, where six roads radiate symmetrically from the green and a stately white church stands proudly above the town. From here you'll proceed to Wilmington, with an old cemetery and church marking the original center of town, and then head north into more wooded, less-developed landscape. You'll pass unspoiled Fosters Pond and Field Pond as you wind through the Harold Parker State Forest. From here it's a smooth run to North Reading, a charming town with a large triangular green, an old clock-towered church, and a striking Victorian building

DIRECTIONS
FOR
THE RIDE

1. Right on North Avenue for almost 0.7 mile to John Street (unmarked) on right. It's immediately after Lakeview Avenue on right.

2. Right for 0.5 mile to end (Route 129). Here the short ride turns left and then right on Route 28, and the long ride turns left but stays on Route 129.

3. Turn left and follow Route 129 for 2.2 miles to traffic light just after the I–93 interchange (West Street). You'll go through the center of Reading at the beginning, passing the green on your left.

4. Right for 0.9 mile to stop sign (merge right on Woburn Street).

5. Bear right for 1.3 miles to Woburn Street (unmarked) on left, immediately after the bridge over I–93. **CAUTION:** Diagonal railroad tracks at the beginning.

6. Left for 0.7 mile to crossroads and stop sign (Route 62, Salem Street).

7. Straight for 0.9 mile to traffic light (Route 125).

8. Straight for 1.4 miles to fork at traffic island (Rattlesnake Hill Road, unmarked, bears right).

9. Bear right and stay on main road for 0.6 mile to end (Rattlesnake Hill Road on left, Old County Road on right). You'll pass a little dam on the right at bottom of hill.

10. Turn right and just ahead bear left at fork where Glenwood Road (unmarked), a newer road, bears right. Go 0.7 mile to second crossroads and stop sign (Route 125).

11. Straight through a pair of stone pillars onto Harold Parker Road (don't bear right on Gould Road past police station). Go 1.5 miles to crossroads and stop sign (Jenkins Road, unmarked). You'll ride through the Harold Parker State Forest, passing Field Pond on your right.

12. Turn right and stay on main road for 2.8 miles to crossroads and stop sign (Route 62). Jenkins Road becomes Haverhill Street.

At the end you'll pass the North Reading town green on your left. A clock-towered church built in 1829 stands at the head of the green.

13. Turn left and stay on main road for 2.8 miles to fork where Route 62 bears left at large grassy traffic island. (Be sure to stay on main road;

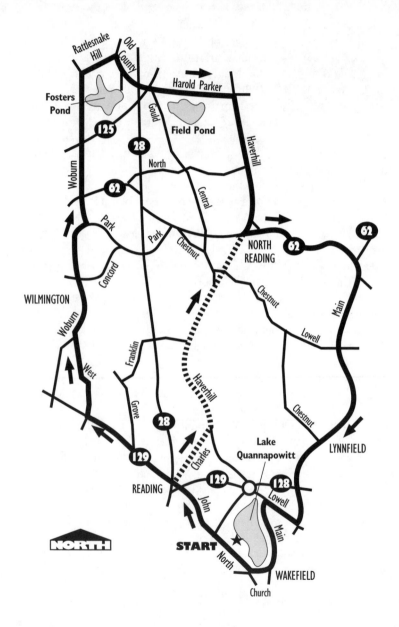

don't bear right on Park Street after 0.3 mile.)

At the beginning you'll pass the Victorian former town hall, now a library, on your left. It was built in 1875. Then you'll parallel the Ipswich River, visible from a few spots on your right.

14. Bear right and stay on main road for 4.6 miles to traffic light (Lowell Street). (Don't bear left on Russell Street after 0.2 mile.) You'll go through the center of Lynnfield after 2.5 miles, passing the green on your left.

15. Right for 0.7 mile to Route 129 East (Main Street) on left, immediately before Lake Quannapowitt on left.

16. Left along lake for 1.1 miles to Church Street, which bears right at traffic light at the Wakefield town green. Notice the fine church at far end of green.

17. Bear right for 0.4 mile to traffic light (North Avenue).

18. Right for 0.7 mile to hotel on right.

Directions for shorter ride

1. Follow directions 1 and 2 for the long ride.

2. Turn left and immediately bear right on Route 129. Then immediately turn right on Route 28 at traffic light. Go less than 0.2 mile to Charles Street, which bears right.

3. Bear right and stay on main road for 1.2 miles to stop sign (merge left on Haverhill Street). Don't bear left on Pearl Street after 0.25 mile.

5. Bear left for 2.4 miles to crossroads and stop sign (Route 62) in the center of North Reading.

6. Follow the directions for the long ride from number 13 to the end, turning right instead of left on Route 62.

that was formerly the town hall. From North Reading you'll parallel the upper reaches of the Ipswich River for a couple of miles and then turn south to Lynnfield, the most affluent of the five communities along the route. The town center is a New England classic, with a handsome white church and a slender triangle of a green surrounding a meeting-house built in 1715. From here it's not far to Wakefield, one of the most visually appealing of the suburbs inside the Route 128 semicircle. The focal point of the community is Lake Quannapowitt, with the center of town at its southern end. In good weather the lakeshore is a giant out-door health club, with a constant flow of walkers, joggers, in-line skaters, and cyclists. You'll enjoy a mile-long ride along the lakefront. At the far end of the lake is a beautifully landscaped park with an old bandstand overlooking the water. Across from the park is the town green, framed by a classic white church, an impressive stone church, and fine old homes. From here, ride a short distance up the other side of the lake back to the start.

Chapter 3:
The Closer Western Suburbs

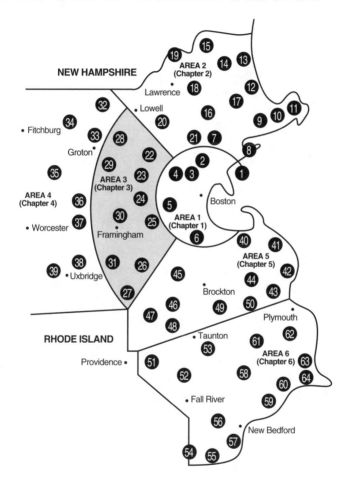

The Minute Man Ride:
Concord–Carlisle–Bedford–Lexington

Number of miles:	24 (18 without Carlisle extension, 11 with Concord–Carlisle loop only)
Terrain:	Gently rolling, with one tough hill.
Road surface:	0.6 mile of dirt road on the 18- and 24-mile rides.
Facilities:	Rest rooms at Old North Bridge in Concord.
Food:	Groceries or snack bars in the towns.
Start:	The 24- and 18-mile rides start at Minute Man National Park, Battle Road Visitor Information Center on Route 2A in Lexington. It's 0.9 mile west of Route 128 (take exit 30B).
	The 11-mile ride starts from the Old North Bridge parking lot on Monument Street in Concord. To get there, exit west from Route 128 onto Route 2A (exit 30B). Go about 3 miles to fork (Route 2A bears left). Bear right for 2.3 miles to end (Monument Street) in center of Concord. Turn right for 0.5 mile to parking lot on right.

This is a tour of four affluent communities northwest of Boston, passing several historic sites related to the battles of Lexington and Concord, the first skirmishes of the Revolution. Between the town centers lies a gently rolling landscape of gentleman farms, some estates surrounded by acres of open land, and gracious Colonial-style homes and farmhouses. The long ride heads farther west to Carlisle, the closest completely unspoiled, classic New England town to Boston.

At the beginning of the ride, you'll skirt Hanscom Field, an Air Force base incongruously dropped in the midst of wealthy suburbs, with jet fighters poised for action in the same spot where musket-armed colonists waited two centuries ago. You'll pass several high-technology firms adjoining the base; then, in a flash, you enter a delightful landscape of horse farms, rolling meadows, and old clapboard homes. If you wish, you can ride on the Battle Road Trail, a dirt bicycle and pedestrian path that attempts to follow the original roadway as it existed in 1775.

From here it's a couple of miles into Concord, a town unique as both a historic and literary center. Nearly a century after the Revolution, Concord was the home at one time or another of the Alcotts, Hawthorne, Emerson, and Thoreau. They are all buried in Sleepy Hollow Cemetery, just outside town. Coming into Concord, you'll pass the Wayside, where the Alcotts and Hawthorne once lived; the Orchard House, another Alcott home; and the Emerson House. Just north of town, a half mile off the route, is Concord's most famous landmark, the Old North Bridge. It's a lovely spot despite the daily onslaught of hundreds of sightseers and schoolchildren on field trips—a simple, gently bowed wooden bridge over the lazy Concord River, replaced several times since the Revolution. Adjacent to the bridge is the Old Manse, built in 1770 by Emerson's grandfather and the residence of both Hawthorne and Emerson, and the North Bridge Visitor Center, housed in an elegant brick mansion.

From Concord it's not far to Bedford, a pleasant residential community with an unusually large and elegant white church in the center of town. The section from Bedford to Lexington passes through gracious, well-to-do residential areas, going past an appealing mixture of tastefully designed newer homes and fine older ones set off by shade trees and broad lawns. Finally you arrive at famed Lexington Green, also called Battle Green, scene of the first American casualties of the Revolution. The large, triangular, tree-shaded green, with a stately white church at its head, is a delightful place to rest. At one corner of the

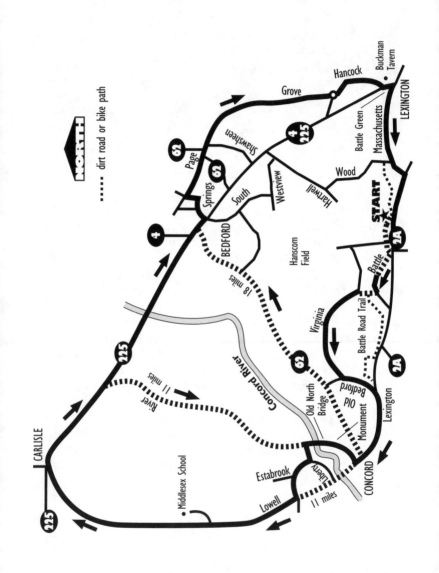

NORTH

dirt road or bike path

CARLISLE

225

225

4

62

62

Page

Springs

BEDFORD

South

Shawsheen

Grove

Hancock

Buckman
Tavern

LEXINGTON

4
225

Battle Green

Massachusetts

Wood

Hartwell

Westview

START

2A

Battle

Hanscom
Field

18 miles

Concord River

River   11 miles

Virginia

Battle Road Trail

62

Old North
Bridge

Bedford

PIO

Monument

Lexington

2A

Middlesex School

Estabrook

Lowell

Liberty

11 miles

CONCORD

DIRECTIONS
FOR
THE RIDE

1. Right (west) on Route 2A for 0.9 mile to a dirt road, blocked off to cars, that bears right. It's 0.2 mile after the road to Hanscom Field on right. The restored William Smith House, a typical home from the Revolutionary era, is on your right at the intersection.

2. Bear right for 0.5 mile to a dirt footpath on the right that passes through a pair of stone pillars. It comes up shortly after pavement resumes, and just as you start to go downhill. You'll pass the Samuel Hartwell House (only the chimney remains) and the Ephraim Hartwell Tavern, a house-plus-tavern from the mid-1700s.

3. Right for 0.2 mile to paved road (Virginia Road, unmarked). **CAUTION:** Walk along the rough, rocky footpath.

After 100 yards you'll see a wider dirt bicycle/pedestrian path (the Battle Road Trail) on your left. If you wish, you can follow it (turn left and just ahead turn right) for about 2 miles to the Willow Pond Kitchen Restaurant on Lexington Road. Resume with direction number 6, going straight on Lexington Road for 1.5 miles instead of bearing right for 1.3 miles.

The path winds through woods at the beginning and farmland at the end, and crosses two marshes over narrow boardwalks with sharp corners. (You should walk your bike along the boardwalks.)

4. Bear slightly left for 1.9 miles to end (Old Bedford Road, unmarked). You'll pass Hanscom Field on your right.

5. Left for 0.5 mile to stop sign (merge right on Lexington Road, unmarked).

6. Bear right for 1.3 miles to Route 62 East on right at small rotary in the center of Concord. Here the 18-mile ride turns right.

You'll pass the Wayside, the Orchard House, and the Emerson House. To visit the Sleepy Hollow Cemetery, turn right on Route 62 East and go 0.25 mile to cemetery on left.

7. Straight for 1 block to end (Monument Street).

8. Right for almost 0.9 mile to Liberty Street on left (sign says TO MINUTE MAN VISITOR CENTER.)

After 0.5 mile you'll see the Old Manse on your left. Immediately after the Manse, a path on the left leads 0.1 mile to the Old North Bridge.

9. Left on Liberty Street for 0.2 mile to end, at traffic island (Estabrook Road on right). The entrance to the North Bridge Visitor Center is on your left just before the intersection. A footpath behind the visitor center leads 0.2 mile through an idyllic meadow to the Old North Bridge.

10. Turn right and stay on main road for almost 0.7 mile to crossroads and stop sign (Lowell Road). Don't turn right on Estabrook Road after 0.25 mile.

11. Right for 4.3 miles to rotary in the center of Carlisle (Route 225 goes straight). You'll pass the Middlesex School, which is worth a look, on the right after 1.4 miles. It's set back 0.3 mile from the road.

Notice the graceful white church on your right just before the rotary. A country store is on your left at the rotary.

12. Straight for 4.2 miles to fork just after yield sign (Routes 4 and 225 bear left). After 0.6 mile you'll pass Kimball Farm Ice Cream, an excellent spot for a treat, on the left.

13. Bear left for 0.3 mile to traffic light just after an impressive church on right (South Road on right, Springs Road on left). This is the center of Bedford.

14. Turn left (**CAUTION** here) and just ahead bear right at fork (still Springs Road). Go less than 0.2 mile to end (merge left at stop sign).

15. Bear left for 0.25 mile to crossroads and stop sign (Pine Hill Road on left, Page Road on right).

16. Right for 0.7 mile to stop sign (merge head-on into Route 62).

17. Straight for 0.2 mile to where Route 62 curves sharply left and Page Road goes straight.

18. Go straight and just ahead bear left at fork (still Page Road). Go 2.8 miles to rotary. You'll climb a long, steady grade, the only real hill on the ride, and enjoy a fast, smooth descent.

19. Go two-thirds around rotary onto Hancock Street (unmarked), passing a garden store on left. Go 1 mile to traffic island immediately after crossing the bikeway. Battle Green is on the far side of the island.

Battle Green, Lexington

20. Bear left at traffic island and stop sign, following the green on your right. Go 1 block to the tip of the green (Massachusetts Avenue, unmarked). The Buckman Tavern is on your left opposite the green.

21. Sharp right for 1.9 miles to crossroads and stop sign (Route 2A). Notice the statue honoring the Minute Men at the far end of the green.

If you wish, you can complete the last 0.8 mile of the ride on the dirt Battle Road Trail. To do so, turn right after 1.4 miles on Wood Street, just after bridge over Route 128. Go 100 yards, turn left on Old Massachusetts Avenue, and just ahead turn right on bikeway for 0.8 mile to parking lot.

22. Right on Route 2A for almost 0.6 mile to parking lot on right.

Directions for shorter ride: 18 miles

1. Follow directions for the long ride through number 6, to Route 62 East in the center of Concord. Here the ride turns right, but if you want to visit the Old North Bridge, continue straight for 1 block to end (Monument Street). Turn right on Monument Street and go 0.5 mile.

2. Right for 4.5 miles to traffic light in center of Bedford just after an impressive church on the right. At the light, South Road turns right and Springs Road turns left.

You'll pass Sleepy Hollow Cemetery on your left after 0.25 mile.

3. Follow directions for the 24-mile ride from number 14 to the end.

Directions for shorter ride: 11 miles

Here's a short, easy ride passing entirely through an idyllic landscape of estates, gentleman farms, and rolling, open meadows and hillsides. On the way to Carlisle, you'll pass the Middlesex School, a preparatory school with beautiful grounds and elegant brick buildings that is worth visiting. Don't miss the beautiful walk from the starting point across the Old North Bridge to the visitor center. It's 0.1 mile to the bridge and then 0.2 mile to the visitor center.

Start: Old North Bridge parking lot on Monument Street in Concord.

1. Left on Monument Street for 0.5 mile to end (Lowell Road) in center of Concord.
2. Right for 5.5 miles to rotary in the center of Carlisle (Route 225 goes straight).

The entrance to Middlesex School is on your right after 2.6 miles, just before a smaller road bears left. The school is set back 0.3 mile from the road.

Notice the graceful white church on your right just before the rotary. A country store is on your left at the rotary.
3. Bear right for 1.6 miles to River Road, which bears right. Kimball Farm Ice Cream, an excellent spot, is on your left after 0.6 mile.
4. Bear right and stay on main road for 3.8 miles to Old North Bridge parking lot on left.

---

green is a fine old statue in honor of the Minute Men, built in 1799. Across the street from the green is the Buckman Tavern, where the Minutemen assembled to await the British, a superbly restored and maintained old tavern with its original furnishings intact.

The long ride heads north from Concord past the Old North Bridge and the visitor center to the elegant, unspoiled rural town of Carlisle. You'll go along a ridge with fine views across broad, open meadows, and then pass the gracious campus of the Middlesex School, an exclusive preparatory school with broad lawns and handsome red-brick buildings. The center of town is a jewel, with a stately white church standing over the green, an old wooden schoolhouse on top of the hill, a fine brick Victorian library, and a delightful country store. From Carlisle it's a smooth ride to Bedford, where you'll pick up the route of the short ride.

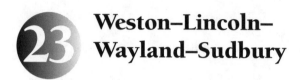

Weston–Lincoln–
Wayland–Sudbury

Number of miles:	26 (13 without Sudbury–Wayland–Weston extension)
Terrain:	Gently rolling, with two short hills. The long ride has an additional hill 0.3 mile long.
Food:	Groceries and restaurants in all the towns except Lincoln.
Note on the route:	0.3 mile of one-way road in the wrong direction where you should walk your bike.
Facilities:	Rest rooms at start and at Walden Pond.
Start:	DoubleTree Guest Suites, at Winter Street and First Avenue in Waltham, just west of Route 128. Entrance is on First Avenue.

This is a tour of the gracious, wealthy communities west of Boston outside the Route 128 semicircle. Bicycling in this area is pure joy as you wind through a neat landscape of horse farms; estates; broad, gently rolling fields; unspoiled ponds; and classic New England town centers along a network of smooth, well-maintained country roads. Walden Pond, where Thoreau built his cabin, is 0.7 mile off the route.

The ride starts off through an office park, but after a half-mile, you'll enter the gracious town of Weston, where the road suddenly begins winding past stone walls and fine houses on impeccably landscaped lots. You'll turn northwest onto Route 117, among the better numbered roads in the Boston metropolitan area for bicycling. After 2 miles you'll cross the town line into Lincoln, one of Boston's most elegant old-money-eyed suburbs, and stay within the town's borders for the rest of the short ride except for the final mile.

Just before turning off Route 117, you'll pass Drumlin Farm, a 200-acre farm with a full contingent of barnyard animals and fowl, run by the Massachusetts Audubon Society. There's an inspiring view from the top of Hathaway Hill on the grounds. Just ahead is the Codman House, a majestic Federal-era mansion maintained by the Society for the Preservation of New England Antiquities. From here you'll head past estates and gentleman farms to the DeCordova Museum, an impressive, castle-like building on top of a hill overlooking Sandy Pond. The museum focuses on contemporary New England art, including video and computer-generated art. The grounds include the largest outdoor sculpture park in New England.

From the museum it's a half-mile to the town center of Lincoln, which is unusual for its lack of commercial establishments. The business section is a mile southwest. A handsome brick library, a stately white church on the hillside, and an old burying ground across the street grace the town center. You finish by pedaling along the shore of the Cambridge Reservoir, a blur when you brush past it on Route 128 but delightful when you cruise alongside it on a bicycle.

The long ride heads farther south to the center of Weston, a community as affluent as Lincoln, with a similar landscape of estates on spacious grounds and large homes nestled amid five-acre wooded lots. The center of town is elegant, with an attractive row of shops, two handsome stone churches, and an elliptical green with the pillared town hall standing over it. You'll pass the old train station, now abandoned, just before the center of town. Next to the station is the proposed Wayside Rail Trail, now a dirt path, which would follow an abandoned Boston and Maine railroad line for about 25 miles from Waltham west to Berlin. All the towns along the route have supported the bikeway except for Weston, which voted against it in 1997, fearful that the pillaging hordes from Waltham and points east would invade the center of town less than a half-mile from the railbed. If the bikeway is built, all those ma-

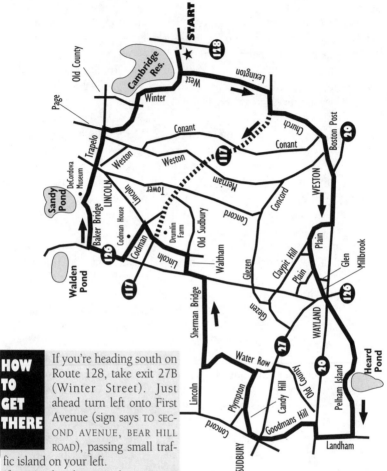

HOW TO GET THERE

If you're heading south on Route 128, take exit 27B (Winter Street). Just ahead turn left onto First Avenue (sign says TO SECOND AVENUE, BEAR HILL ROAD), passing small traffic island on your left.

If you're heading north on Route 128, take exit 27B (Winter Street). Turn right at end of ramp and just ahead right again, crossing over Route 128. Take first left onto First Avenue (sign says TO SECOND AVENUE, BEAR HILL ROAD), passing small traffic island on your left.

DIRECTIONS
FOR
THE RIDE

1. Left on Winter Street for 0.1 mile to West Street on left at traffic light. It's safest to walk on the sidewalk on the left side of the road because you can't turn left directly onto the roadway.

2. Left for 1.4 miles to end (Route 117). West Street becomes Lexington Street.

3. Right for 0.2 mile to Church Street on left (sign says TO WESTON CENTER). Here the short ride goes straight.

4. Left for 1.2 miles to yield sign (merge right on Boston Post Road, unmarked) in Weston.

After 1 mile you'll pass the abandoned train station on your left on the far side of a railroad bridge. The proposed Wayside Rail Trail runs beneath the bridge. At the end, notice the town hall on your right on the far side of the green, and the stone church on your left.

5. Bear right and stay on main road for 0.9 mile to stop sign (merge right on Route 20).

6. Bear right for 0.9 mile to Plain Road on right. **CAUTION:** Route 20 is busy.

7. Right for 0.9 mile to fork (Claypit Hill Road bears right, Plain Road bears left).

8. Bear left for almost 0.5 mile to another fork (Plain Road bears right, Glen Road bears left).

9. Bear left and just ahead bear right on Millbrook Road. Go 0.4 mile to crossroads and stop sign (Routes 126 and 27) in the center of Wayland.

Notice the bell-towered church to your left and the pillared house on the far right side of the intersection. The small white building on the far left corner is a former law office built around 1826.

10. Go straight and just ahead cross Route 20 diagonally onto Pelham Island Road (**CAUTION** here). Go 2.5 miles to end (Landham Road, unmarked). You'll cross the Sudbury River and then ride along Heard Pond on your left.

11. Right for 0.6 mile to end (Route 20).

12. Right for 0.2 mile to Goodmans Hill Road on left.

13. Left for 1.6 miles to end (Concord Road, unmarked). You'll climb a fairly steep hill for 0.3 mile—the only tough climb on the ride.

14. Right for 0.4 mile to Candy Hill Road on right. At the beginning you'll go through the center of Sudbury at traffic light, passing a traditional white church on your left and the town hall on your right.

15. Right for 0.3 mile to stop sign at bottom of hill (merge right on Plympton Road, unmarked). **CAUTION:** Watch for sand at the intersection.

16. Bear right for 0.8 mile to end, at traffic island (Water Row Road, unmarked).

17. Left for 1.4 miles to end (Lincoln Road, unmarked) at traffic island with an old stone milepost.

18. Right for 1.9 miles to end (Route 126).

After 0.5 mile, Weir Hill Road on the left leads 0.3 mile to the Great Meadows National Wildlife Refuge, where foot trails skirt the marshes along the Sudbury River.

19. Left for 0.5 mile to Waltham Road on right at grassy traffic island.

20. Right for 0.2 mile to crossroads (Lincoln Road).

21. Left for less than 0.8 mile to crossroads and stop sign (Route 117). Here the ride goes straight, but if you turn right for 0.2 mile, you'll come to Drumlin Farm on your right.

22. Straight for 0.3 mile to crossroads (Codman Road).

23. Left for 0.6 mile to end (Route 126). You'll pass the Codman House on your right, set back 0.1 mile off the road.

24. Right for 0.8 mile to Baker Bridge Road (unmarked) on right. Here the ride turns right, but if you go straight for 0.7 mile, you'll come to Walden Pond on your left. There's a beach, and a footpath circles the pond. A replica of Thoreau's cabin, a tiny structure about 16 feet long and 11 feet wide, stands across the road.

25. Right (left if you visited Walden Pond) for 1.1 miles to end (Sandy Pond Road, unmarked). After 0.5 mile you'll pass a stark, square house on your right designed by Walter Gropius in 1938. You'll climb two short hills.

26. Right for 0.6 mile to crossroads and stop sign (Lincoln Road) at five-

way intersection in the center of Lincoln. You'll pass the DeCordova Museum on your left. At the crossroads, notice the handsome brick library on the far left corner.

27. Cross Lincoln Road onto Trapelo Road, bearing left as you go through the intersection. (Don't go straight onto Weston Road.) Go 0.9 mile to crossroads (Page Road on left, Winter Street on right).

28. Right for almost 1 mile to crossroads (sign says DO NOT ENTER if you go straight).

29. Straight for 1.6 miles to hotel on right. The first 0.3 mile is one-way in the wrong direction; walk your bike. This is a beautiful ride along the Cambridge Reservoir.

Directions for shorter ride

1. Follow directions for the long ride through number 3.

2. Straight for 3.8 miles to fourth crossroads (Lincoln Road). It's just past Drumlin Farm on left. **CAUTION:** Dangerous diagonal railroad tracks after 3 miles. Please walk across them.

3. Right for 0.3 mile to crossroads (Codman Road).

4. Follow directions for the long ride from number 23 to the end.

---

rauding cyclists will have to detour through downtown Weston on roads, where they will wreak even more havoc than if they had stayed on the bike path.

From Weston the route turns west to Wayland, another attractive town with a large, graceful white church and a fine brick library. After you leave Wayland, you'll head past unspoiled Heard Pond to the beautiful rural town of Sudbury. In the center of town are two fine old churches facing each other across the road and an impressive, pillared town hall. Idyllic back roads lead you back to Lincoln, where you'll rejoin the short ride near Drumlin Farm.

24 Weston–Wellesley–Wayland

Number of miles:	29 (18 without Wellesley extension)
Terrain:	Gently rolling, with a few moderate hills.
Note on the route:	0.3 mile of one-way road in the wrong direction where you should walk your bike.
Food:	Groceries and restaurants in the towns.
Start:	M.D.C. Duck Feeding Area parking lot in Weston, on the west bank of the Charles River. It's immediately north of Route 30 and immediately east of Route 128.

This is a tour of three wealthy, gracious communities west of Boston just outside the Route 128 semicircle. The region is a pleasure for bicycling, with smooth roads winding past seminaries, colleges, and stately older brick and wooden homes. Highlights of the ride are two colleges in Wellesley—Babson College, where you'll visit the largest revolving globe in the world and a giant relief map of the country, and Wellesley College, which has one of the most beautiful campuses in the state.

You'll start by going through Weston, one of Boston's most affluent suburbs, with estates on spacious grounds and large homes on five acre lots. You'll pass Regis College, a Catholic women's school with a handsome main building, a tall stone tower on a hilltop, and a postal museum on the campus. The town center is a New England jewel, with an attractive row of shops, two stone churches, and a pillared town hall standing over the large elliptical green. From Weston you'll ride through

1. Head out of parking lot for 100 yards to first left (sign says TO ROUTES 30 AND I–95).

2. Left under highway and just ahead left at end. Go less than 0.2 mile to yield sign (merge right on Route 30).

3. Bear right for 0.4 mile to Newton Street, which bears right at second traffic light.

4. Bear right for 1.8 miles to Wellesley Street, which turns sharply left at traffic island. It's just after Ash Street, which also turns sharply left.

5. Sharp left for 1.5 miles to traffic light (Route 30). Here the short ride turns right.

You'll pass the Case Estate of Arnold Arboretum, 112 acres of nurseries and cultivated plants, on your right. Then you'll pass Regis College.

6. Straight for 0.8 mile to Glen Road on left. It is the first left after you pass under the Massachusetts Turnpike.

7. Left for 1 mile to crossroads and stop sign (Oak Street on left, Cliff Road on right). You'll pass the Norumbega Reservoir on your left.

8. Right for 1.7 miles to end (Route 16).

9. Jog right and immediately left on Abbott Road (**CAUTION** here). Stay on main road for 0.8 mile to end (Forest Street, unmarked).

10. Left for less than 0.2 mile to diagonal crossroads and stop sign (Wellesley Avenue).

Here the ride turns sharply right, but if you would like to visit the map at Babson College, continue straight for 0.2 mile to the college entrance on right. The map is in Coleman Hall. Turn right into the college and take second left to end.

11. Turn sharply right. (Bear left if you visited the map.) Stay on main road for 1.4 miles to end, at traffic light (Routes 16 and 135, Washington Street).

12. Left for less than 0.2 mile to a fork where Route 16 bears left and Route 135 bears right, in the center of Wellesley. You'll pass the ornate stone town hall on the right.

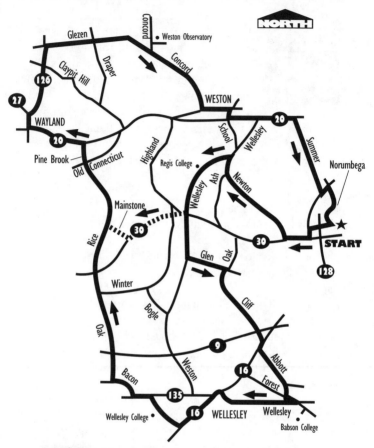

NORTH

Glezen
Concord
Weston Observatory
Claypit Hill
Draper
Concord
126
27
WESTON
20
WAYLAND
20
School
Wellesley
Summer
Pine Brook
Old Connecticut
Highland
Regis College
Ash
Newton
Norumbega
Mainstone
Wellesley
30
START
Rice
30
128
Glen
Oak
Winter
Bogle
Cliff
Oak
9
Abbott
Bacon
Weston
16
Forest
135
16
WELLESLEY
Wellesley
Wellesley College
Babson College

HOW TO GET THERE
From Route 128 South take exit 24 (Route 30). Cross Route 30 at traffic light and go 0.1 mile to second right. Turn right and just ahead right again into parking lot.

From Route 128 North take exit 24. Turn left on Route 30 and just ahead right at traffic light. Go 0.1 mile to second right. Turn right and just ahead right again into parking lot.

From Massachusetts Turnpike follow signs to I–95 North and Route 30. Turn left on Rotue 30 and follow directions for Route 128 North.

13. Bear left (**CAUTION** here) for 0.6 mile to the entrance to Wellesley College on right at traffic light.

14. Right for 0.8 mile to end (Route 135). You'll see Lake Waban on your left as soon as you enter the college. Side roads on the left lead down to the lakeshore.

15. Left for 0.4 mile to Bacon Street (unmarked) on right.

16. Right for 0.5 mile to Oak Street on right, at traffic light.

17. Right for 2.3 miles to crossroads and stop sign (Route 30). **CAUTION** crossing Route 9 at traffic light after 0.7 mile.

18. Straight for 2.5 miles to end (Old Connecticut Path, unmarked).

19. Jog right and immediately left (almost straight) onto Pine Brook Road. It is one-way in the wrong direction; walk your bike. Go 0.3 mile to end (Route 20).

20. Left for 1 mile to traffic light (Routes 27 and 126) in the center of Wayland. The small white building on the far right corner is a former law office built around 1826.

21. Turn right and just ahead bear right on Route 126. Go 1.3 miles to second crossroads (Glezen Lane). Notice the graceful library on your right at the beginning.

22. Turn right and stay on main road for 3.6 miles to end, at a T-inter- section in Weston.

After 2 miles you'll pass the Campion Center, an impressive domed building, on your left. It is a Jesuit spiritual center and retirement home. Just north of it is the Weston Observatory, in front of which are rocks with fossils and dinosaur footprints. To get there, turn sharply left on Concord Street (unmarked) just before the Campion Center and then immediately right.

23. Left for 0.4 mile, through the center of Weston, to School Street on right. It's opposite a stone church on the left. Notice the pillared town hall to the left on the far side of the green.

24. Right and just ahead left at traffic light on Route 20 (**CAUTION** here). Go 1 mile to Summer Street on right, just after the Gifford School on left.

25. Right for 1.4 miles to a yield sign where you merge head-on into a larger road. You will turn sharply left here.

Wellesley College

26. Sharp left for 0.2 mile to crossroads (Norumbega Road on right). You come to it while you're going downhill.

27. Right for 0.8 mile to Duck Feeding Area parking lot. You'll pass a stone tower on the left at the beginning (don't bother going into it—there's no view from the top and the odor is foul). Then you'll follow the Charles River on your left.

Directions for shorter ride

1. Follow directions for the long ride through number 5.

2. Right for 1.6 miles to Mainstone Road on right, just after Natick town line. You'll pass an old cemetery on your right at the beginning.

3. Right for 0.8 mile to end (Rice Road, unmarked). You'll climb steeply for 0.25 mile near the beginning.

4. Right for 1.3 miles to end (Old Connecticut Path, unmarked).

5. Follow directions for the long ride from number 19 to the end.

Wayland, the next town to the west. Wayland is a little more rural, with some extensive sections of woods and rolling pastureland. The center of town boasts a fine white church and brick library. The return trip passes the Weston Observatory (part of Boston College), where there are rocks containing the imprint of fossils and dinosaur feet.

The long ride heads south into Wellesley, a more densely populated but equally elegant suburb. You'll visit Babson College, a top-rated business school with a fascinating attraction—a relief map of the United States, 65 feet long and 40 feet wide, viewed from a balcony above. The map was built from 1937 to 1940 with painstaking attention to detail. The largest revolving globe in the world, 28 feet in diameter, is outside the building. There is no admission charge. From Babson you'll go through the center of Wellesley, with its Gothic-style town hall and an attractive row of smart shops. Just ahead is the centerpiece of the town, Wellesley College. The rolling, elm-shaded campus, bordering the shore of Lake Waban, is a delight to bike through as you pass its dignified ivy-covered buildings. After leaving the college you'll join the route of the short ride, going through Wayland and then back through Weston.

Charles River Tour:
Westwood–Dover–Sherborn–South Natick–Needham–Dedham

Number of miles:	31 (20 without Sherborn–South Natick extension, 14 with shortcut bypassing Dover)
Terrain:	Gently rolling, with two hills on the 31-mile ride.
Food:	None on two shorter rides until near end. Grocery in South Natick.
Start:	Holiday Inn, Route 1 in Dedham, just north of Route 128. Take exit 15A. Park at west side of the lot near Route 1A.

The valley of the Charles River upstream from Newton provides relaxed and scenic cycling. The river flows peacefully past landed estates, broad meadows, and graceful old communities as it follows a west-to-east course from South Natick to Dedham. Country roads crisscross the region, with its gentleman farms, horses grazing in pastures set off by stone walls and white wooden fences, and stately old homes.

The ride heads through Westwood, an affluent mansion-dotted community, and then into the old-moneyed enclave of Dover, which is a paradise for biking. After paralleling the Charles through Dover, you'll cross the river into Needham. Most of Needham is a bedroom suburb, but the southern rim of the town along the river shares Dover's gracious landscape. From Needham you'll go into Dedham, a handsome town with distinguished public buildings gracing its center. Approaching downtown you'll pass fine old Colonial-style homes and two graceful white churches. Just ahead are stately granite courthouses and the handsome stone public library, built in 1873. After passing a Gothic-style

DIRECTIONS
FOR
THE RIDE

1. Left (south) on Route 1A for 0.3 mile to Gay Street (unmarked) on right at the Westwood town line.

2. Right for 1.6 miles to Fox Hill Street, which bears right up a gradual hill.

3. Bear right for 0.9 mile to end (Route 109). **CAUTION:** Watch for potholes.

4. Right for 0.4 mile to Summer Street on left (sign may say TO DOVER, 4 MILES).

5. Left (**CAUTION** here) for 1.2 miles to end (Westfield Street).

6. Left for 0.2 mile to Wilsondale Street, a narrow lane that bears left.

7. Bear left and stay on main road for 1.6 miles to end (Dedham Street, unmarked).

8. Left for 0.4 mile to Mill Street on right at top of little hill.

9. Right for 0.4 mile to end. The road runs along the Charles River on your right.

10. Right for less than 0.2 mile to Fisher Street on left, immediately after the bridge over the Charles River. Here the 14-mile ride goes straight. You'll pass a beautiful little dam on your right.

11. Left for 0.4 mile to end. **CAUTION:** Bad diagonal railroad tracks after 0.1 mile.

12. Left for 0.3 mile to Claybrook Road on right, just after recrossing the Charles. You are now in Dover.

13. Right for 1.6 miles to crossroads and stop sign. You can catch glimpses of the Charles on your right.

14. Straight for 0.4 mile to end (merge right on Pleasant Street).

15. Bear right for 0.5 mile to Dover Road on right. Here the 20-mile ride turns right and the long ride goes straight. You'll pass Lookout Farm, an excellent fruit and vegetable stand, on your left.

16. Straight for less than 0.2 mile to Glen Street (unmarked) on left.

17. Left for 2.4 miles to stop sign at bottom of hill (merge right on Farm Street, unmarked).

18. Bear right for 0.5 mile to fork where Bridge Street bears right at traffic island.

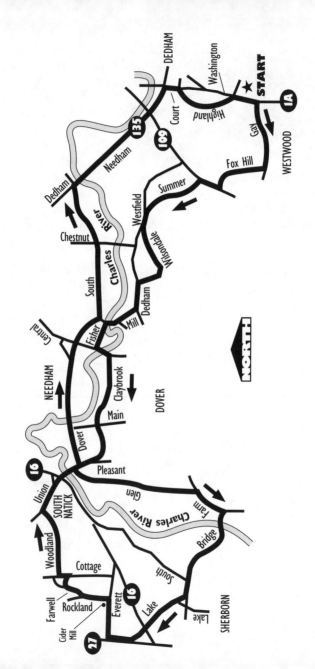

19. Bear right for 1.7 miles to second right (Lake Street) at traffic island. You will cross the Charles into Sherborn and pass a magnificent old dairy farm on the right.

20. Right for 0.9 mile to crossroads and stop sign (Route 16, Eliot Street).

21. Straight for 0.4 mile to end (merge right on Route 27).

22. Bear right for almost 0.3 mile to Everett Street on right.

23. Right for almost 0.9 mile to Rockland Street on left, just before top of hill.

24. Left for 0.6 mile to fork (Farwell Street bears right). Just after you turn onto Rockland Street, you'll see a cider mill on your left. It's a great rest stop during apple season.

25. Bear right for 0.5 mile to end (Fay Way, unmarked).

26. Zigzag right, immediately left at end, and then immediately right on Woodland Street. Go 1.3 miles to end (Union Street, unmarked). **CAUTION:** The end comes up suddenly at bottom of sharp hill.

27. Right for 0.5 mile to traffic light (Route 16) in South Natick. Notice the ornate Victorian library on the far right-hand corner.

28. Straight onto Pleasant Street for 0.4 mile to Dover Road on left, just after Phillips Street on left. You'll cross the Charles River, where there's a little dam on your right.

29. Left for 2.3 miles to crossroads and stop sign (Central Avenue). After 0.6 mile you'll cross the Charles again into Needham.

30. Straight for 0.6 mile to end (South Street). **CAUTION:** Diagonal railroad tracks just before end.

31. Left for 1.3 miles to stop sign and blinking light (Chestnut Street).

32. Straight for 1 mile to traffic light (Dedham Avenue, Route 135).

33. Right for 2.3 miles to traffic light (Route 109) at the Dedham green. At the beginning of this section, you will cross the Charles once more, into Dedham.

34. Straight for 0.4 mile to another light (Court Street, unmarked). This is the center of Dedham. The granite buildings on the far side of the intersection are courthouses.

35. Right for 0.2 mile to second crossroads (School Street on left, Highland Street on right). Notice the classic white church on your right just

after you turn right, and the magnificent stone church just before Highland Street.

36. Turn right and stay on main road for almost 1 mile to stop sign (merge right on Route 1A). Don't bear right on Sandy Valley Road after 0.5 mile.

37. Bear right for 0.1 mile to Holiday Inn on left, set back from the road. **CAUTION** turning left to the Inn.

Directions for shorter ride: 20 miles

1. Follow directions for the 31-mile ride through number 15. Here the ride turns right, but if you go straight for 0.3 mile, you'll come to the dam in South Natick.

2. Right for 2.3 miles to crossroads and stop sign (Central Avenue). After 0.6 mile you'll cross the Charles into Needham.

3. Follow directions for the 31-mile ride from number 30 to the end.

Directions for shorter ride: 14 miles

1. Follow directions for the 31-mile ride through number 10.

2. Straight for 1.4 miles to stop sign and blinking light (Chestnut Street).

3. Follow directions for the 31-mile ride from number 32 to the end.

stone church, it's a short ride back to the starting point.

The long ride heads farther upriver through the elegantly rural town of Sherborn, and then to the attractive village of South Natick. Most of Natick is an uninspiring bedroom community near busy Route 9 but the southern part of the town near the Charles is beautiful and quite rural. Gracing South Natick are a pair of handsome churches, a Victorian library, and a dam across the Charles.

The Upper Charles River:
Walpole–Millis–Medfield–Sherborn–Dover

Number of miles:	30 (16 without Millis–Sherborn–Dover extension)
Terrain:	Delightfully rolling, with lots of little ups and downs.
Food:	Grocery and restaurants in Medfield. Lunch counter in Dover. Ice cream shop in Westwood. Grocery and pizza in East Walpole.
Start:	Main Street Shopping Center, Route 1A in Walpole, immediately north of Route 27.

The wealthy, woodsy suburbs southwest of Boston, halfway between the city and the northeastern corner of Rhode Island, provide ideal cycling on an impressive network of well-maintained, winding country lanes. The region is far enough from Boston to be rural rather than suburban. The landscape has a trim, prosperous look to it, with stone walls; old, well-maintained farmhouses framed by shade trees; spacious homes nestled on five-acre, pine-studded lots; and some estates in Dover. Coursing through the region are the upper reaches of the Charles River, a favorite canoeing run.

You'll start from Walpole, an attractive residential community with a brick Victorian town hall opposite its green. You'll quickly head into undeveloped countryside as you cross the Charles into Millis and recross it into Medfield, both well-scrubbed, upper-middle-class communities. The return leg to Walpole brings you through forests with a few well-designed, spacious homes set back from the road among the trees.

The long ride heads farther north into Sherborn, one of Boston's

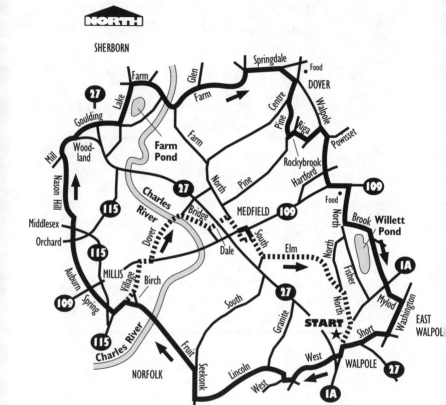

DIRECTIONS
FOR
THE RIDE

1. Right on Route 1A and immediately cross Route 27. Go 0.1 mile to traffic light (West Street, unmarked, bears right). Notice the Victorian town hall on the left just before the fork.

2. Bear right and stay on main road for 1.1 miles to crossroads, at yield sign (Norfolk Street on left, West Street on right).

3. Right for 0.2 mile to Lincoln Road on right, immediately after railroad overpass.

4. Turn right and stay on main road for 2.2 miles to end (Seekonk Street).

5. Right for 0.6 mile to Fruit Street, which bears left up a little hill.

6. Bear left and stay on main road for 2.8 miles to crossroads and stop sign (Village Street). Here the short ride turns right. You'll cross the Charles River into Millis after 1.9 miles.

7. Left for 0.2 mile to first right, Spring Street.

8. Right for 0.8 mile to second crossroads and stop sign (Route 109), in Millis.

9. Straight for 0.4 mile to fork (Curve Street bears right, Ridge Street bears slightly left). **CAUTION** crossing Route 109 and at bumpy railroad tracks just ahead.

10. Bear left for 0.5 mile to stop sign (merge left; Union Street is on right).

11. Bear left (still Ridge Street) for 3 miles to end (merge right on Mill Street). You'll go straight at two crossroads and stop signs in the first mile.

12. Bear right for 0.6 mile to fork where Woodland Street bears right and West Goulding Street bears left.

13. Bear left for 0.5 mile to end (Route 27).

14. Jog left and immediately right (almost straight) for 0.6 mile to Lake Street, which turns sharply left at top of hill. **CAUTION:** Diagonal railroad tracks after 0.25 mile.

15. Sharp left for 1.1 miles to crossroads and stop sign (Farm Road). You'll pass Farm Pond on your right.

Horse farm, Wrentham

16. Right for 1.7 miles to end (Farm Street). You'll cross the Charles into Dover near the end.

17. Left for 2 miles to crossroads (Pegan Lane on left, Springdale Avenue on right). A sign may point right TO DOVER, NEEDHAM.

18. Right for 0.8 mile to fork just before railroad tracks (Dedham Street bears left, Springdale Avenue bears right).

19. Bear right for 0.2 mile to traffic light (Centre Street) in the center of Dover. There's a lunch counter at the Dover Pharmacy, on the far left side of the intersection.

20. Right for 0.4 mile to Pine Street, a smaller road that bears left.

21. Bear left for 1.1 miles to Rockybrook Road on left. It's just after a dirt path on the right that leads 0.7 mile to a fire tower.

If you visit it, follow the main path to the tower (bear left at the first fork and right at the second one). There are some short, very steep sections. **CAUTION:** Watch for loose gravely spots and wooden beams across the path to control erosion. Coming back, bear left at fork halfway down.

22. Turn left and just ahead bear right at fork on Riga Road. Go 0.3 mile to end (Cedar Hill Road, unmarked).

23. Left for 0.4 mile to end (Walpole Street, unmarked).

24. Right for 1 mile to crossroads and stop sign (Hartford Street).

25. Straight for 0.5 mile to end (County Street, Route 109).

26. Left for 0.5 mile to North Street on right. The Bubbling Brook, a great spot for ice cream, is on your right at the intersection.

27. Right for 1 mile to Brook Street on left. The farmland on your right belongs to the Norfolk County Agricultural Laboratory.

28. Left for 0.8 mile to rotary. You will go along Willett Pond on your right.

29. Bear slightly right along pond for 1.1 miles to crossroads and stop sign (Route 1A). Here the ride goes straight, but you can cut 2 miles off the route by turning right on Route 1A (a busy, unattractive road) for 1.8 miles to shopping center on right.

30. Straight for 1 mile to end (Washington Street, unmarked) in South Norwood.

31. Right for 1.2 miles to crossroads (Polly Lane on left, Short Street on right). You'll pass an unusual wooden clock tower on your left after 0.7 mile and go through East Walpole.

32. Turn right and stay on main road for 1.8 miles to traffic light (Route 1A) in Walpole. (Don't bear right after 0.3 mile). You'll pass an equestrian statue on your right after 0.4 mile.

33. Straight and immediately right into driveway of shopping center.

Directions for shorter ride

1. Follow directions for the long ride through number 6.

2. Right for 0.8 mile to stop sign (merge right on Route 109).

3. Bear right for 0.3 mile to Dover Road on left.

4. Left (**CAUTION** here) for 1.2 miles to Bridge Street on right, just after you cross the Charles River. (Ignore another Bridge Street on right before you cross the river.)

5. Right for 0.6 mile to Dale Street (unmarked) on left. It's your fourth left, opposite house number 20 on right.

6. Left for 0.7 mile to end (North Street, unmarked). You'll cross Route 27 at a traffic light.

7. Right for 0.4 mile to end (Route 109) in the center of Medfield.

8. Straight onto Pleasant Street for 0.5 mile to end.

9. Left and just ahead right at end (South Street, unmarked). Go 0.3 mile to Elm Street on left, just before railroad tracks.

10. Turn left and stay on main road for 2.9 miles to end (merge right at stop sign).

11. Bear right and stay on main road for 0.6 mile to end (Route 1A).

12. Right for 0.4 mile to shopping center on right. **CAUTION:** Route 1A is very busy.

most unspoiled suburbs and a paradise for bicycling. You'll ride beside pretty Farm Pond, pass a sweeping dairy farm, and cross the Charles again into Dover, the closest truly rural and unspoiled town to Boston and one of the city's most upper-crust, old-moneyed suburbs. You'll pass several estates with mansions surrounded by acres of rolling meadows. For a side trip, you can follow a dirt road 0.7 mile to an unfenced fire tower at the top of Snow Hill. The tall buildings of downtown Boston, about 15 miles away, are clearly visible from the top. The return run to Walpole brings you through a large stretch of open farmland and then along beautiful Willett Pond. The fascinating mill village of East Walpole, with a mixture of old brick factories and some fine wooden houses, is two miles before the end.

27 Plainville–Cumberland, Rhode Island–Wrentham

Number of miles:	28 (11 without Cumberland–Wrentham loop)
Terrain:	Rolling to hilly. There's a tough climb at the beginning and some exhilarating descents.
Food:	Country store in Cumberland. Country store in Wrentham. Burger King at end.
Start:	Burger King, junction of Routes 106 and 152 in Plainville.

This ride explores the rural, largely wooded area surrounding the northeastern corner of Rhode Island. You can amble along at a leisurely pace to savor the beauty of the narrow, twisting back roads. The long ride includes an enjoyable spin along the Diamond Hill Reservoir, a large pond just across the Rhode Island border.

The ride starts from Plainville, a pleasantly rural town consisting mainly of woods, farmland, and orchards. The short ride stays almost entirely within the town's boundaries, following small roads with very little traffic. A steep climb at the beginning is counterbalanced by a long, steady descent to Whiting Pond. You'll climb again, more gradually this time, past horse farms and onto a ridge with a fine view, and enjoy a swooping descent to Route 1A.

The long ride heads farther west into Cumberland, Rhode Island, a lovely rural town in the northeast corner of that state. As you pedal along a narrow lane, you'll descend a short hill, and suddenly the Diamond Hill Reservoir will unfold before you. The reservoir, which provides water for the city of Pawtucket, is completely undeveloped and

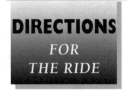

DIRECTIONS
FOR
THE RIDE

1. Left from side entrance onto Route 106 (not Route 152) for 0.3 mile to crossroads (George Street).

2. Left and just ahead right at end. Go 1.5 miles to traffic light (Routes 1 and 1A).

There's a steep hill at the beginning. At the top you'll pass World War I Memorial Park on your left; there's a small zoo here and a good view from the base of a fire tower.

3. Straight across Route 1 at traffic light, and then immediately right on Route 1A. Be sure you're on Route 1A and not Route 1. Go 100 yards to Whiting Street on left.

4. Left for 1.1 miles to end. The road turns sharply and changes its name several times, but stay on it to the end. You'll pass a small dam and Whiting Pond on your left at the beginning.

5. Right for 0.3 mile to second left (Warren Street), just after country club on left.

6. Left for 1.2 miles to end (High Street, unmarked). This stretch is a steady climb, with a steep pitch at the beginning.

7. Right for 0.3 mile to Rhodes Street on left at bottom of little hill. Here the short ride goes straight.

8. Left for 1.3 miles to end (Burnt Swamp Road, unmarked).

Most of this section is downhill. You'll pass a branch of the Wentworth Institute, an engineering school with its main campus in Boston. At the end you're in Cumberland, Rhode Island.

9. Right for 0.3 mile to end (Reservoir Road on left).

10. Left for 2.5 miles to end (Route 114). You'll ride along the Diamond Hill Reservoir. At the end, there's a country store on the far side of the intersection.

11. Left for 0.6 mile to traffic light (Route 120, Nate Whipple Highway).

12. Right for 2.5 miles to end (Route 122, Mendon Road). You'll pass Sneech Pond on your right near the end.

13. Right for 0.2 mile to West Wrentham Road on right at traffic light.

14. Right for 2.4 miles to traffic light (Route 114, Pine Swamp Road).

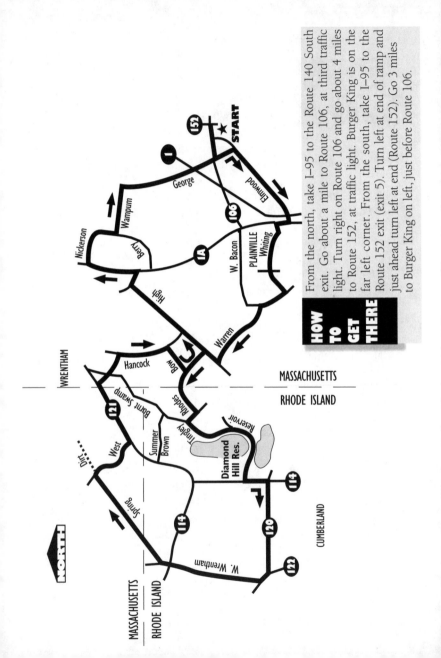

HOW TO GET THERE

From the north, take I-95 to the Route 140 South exit. Go about a mile to Route 106, at third traffic light. Turn right on Route 106 and go about 4 miles to Route 152, at traffic light. Burger King is on the far left corner. From the south, take I-95 to the Route 152 exit (exit 5). Turn left at end of ramp and just ahead turn left at end (Route 152). Go 3 miles to Burger King on left, just before Route 106.

There's a tough hill on the first half of this section and a relaxing descent at the end.

15. Go straight and just ahead bear right at fork (still West Wrentham Road). Go 2 miles to crossroads and stop sign (West Street, unmarked). **CAUTION:** Watch for sandy spots. West Wrentham Road becomes Spring Street at the Massachusetts line, after 0.5 mile.

16. Right for 0.9 mile to end (Route 121).

17. Left for 1.2 miles to Hancock Street on right. There's a country store at the intersection. This is Sheldonville, a village in Wrentham.

18. Right for 0.7 mile to end, at top of steep hill.

19. Right for 1.1 miles to Bow Street, a small lane on right (sign may say TO WENTWORTH).

20. Right for 0.5 mile to end (Rhodes Street, unmarked).

21. Left for 0.6 mile to end (High Street, unmarked). You'll climb steadily, but you will be rewarded for your efforts.

22. Left for 1.4 miles to end, at stop sign. There's a fine view to your left at the beginning; then you'll enjoy a fast descent.

23. Right for 0.2 mile to end (Route 1A).

24. Left for 0.7 mile to Nickerson Street on right, just after traffic light. There's an outlet mall to your left at the light.

25. Right for 0.7 mile to Wampum Street on left.

26. Turn left and stay on main road for 1.9 miles to Route 1, at stop sign.

27. Straight (**CAUTION** here) for 0.5 mile to crossroads and stop sign (Route 106).

28. Left for 0.3 mile to Burger King on right, immediately before traffic light. The Burger King is set back from the road.

Directions for shorter ride

1. Follow directions for the long ride through number 7.

2. Straight for 1.4 miles to end, at stop sign. There's a fine view to your left at the beginning; then you'll enjoy a fast descent.

3. Follow directions for the long ride from number 23 to the end.

surrounded by low, wooded hills. The road hugs the shore and crosses a causeway with water on both sides. After leaving the watershed, the route ascends gradually onto a ridge with fine views and descends to the Wrentham, Massachusetts, border.

Wrentham is a gracious community on the outer fringe of the Boston metropolitan area, far enough away from the city to be more rural than suburban. Spring Street, a narrow winding lane, bobs up and over several sharp hills, none long enough to be discouraging. Horse pastures and fine wooden houses greet you at each bend. Soon you'll arrive in Sheldonville, a village within Wrentham with an old church and a good country store. Just ahead you'll climb sharply onto a ridge and rejoin the short ride just before the exhilarating descent to Route 1A.

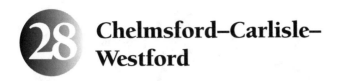

28 Chelmsford–Carlisle–Westford

Number of miles:	27 (13 without Westford extension)
Terrain:	Rolling, with a few moderate hills and one tough one.
Food:	Grocery in Carlisle. Grocery and pizza shop in Westford. Convenience store and pizza shop at end. Ice cream shops in Carlisle and Westford, each 0.6 mile off the route.
Start:	Small shopping center on the east side of Route 4 in Chelmsford, 1.4 miles south of the center of town. It's just south of Mill Road.

This ride takes you exploring in three attractive towns on the outer edge of suburban Boston. You start from the outskirts of Chelmsford, a pleasant, middle-class suburb of Lowell with an attractive town center. The first few miles go through residential areas, passing the Middlesex County House of Correction in Billerica, an ornate Victorian building that appears inviting from the outside. The landscape becomes graciously rural as you cross the town line into Carlisle. Carlisle is one of the closest truly unspoiled towns to Boston, with a strict no-growth policy. Narrow lanes weaving past farms, estates, and woodland provide a paradise for biking. The center of town is a jewel, with a magnificent old church fronting the green, a fine brick Victorian library, and an old wooden schoolhouse on top of a hill.

From Carlisle to Westford, the rural landscape of gentleman farms, woodland, and an occasional orchard continues. Westford is an unspoiled hilltop town with a large green framed by a classic white

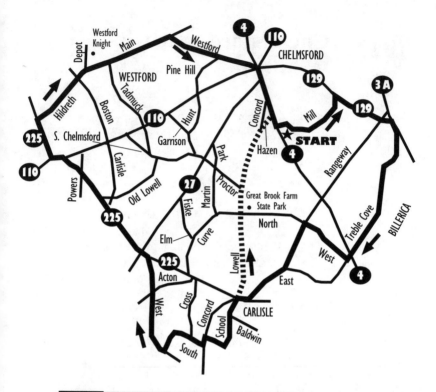

HOW TO GET THERE

If you're heading north on Route 3, take exit 29 (Route 129). Turn right at end of ramp for 0.3 mile to Mill Road on left at traffic light. Turn left for 1.8 miles to shopping center on left.

If you're heading south on Route 3 from Nashua, take exit 32 onto Route 4 South. Go 3.4 miles to shopping center on left.

If you're heading north on I–495, take exit 33 (Route 4). Turn right at end of ramp for 1.9 miles to shopping center on left.

If you're heading south on I–495, take exit 34 (Route 110). Bear right at end of ramp for 0.7 mile to the center of Chelmsford. Go straight on Route 4 South for 1.4 miles to shopping center on left.

DIRECTIONS

FOR

THE RIDE

1. Right on Mill Road for 1.8 miles to end (Route 129).

2. Right for 1.3 miles to end (merge right on Route 3A).

3. Bear right and just ahead turn right at traffic light on Treble Cove Road. Go 2.9 miles to crossroads and stop sign (Route 4, Nashua Road). You'll pass the Middlesex County House of Correction on your right and Winning Pond on your left toward the end.

4. Straight and just ahead right on West Street. Go 1 mile to crossroads and stop sign (Rutland Street). The land becomes rural as you enter Carlisle.

5. Left for 0.9 mile to stop sign (merge right on East Street).

6. Bear right for 1.1 miles to stop sign (merge right on Route 225). Here the ride bears right, but if you turn sharply left for 0.6 mile you'll come to Kimball Farm Ice Cream, a great spot for a snack, on your left.

7. Bear right for 0.1 mile to rotary in the center of Carlisle. Here the short ride turns right. Notice the handsome brick library on your left, built in 1895. There's a country store on your right at the rotary.

8. Go straight and then immediately bear left uphill on School Street (unmarked), passing church on left. (Don't bear left on Concord Street, which is immediately after School Street.) Go 2 miles to end.

The church was built in 1811. Just beyond it there's a fine old wooden school on your left, at the top of the hill.

9. Left and just ahead right on South Street. Go 0.3 mile to fork (Cross Street bears right).

10. Bear left (still South Street) for 1 mile to end at traffic island (merge left on West Street). You will turn sharply right here.

11. Sharp right for 1.5 miles to fork where Acton Street bears right and West Street bears slightly left.

12. Bear left for 0.7 mile to end (merge left on Route 225).

13. Bear left (**CAUTION** here) and stay on Route 225 for 2.8 miles to end, at stop sign (merge left on Route 110).

14. Bear left for 0.3 mile to where Route 225 (Concord Road) turns

Farm in Carlisle

right and Route 110 goes straight. Here the ride turns right, but if you go straight for 0.6 mile, you'll come to Kimball Farm Ice Cream on your left.

15. Right for 0.7 mile to Hildreth Street (unmarked) on right at a small traffic island. It's shortly after Tallard Road on left.

16. Right for 1.6 miles to traffic island with a monument in the center of Westford. This stretch is a gradual climb with a steep section toward the end.

17. Bear right and immediately go straight at crossroads onto Lincoln Street, passing the green on your left. Go 0.3 mile to fork where Depot Street bears left and Main Street bears right.

Notice the elegant white church and the handsome beige-brick library on the far side of the green. Just beyond the green on your right is the town hall and a wooden Victorian schoolhouse, now a community center.

When you get to the fork, the ride bears right, but if you bear left for 0.2 mile, you'll come to the Westford Knight on your right just as you start to go downhill—watch for a stone marker and five small stone pillars connected by chains. If you come to Abbott School, you've gone 0.1 mile too far.

18. Bear right for 2.9 miles to Westford Street, which bears right just beyond a ballfield and fire station on your right. There's a fast descent out of Westford.

19. Bear right and stay on main road for 2.1 miles to stop sign in the center of Chelmsford.

Just before the green you'll pass an unusual Gothic church on your left and then an old cemetery with weathered slate tombstones on your right. Notice the fine Victorian town hall on your left and the monument in the center of the green.

20. Bear slightly right onto Route 4 South. **CAUTION:** Busy intersection. Go 1.5 miles to shopping center on left, just after Mill Road (unmarked) on left.

Directions for shorter ride

1. Follow the long ride through direction number 7.
2. Right onto Lowell Street (unmarked), passing country store on right. Go 3.4 miles to fork where the main road bears left and Hazen Road bears right. To visit Great Brook Farm State Park, turn right after 1.8 miles on North Road. Go 0.3 mile to park entrance on left.
3. Bear right for 0.3 mile to end (Route 4).
4. Right for 0.2 mile to shopping center on left.

church, a fine turn-of-the-century library, and gracious old homes. Just off the route on the edge of town sits the Westford Knight, one of New England's unsolved mysteries. It is an outline of a medieval knight, complete with shield and sword, drawn on a rock. It was noticed by the earliest settlers, and its origin remains unknown. One theory is presented on a nearby stone marker. The return to Chelmsford passes farms and orchards and then becomes more residential but remains pleasant after you cross the Chelmsford town line. You'll bicycle through the town center shortly before the end of the ride. Several churches, an old cemetery with slate tombstones from the early 1800s, and the Victorian town hall frame the green, with a monument in the middle.

The short ride bypasses Westford, taking a more direct route from Carlisle back to Chelmsford along a rolling secondary road. You'll pass Great Brook Farm State Park, an extensive natural area with woods, fields, a working dairy farm, an ice cream stand, and 10 miles of trails suitable for mountain biking.

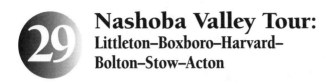

Nashoba Valley Tour:
Littleton–Boxboro–Harvard–Bolton–Stow–Acton

Number of miles:	33 (18 without Harvard–Bolton–Stow extension)
Terrain:	Very rolling, with one long, gradual hill and several shorter ones on the longer ride.
Food:	Groceries or restaurants in all the towns except Boxboro.
Start:	Nagog Park, a shopping center on Route 119 in Acton, at the Littleton town line. It's between Routes 27 and 110, and it's about 3 miles east of I–495.

The Nashoba Valley is the nickname for the rolling, rural, apple-growing country northwest of Boston near I–495. The Nashua Valley would be a more accurate name because the Nashua River flows along the region's western edge. The area is just far enough away from Boston to be rural rather than suburban, and it is dotted with graceful, unspoiled New England towns. Abounding with narrow lanes twisting past orchards and old farmhouses, the Nashoba Valley provides superb biking that is a bit challenging because of the numerous ups and downs in the landscape. On the longer ride, a scenic and historic highlight are the Fruitlands Museums, set on a broad hillside with an outstanding view.

At the start of the ride, you'll immediately head into Littleton along the shore of undeveloped Nagog Pond and then get into rolling orchard country. Once through the tiny center of Littleton, you'll ascend onto a long, high ridge capped with orchards that leads into Harvard. At the

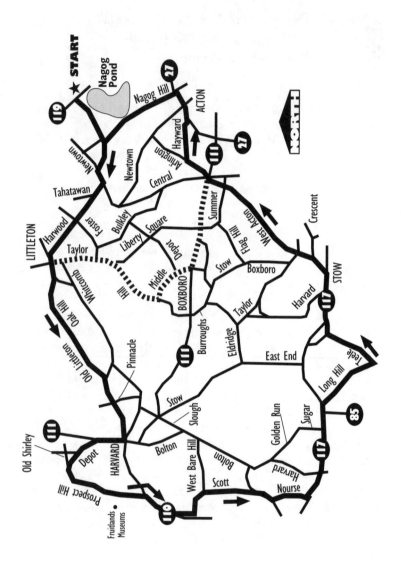

1. Right on Route 119 and immediately left onto Nashoba Road. Go 1.8 miles to end, at second stop sign (merge left). You'll go along Nagog Pond on your left at the beginning.

2. Bear left and just ahead bear right on Harwood Avenue. Go 0.6 mile to fork where Tahatawan Road bears right and the main road goes straight.

3. Straight for 2.1 miles to end, in Littleton. Here the short ride turns left and immediately left again on Taylor Street.

Notice the old railroad station on your left at the intersection. The commercial center of town, Littleton Common, is 2 miles east at the junction of Routes 110 and 27.

4. Left for less than 0.2 mile to fork where Oak Hill Road bears right.

5. Bear right and stay on main road for 3.1 miles to crossroads and stop sign (Pinnacle Road). Don't bear left after 2.7 miles on Old Schoolhouse Road, (unmarked). Most of this stretch is a gradual climb.

6. Straight for 1.4 miles to Route 111, at blinking light in the center of Harvard. Notice the stately brick library on right.

7. Right for 0.3 mile to Depot Road, which bears left while you're going downhill.

8. Bear left and stay on main road for 1.1 miles to stop sign (merge left onto Prospect Hill Road, unmarked). Don't bear right on Craggs Road after 0.7 mile. At the stop sign Old Shirley Road (unmarked) is on your right.

9. Bear left for 1.9 miles to end (Route 110). Fruitlands is on your right just past the top of the hill.

10. Right for 1.3 miles to West Bare Hill Road on left. It comes up while you're going downhill.

11. Left for less than 0.5 mile to fork (West Bare Hill Road bears left, Scott Road bears right).

12. Bear right for 1.3 miles to end (merge right at stop sign). Scott Road becomes Bare Hill Road at the Bolton town line.

13. Bear right for 0.3 mile to Nourse Road on left.

14. Left for 1 mile to end (Route 117).

15. Left for 2.1 miles to Long Hill Road, which bears right shortly after Route 85 on right.

You'll go through the center of Bolton. Notice the ornate stone library on your right as you come into town. To visit the Nashoba Valley Winery, turn right after 0.7 mile on Watoquadoc Hill Road at blinking light. Go 0.4 mile to winery on left, while climbing steep hill.

16. Bear right and stay on main road for 1.5 miles to diagonal crossroads (Teele Road). It comes up while you're going downhill.

17. Sharp left for 1.5 miles to end, at traffic island (Old Bolton Road).

18. Right for 0.4 mile to stop sign (merge right on Route 117).

19. Bear right for 1.7 miles to Crescent Street (unmarked), which bears left at the Stow town hall (sign may say TO ACTON).

20. Bear left for 0.3 mile to fork where Crescent Street bears right and West Acton Road bears left. Notice the fine church and library on your right at the beginning.

21. Bear left for 0.2 mile to a three-way fork.

22. Straight for 2.3 miles to second stop sign (merge left on Central Street).

23. Bear left for 0.2 mile to traffic light (Route 111, Massachusetts Avenue). This is West Acton.

24. Go straight and immediately turn right on Arlington Street. Go 0.5 mile to Hayward Road, which turns right uphill.

25. Right for 1.3 miles to end (Route 27).

26. Left (**CAUTION** here) for 0.7 mile to crossroads just beyond the center of Acton (Nagog Hill Road).

27. Left for 2.4 miles to crossroads and stop sign at top of hill (Nashoba Road, unmarked). You'll climb a step-like hill with some steep sections and then enjoy a fast downhill to Nagog Pond.

28. Right for 1.2 miles to end (Route 119). You'll go along Nagog Pond on your right.

29. Jog right and immediately left into shopping center at traffic light.

Directions for shorter ride

1. Follow directions for the long ride through number 3.
2. Left and immediately left again at crossroads onto Taylor Street. Go 1.9 miles to Hill Road, which bears right at a small green. It's just past the top of a long, steady hill.
3. Bear right for 1.8 miles to Middle Road on left, just before you go downhill.
4. Left for 1.1 miles to crossroads and stop sign (Route 111). There's a fast descent at the beginning. Just before the intersection, the Boxboro town hall is on your left.
5. Left for 2.1 miles to traffic light at bottom of hill (Central Street). This is West Acton.
6. Jog left and immediately right on Arlington Street. Go 0.5 mile to Hayward Road, which turns right uphill.
7. Follow directions for the long ride from number 25 to the end.

---

highest point is an astronomical observatory belonging to Harvard University (the names of the town and the university are coincidental and confusing to newcomers) and a fire tower.

Harvard is one of the most graceful and classically elegant of the outer Boston suburbs, and strict zoning laws will keep it that way for the foreseeable future. No tract housing mars the landscape; instead you'll find only gentleman farms with broad fields, orchards, weathered barns, and widely spaced newer homes tastefully integrated with the wooded landscape on large lots. The town center is a jewel, with a fine old brick library, a general store, a large sloping green, and a classic white church on a little hill at the head of the green.

Just outside town you'll ascend Prospect Hill, a magnificent open ridge with a spectacular view to the west. On a clear day you can see Mount Wachusett and even Mount Monadnock, 40 miles away. At the top of the ridge are the Fruitland Museums, a group of buildings with an eighteenth-century farmhouse, a Shaker house, a museum of American Indian relics, and a gallery of early American portraits and landscape paintings. The farmhouse contains a museum of the Transcendentalist movement, with memorabilia of the Alcott family, Emerson, Thoreau, and its other leaders, along with period furnishings and early farm implements. The Shaker house was moved several miles from a smaller Shaker village built during the 1790s. The rest of the village is 2 miles off the route.

From Harvard you'll proceed on winding lanes to Bolton, another delightful rural town with a cluster of antiques shops and an ornate stone library. The Nashoba Valley Winery, perched on a hillside with a glorious view and open for tours and tastings, is on the edge on town just off the route. The ride continues east to Stow, another unspoiled community consisting mainly of orchards, wooded hills, and farms along the Assabet River, a favorite of canoeists. From Stow you'll return to the start through the length of Acton, the most populous of the towns on the ride but still essentially rural. The center of town is another New England classic, with a fine, white, clock-towered town hall, graceful old church, and a small green with a tall obelisk honoring the leader of the Acton Minute Men. The homestretch takes you through woods, old farms, and back along the shore of Nagog Pond.

The short ride bypasses Harvard, Bolton, and Stow by cutting across Boxboro, which is circled by the long ride but never actually touched. Boxboro, a rural wooded town like Bolton and Stow, is unique in that it has no distinct town center.

Wayside Inn Ride:
Framingham–Southboro–Sudbury

Number of miles:	24 (15 with shortcut bypassing Wayside Inn)
Terrain:	Gently rolling with several short, steep hills.
Food:	Grocery and pizza shop just off the route in Southboro. Pizza when you cross Route 20 in Marlboro.
Facilities:	Rest rooms next to Wayside Inn.
Start:	Shopping center at Franklin Street and Mount Wayte Avenue in Framingham, about a mile south of Route 9.

Midway between Boston and Worcester, delightful bicycling abounds in the region lying around the Sudbury Reservoirs, a long chain of lakes surrounded by rolling hills, orchards, and open farmland. The landscape is rural in a prosperous, well-scrubbed sort of way, with gentleman farms, horse paddocks, and rambling, well-maintained old New England farmhouses set off by spreading shade trees and stone walls. A network of smooth secondary roads, many going along the lakeshores, gets you away from the traffic. A historic highlight of the ride is the Wayside Inn in Sudbury, the oldest continuously operating inn in the country, built around 1700 and visited by Longfellow during the mid-1800s. The poet was fascinated and celebrated it in his famed poems, *Tales of a Wayside Inn*. Sixty years later another captivated visitor, Henry Ford, decided to construct elements of a New England village next to the inn, so he added an operating gristmill, a little red schoolhouse, and a classic white church.

The ride starts from Framingham, one of Boston's most populous

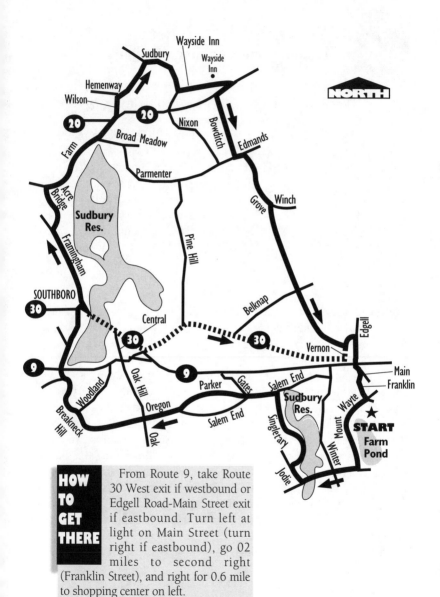

NORTH

Wayside Inn

Sudbury

Wayside Inn

Hemenway

Wilson

20

20

Farm

Nixon

Bowditch

Edmands

Broad Meadow

Parmenter

Winch

Grove

Acre Bridge

Sudbury Res.

Framingham

Pine Hill

SOUTHBORO

30

Central

Belknap

30

30

Edgell

Vernon

9

9

Parker

Gates

Salem End

Main

Franklin

Woodland

Oak Hill

Oregon

Salem End

Sudbury Res.

Mount Wayte

Breakneck Hill

Oak

Singletary

Winter

★ START Farm Pond

Jodie

HOW TO GET THERE From Route 9, take Route 30 West exit if westbound or Edgell Road-Main Street exit if eastbound. Turn left at light on Main Street (turn right if eastbound), go 02 miles to second right (Franklin Street), and right for 0.6 mile to shopping center on left.

1. Left on Mount Wayte Avenue for 1.1 miles to end (Fountain Street). You'll pass Farm Pond on your left.

2. Right for 0.9 mile to Jodie Road on right, just after bridge. You'll pass Reservoir Number 2, one of several lakes composing the Sudbury Reservoirs system, on your right just before the intersection.

3. Right for 0.2 mile to Singletary Lane on right, halfway up the hill.

4. Right for 1.4 miles to end (Salem End Road, unmarked). You'll follow Reservoir Number 2 on your right.

5. Left for 0.4 mile to fork where Gates Street bears right.

6. Bear right and just ahead bear left at another fork on Parker Road. Go 1.3 miles to stop sign (merge right on Oregon Road, unmarked).

7. Bear right and stay on main road for 1.6 miles to second stop sign (merge right on Woodland Road, unmarked).

8. Bear right under Massachusetts Turnpike, and bear left on far side of underpass on Breakneck Hill Road. Go 0.9 mile to fork (Mount Vickery Road bears left).

9. Bear right and just ahead cross Route 9 at traffic light (**CAUTION** here). Go 0.4 mile to fork where Latisquama Road bears left and White Bagley Road bears right. You'll follow the Sudbury Reservoir on your right.

10. Bear right for 0.5 mile to end (Route 30). Here the short ride turns right and immediately right again at end.

11. Left for 1.6 miles to Acre Bridge Road, which bears right.

12. Bear right for 0.7 mile to stop sign where the main road bears left and Farm Road (unmarked) turns right.

13. Turn right and stay on main road for 1.9 miles to traffic light at Route 20. (Don't bear right on Broad Meadow Road after 1.5 miles.) You'll pass Marlboro Airport, the oldest commercial airport in Massachusetts, on your right near the end.

14. Bear left across Route 20 onto Wilson Street. Stay on main road for 1.9 miles to end (Sudbury Street). You'll climb steeply for 0.2 mile near the beginning.

The gristmill next to the Wayside Inn, Sudbury

15. Right for 1.4 miles to end (Wayside Inn Road).

16. Left for 1 mile to end (Route 20). You'll pass the gristmill, the chapel, the little red schoolhouse, and finally the Wayside Inn itself.

17. Sharp right for 0.4 mile to second left, Bowditch Road.

18. Turn left and stay on main road for 1.4 miles to end at Edmands Road. (Don't bear right on smaller road after 0.25 mile.) You'll climb and then descend steeply. **CAUTION:** The end comes up suddenly at bottom of steep hill.

19. Turn left and then immediately bear right on Grove Street (unmarked). Stay on main road for 2 miles to crossroads and stop sign (Belknap Road).

20. Straight for 0.9 mile to end (Vernon Street), opposite the Framingham town green.

21. Left for 0.1 mile to end (Edgell Road). Notice the two impressive brick churches facing each other across the road at the head of the green.

22. Turn right. After 0.2 mile you'll cross the overpass above Route 9. (**CAUTION** here—busy intersections.) Continue 0.2 mile to second right, Franklin Street.

23. Right for 0.6 mile to Mount Wayte Avenue, at traffic light. The shopping center is just past light on right.

Directions for shorter ride

1. Follow directions for the long ride through number 10.

2. Right and then immediately right again at end (still Route 30). Go 0.3 mile to blinking light where main road curves left.

3. Curve left for 0.8 mile to traffic light (Route 30 turns left).

4. Left for 3.5 miles to stop sign (Vernon Street on left). **CAUTION:** Bumpy railroad tracks on far side of bridge over Massachusetts Turnpike after 2.9 miles. There's an excellent bagel shop on your left at the stop sign.

5. Left for 0.2 mile to end (Edgell Road) at grassy traffic island. You'll go along the Framingham town green. Notice the two impressive brick churches facing each other across the road at the head of the green.

suburbs, with 65,000 residents. Framingham is a city of three faces: partly an old industrial town with dreary rows of old wooden houses, partly a bedroom suburb with tract houses and modern apartment complexes, and partly a gracious rural town with lakes, horse farms, and a classic New England green. This ride goes through the third face. At the beginning you'll head along two ponds and proceed west into Southboro, a gracious, well-to-do community with gentleman farms spreading across rolling hillsides, the prestigious St. Mark's preparatory school, and a classic New England village center. The school and center of town are about a mile off the route. After two delightful runs along the lake, it's not far to the Wayside Inn.

Approaching the inn you first come to the gristmill, a masterpiece of historical reconstruction built for Ford in 1929. It is an authentic, working reproduction of an eighteenth-century stone mill, with a massive water wheel 18 feet in diameter. Just past the mill is the Martha-Mary Chapel, a replica of a New England church that somehow looks more sterile than the real one. It is now used only for weddings. Next to the chapel is the Redstone School, an actual one-room little red schoolhouse that was moved in 1926 from Sterling, 20 miles to the west, and used as a public school until 1951. This is the school that Mary and her little lamb went to. Just past the school is the inn itself, a graceful gambrel-roofed building all but overshadowed by the attractions leading up to it.

The return to Framingham takes you back through the city's third face, passing horse farms and gracious old Colonial-style homes. At the end you'll go by the handsome green, framed by two stately brick churches facing each other across the road and an ornate, steep-gabled Victorian library.

Holliston–Hopkinton

Number of miles:	29 (19 without western loop, 10 if you do the western loop only)
Terrain:	Rolling, with several hills.
Food:	Grocery and restaurant in Hopkinton. Country store in Southville. Burger King at end.
Start:	Tage Inn on Beaver Street in Milford. It's just north of Route 109 and just west of I–495. To do just the western loop, start at the junction of Routes 135 and 85 in the center of Hopkinton.

This ride will take you exploring two wooded, wealthy communities on the outer edge of Boston's suburbia, midway between Boston and Worcester and a little south of both. The landscape is rural rather than suburban, consisting mainly of wooded hills, some open farmland and orchards, and several unspoiled lakes. A wide-ranging network of narrow country roads provides superb bicycling if you're willing to tackle a few hills. The ride consists of a figure-eight with Hopkinton at the center. You may ride either loop or both.

The eastern loop heads through woods and past small farms to the center of Hopkinton, located on a broad hilltop. Hopkinton becomes known to the world on Patriot's Day, the third Monday in April, when the Boston Marathon starts here at noon. From Hopkinton you'll traverse large expanses of farmland and pass the undeveloped Ashland Reservoir. Then you'll ascend onto a long ridge with orchards on the top and fine views of the surrounding hills and valleys. The return leg

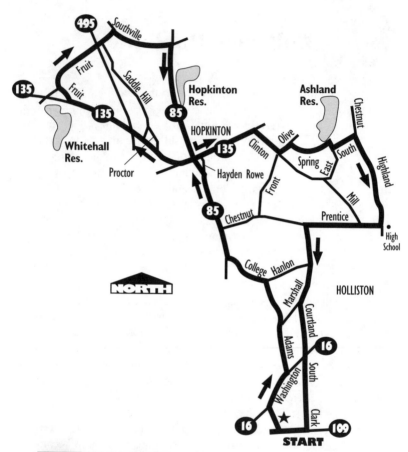

HOW TO GET THERE

To get to the inn from I–495, take exit 19 (Route 109). Follow Route 109 West to traffic light just ahead (Beaver Street). Turn right and go 0.1 mile to inn on right.

DIRECTIONS
FOR
THE RIDE

1. Right for 0.3 mile to traffic light (Route 16).
2. Right for 0.9 mile to Adams Street (unmarked), a small road that bears left.
3. Bear left and stay on main road for 1.9 miles to end (Hanlon Road). Don't bear right on Marshall Street (unmarked) after 0.9 mile.
4. Left for 0.9 mile to end (Route 85).

5. Turn right and stay on Route 85 for 2.4 miles to traffic light (Route 135, Main Street). This is the center of Hopkinton. Here the 19-mile ride turns right and the 29-mile ride turns left.

6. Left for 0.4 mile to traffic light where Route 135 bears right. You'll pass the former brick high school (now offices), built in 1894, on the left.

7. Bear right for 2.5 miles to Fruit Street, which bears right. After 2 miles you'll go through the gracious village of Woodville (part of Hopkinton) and pass a small dam on your left. The Whitehall Reservoir is just past Fruit Street on the left.

8. Bear right for 0.3 mile to fork (Cunningham Street bears left).

9. Bear right (still Fruit Street) for 2.3 miles to end at grassy traffic island.

10. Right for 1.5 miles to Route 85, at traffic light. You'll go through the tiny village of Southville, a part of Southboro. An old-fashioned country store is on the right just before the light.

11. Right for 2.9 miles to traffic light (Route 135, Main Street), back in the center of Hopkinton. You'll pass Hopkinton State Park and the Hopkinton Reservoir on your left. There's a tough hill leading into town.

12. Left for 1.7 miles to Clinton Street on right (sign may say LABORERS TRAINING CENTER). Notice the handsome stone library on your right at the beginning.

13. Right for 0.6 mile to Olive Street on left at traffic island.

14. Left for 0.2 mile to Spring Street on right.

15. Right for 0.9 mile to South Street (unmarked) on left, shortly after you pass the Ashland Reservoir on left. It comes up while you're climbing a steep hill.

16. Left for 0.4 mile to end (Chestnut Street on left, Highland Street on right). Both roads are unmarked.

17. Right for 2 miles to Prentice Street on right.

18. Right for 1.6 miles to Marshall Street (unmarked) on left.

19. Left for 1.7 miles to fork where Marshall Street bears right and Courtland Street bears left.

20. Bear left for 0.7 mile to crossroads and stop sign (Route 16, Washington Street). Just before the intersection you'll pass Weston Pond on your left.

21. Straight for 1.8 miles to end (Route 109).

22. Right for 0.7 mile to traffic light (Beaver Street, unmarked, on right).

23. Right for 0.1 mile to inn on right.

Directions for shorter ride: 19 miles

1. Follow directions for the long ride through number 5.

2. Right for 1.7 miles to Clinton Street on right (sign may say LABORERS TRAINING CENTER). Notice the handsome stone library on your right at the beginning.

3. Follow directions for the long ride from number 13 to the end.

Directions for shorter ride: 10 miles

(Start from junction of Routes 135 and 85 in the center of Hopkinton.)

1. Head west on Route 135 for 0.4 mile to traffic light where Route 135 bears right. You'll pass the former brick high school (now offices), built in 1894, on your left.

2. Follow directions for the 29-mile ride from numbers 7 through 11.

---

brings you through a rural landscape along winding lanes through woods, past old barns and farmhouses, and along Weston Pond.

The western loop passes through a landscape that is similar but a little more wooded. You'll ride through the well-kept villages of Woodville and Southville and then along the Hopkinton Reservoir, adjoining Hopkinton State Park. The reservoir is surrounded by round, green hills.

Chapter 4:
The Outer Western Suburbs

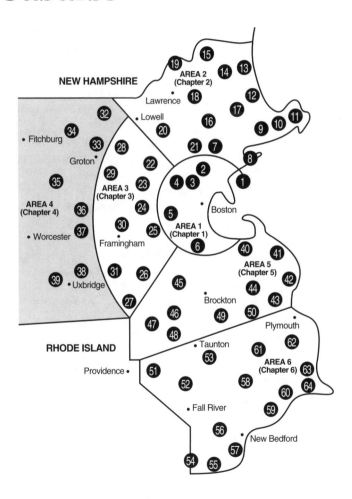

Westford–Dunstable–Tyngsboro

Number of miles:	26 (13 without Dunstable–Tyngsboro extension)
Terrain:	Rolling, with two tough hills.
Food:	Groceries and snack bars in the towns. Burger King and McDonald's near end on Route 110 just east of Boston Road. (Turn left from Boston Road onto Route 110).
Start:	Westford town green, about a mile northwest of I–495. Park on Lincoln Street or in the public parking lot behind the town hall (also on Lincoln Street) if there is no on-street parking.

Just west of Lowell, along the west bank of the Merrimack River, is a delightful biking area of gentle wooded hills, small farms, and unspoiled small towns. As you head west of Lowell, the countryside quickly becomes rural because you're just far enough from Boston to make commuting impractical. Westford actually lies on the fringe of the metropolitan area, but it is a well-to-do community with a no-growth policy and is very much a small town.

The ride starts from Westford, one of the many gracious, still-unspoiled towns that dot the countryside northwest of Boston along I–495. The hilltop village center is exceptionally appealing, with a large tree-studded green framed by a graceful white church, the stately white wooden town hall, and a turn-of-the-century beige-brick library. Just beyond the green is an ornate wooden Victorian schoolhouse, now a

1. Follow Lincoln Street for 0.25 mile to fork where Main Street bears right and Depot Street bears left.

2. Bear left and stay on the main road for 1 mile to fork immediately after railroad tracks (Plain Road bears right). **CAUTION:** Long, steep descent—keep your speed under control.

The Westford Knight will be on your right after 0.2 mile, just as you start to go downhill. Watch for a stone marker and five small stone pillars connected by chains. If you come to Abbott School, you've gone 0.1 mile too far.

3. Bear left (still Depot Street) and stay on main road for 1.1 miles to fork (Dunstable Road bears left).

4. Bear left and stay on main road for 3.2 miles to Chestnut Road on right at bottom of hill. Here the short ride turns right.

You'll go straight at 3 crossroads, passing Long-Sought-for Pond on your right just before the second one.

5. Straight for 1.9 miles to end (Route 113).

6. Left for 0.2 mile to High Street on right, opposite the church in the center of Dunstable. Notice the fine brick library on your right. Here the ride turns right, but there's a country store just ahead on Route 113.

7. Right for 0.8 mile to fork where Thorndike Street bears right and High Street bears left.

8. Left for 1.8 miles to end (Ridge Road). **CAUTION:** Sandy spots. At the end you're in Nashua, New Hampshire, a city promoting the development of condominiums and subdivisions.

9. Right for 1 mile to East Dunstable Road on right. There's a tough hill midway along this stretch.

10. Right for 1.4 miles to end.

11. Left for 0.6 mile to end (Route 113).

12. Left for 0.5 mile to Locust Avenue on left, shortly before the Route 3 overpass.

13. Turn left and stay on main road for 0.9 mile to crossroads and stop

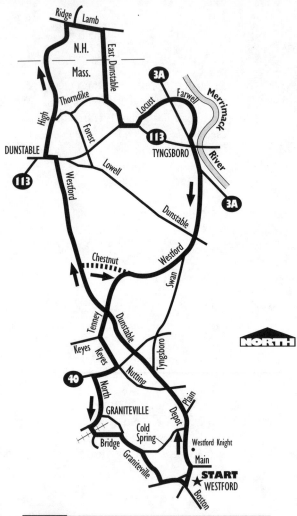

HOW TO GET THERE

From I–495, take the Boston Road exit (exit 32). Turn left at the end of the ramp if you were heading north on I–495; turn right if you were heading south. Go about a mile to Lincoln Street on right at the green, and turn right.

sign (Route 3A, Middlesex Road). Don't bear right on Old Kendall Road at the beginning.

You'll pass Locust Pond on your right. Just before the end there may be a barricade to keep out cars. Walk around it on the left.

14. Straight for 1.4 miles to end (merge left on Route 3A) in Tyngsboro. Notice the fine brick library on the far side of the intersection.

15. Bear left for 0.4 mile to Westford Road, which bears right at second traffic light. Notice the small dam on your right immediately before the first light.

16. Bear right for 1.7 miles to fork (Swan Road bears slightly left, Westford Road bears right).

17. Bear right for 0.9 mile to another fork (Chestnut Road bears slightly right, Westford Road bears left).

18. Bear left for 1.5 miles to crossroads (Dunstable Road, unmarked).

19. Straight (**CAUTION** here—no stop sign) for 0.7 mile to fork, at traffic island (Keyes Road bears both right and left).

20. Bear left for 0.6 mile to end (Route 40). You'll pass Keyes Pond on your right.

21. Right for 0.6 mile to North Street on left (sign may say TO FORGE VILLAGE).

22. Left for 1.1 miles to a small road that turns left under a narrow railroad bridge. It's just after a millpond on the left.

Notice the turreted Victorian mansion on your right opposite the pond. This is Graniteville, a mill village in Westford.

23. Left and then immediately left again on Bridge Street. Go 0.5 mile to end at stop sign.

24. Right for 0.4 mile to fork where Cold Spring Road bears left and Graniteville Road (unmarked) bears right.

25. Bear right for 0.8 mile to end at top of long hill.

26. Left for less than 0.2 mile to fork at the Westford green (Boston Road bears right).

27. Bear right for 100 yards to crossroads (Lincoln Street). The starting point is to your left.

Directions for shorter ride

1. Follow directions for the long ride through number 4.
2. Right for 1.2 miles to stop sign (merge left on Westford Road). You will turn sharply right here. **CAUTION:** Watch for potholes and cracks.
3. Sharp right for 1.5 miles to crossroads (Dunstable Road, unmarked).
4. Follow directions for the long ride from number 19 to the end.

---

community center. On the edge of town sits the Westford Knight, one of New England's unsolved mysteries. It is an outline of a medieval knight, complete with shield and sword, drawn on a rock. It was noticed by the earliest settlers, and its origin remains unknown. One theory is presented on a nearby stone marker.

From Westford you'll enjoy a long descent and then proceed on wooded backroads to Dunstable, a graceful picture-postcard town with a traditional old church, little village green, and a fine brick library. From Dunstable you'll hug the Massachusetts–New Hampshire border to Tyngsboro, another small town lying directly along the west bank of the Merrimack. Its major landmark is the graceful steel-arched bridge across the Merrimack. Until 1960 Tyngsboro sat on the main road from Boston to New Hampshire; then Route 3 was built, bypassing the town, and it became nearly forgotten. (Many residents moved from Tyngsboro to New Hampshire, which has no sales or income tax.)

From Tyngsboro you'll return to Westford along winding lanes through the handsome mill village of Graniteville, which is part of Westford. Graniteville is accurately named, with a handsome bell-towered granite mill standing above a delightful little millpond. Since Westford sits on top of a hill, you'll have a climb at the end of the ride.

Covered-Bridge Ride:
Groton–Pepperell–
Hollis, New Hampshire–Ayer

33

Number of miles:	30 (20 without Hollis extension)
Terrain:	Rolling, with one long hill.
Food:	Groceries and snack bars in the towns.
Start:	Victory Super Market on Route 2A in Ayer, 0.8 mile north of the center of town. It's just north of the fork of Routes 2A and 111.

The valley of the Nashua River, midway between Fitchburg and Lowell, is a bicyclist's paradise of country roads traversing broad farms and orchards and winding through rolling hills. The region is one of the major apple-growing areas of the state. Adding variety to this refreshingly rural landscape are the three gracious New England towns of Groton, Pepperell, and Hollis, New Hampshire. In Pepperell you'll bike over the only original-style covered bridge in the eastern half of the state.

The ride starts on the outskirts of Ayer and immediately heads through rolling orchards and farmlands to the classic New England town of Groton, one of the most elegant in the state. Just over the town line is the stately, meticulously landscaped campus of the Groton School, one of the most prestigious preparatory schools in the country. The most prominent landmark of the campus is the graceful Gothic-style stone chapel. A fine green, several graceful old churches, and the handsome brick buildings of Lawrence Academy, another prep school, dignify the center of town. Surrounding the town are broad acres of gentleman farms, estates, and orchards spreading over the rolling hills.

From Groton it's several miles along backroads to Pepperell, another classic town with a handsome old white church and town hall and an

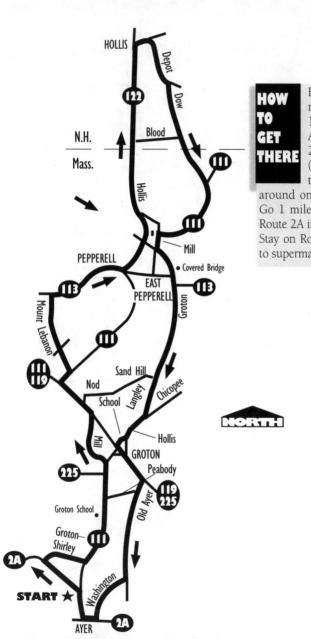

HOW TO GET THERE

From Route 2, exit north onto Routes 110 and 111 toward Ayer (exit 38B). Go 2 miles to rotary (Route 2A). Go three-quarters around onto Route 2A West. Go 1 mile and turn right on Route 2A in the center of Ayer. Stay on Route 2A for 0.8 mile to supermarket on left.

HOLLIS

Depot

Dow

122

N.H.

Mass.

Blood

111

Hollis

111

Mill

PEPPERELL

Covered Bridge

113

EAST PEPPERELL

113

Mount Lebanon

111

Groton

111 119

Sand Hill

Nod

School

Langley

Chicopee

Hollis

GROTON

NORTH

Mill

Peabody

225

119 225

Groton School

Old Ayer

111

Groton–Shirley

2A

START ★

Washington

AYER

2A

DIRECTIONS
FOR
THE RIDE

1. Left (northwest) on Route 2A for 0.8 mile to Groton-Shirley Road (unmarked) on right, just after army training facility on left. **CAUTION:** Diagonal railroad tracks after 0.5 mile.

2. Right for 0.9 mile to end (Route 111). You'll pass a state-run pheasant farm on your left; it is not open to the public. **CAUTION:** More diagonal railroad tracks at the beginning.

3. Left for 2.2 miles to Mill Street, which bears left at small green. It's shortly after Route 225 West on left.

You'll pass the Groton School on your left after 1 mile. It's worth making a loop around the grounds to catch the flavor of this gracious and distinguished school.

4. Bear left for 1.1 miles to end (merge left on Routes 111 and 119).

5. Bear left for 0.8 mile to where Route 111 (River Road) turns right.

6. Right for 0.3 mile to Mount Lebanon Street on left.

7. Left for 2 miles to end (Townsend Street, Route 113). After the crossroads you'll climb steeply for 0.4 mile and have a fine view from the top.

8. Right for 1.4 miles to Route 111, at rotary. You'll go through the center of Pepperell. Notice the handsome brick library on the right.

9. Bear left on Route 111 North for 0.7 mile to where Route 111 turns right and Hollis Street (unmarked) goes straight. Here the short ride turns right.

You'll cross the Nashua River, which flows over a low dam on your left, immediately before the intersection.

10. Straight for 4.6 miles to a road that turns right down a short hill in Hollis, New Hampshire. It's shortly after high school on left.

You'll pass a great ice cream shop on your right near the beginning. The small white building on the far side of the intersection in Hollis was originally a firehouse built in 1859. It is occasionally opened as a museum by the Hollis Historical Society.

11. Bear right and then immediately bear right again (sign may say TO ROUTES 111, 111A). Go 100 yards to stop sign (merge right). Notice the

inviting domed library on your left. At the stop sign there's a country store to your left.

12. Bear right for 0.8 mile to fork where the main road curves left and Dow Road bears right.

13. Bear right for 2.6 miles to end (merge right on Route 111). **CAUTION:** Bumps and potholes on the last 0.7 mile, after crossing back into Pepperell.

14. Bear right for 1.8 miles to crossroads and blinking light (Mill Street).

15. Left for 0.2 mile to crossroads and stop sign (Groton Street).

16. Left for 3.8 miles to end at stop sign (merge right on Hollis Street).

You'll cross the covered bridge over the Nashua River at the beginning. Just ahead is East Pepperell. The commercial area is to your right on Route 113 West; you can obtain food here.

17. Bear right for 0.5 mile to School Street, which bears right.

18. Bear right and just ahead bear left at fork. Go 100 yards to crossroads and stop sign in Groton.

19. Left for 0.9 mile to Old Ayer Road (unmarked), which bears right at a small green.

20. Bear right and stay on main road for 2.4 miles to fork immediately after the road passes under power lines (Groton-Harvard Road bears left, Washington Street bears right uphill).

21. Bear right and stay on main road for 1.1 miles to end (Route 2A, Main Street), in the center of Ayer. (Don't bear right on Howard Street, unmarked, after almost 0.6 mile.)

22. Right and just ahead right again on Routes 2A and 111 (Park Street). Go 0.6 mile to fork where Route 111 bears slightly right and Route 2A bears left.

23. Bear left, and supermarket is just ahead on left.

Directions for shorter ride

1. Follow directions for the long ride through number 9.

2. Right for 0.2 mile to crossroads and blinking light (Mill Street).

3. Right for 0.2 mile to crossroads and stop sign (Groton Street).

4. Follow directions for the long ride from number 16 to the end.

ornate, pillared red-brick library. Just outside town you'll cross the Nashua River over the covered bridge, actually a replica of the original that was rebuilt in 1962. The return trip loops back through Groton across more inspiring rolling estate and orchard country to the center of Ayer, which is an old mill town trying to rebound. When the main line of the Boston and Maine Railroad between Boston, Fitchburg, and Albany declined, the town declined with it. Ayer became primarily an extension of Fort Devens, the large military base just outside town that closed in 1994. The former base is now being converted into a business and industrial park. Although a bit worn, the downtown area is still fascinating, with an ornate Victorian town hall and an old, arcaded commercial block.

The long ride heads north out of Pepperell along a broad, open ridge to Hollis, New Hampshire, just across the Massachusetts border. Hollis is a delightful old town with a classic New England church and green and a handsome white, pillared library. From Hollis you'll head back toward Pepperell through broad farms and orchards and pick up the route of the short ride just in time to go over the covered bridge.

34 Shirley–Lunenburg Townsend–West Groton

Number of miles:	29 (16 without Townsend extension)
Terrain:	Rolling, with one long hill. The long ride has two additional hills.
Food:	Groceries and restaurants in the towns.
Start:	Front Street, in the center of Shirley.

Just east of Fitchburg is a prime area for biking. It has rolling hills and open ridges with fine views, crisscrossed by a network of lightly traveled secondary roads and winding rural lanes. The unspoiled classic New England towns of Shirley Center, Lunenburg, and Townsend are an attractive change of pace from the otherwise rural landscape.

The ride starts from Shirley, a small, somewhat tired-looking town that seems as though it's seen happier days. There's not much keeping the town going except the nearby business and industrial park on the grounds of the former Fort Devens military reservation. A couple of miles north is the town's better half, Shirley Center, one of the finest traditional villages in the outer western suburbs. The small green is framed by an elegant old white church, pillared town hall, old cemetery, and gracious old wooden homes. You'll go through Shirley Center near the end of the ride.

From Shirley you'll ride through spectacular rolling ridge country to the stately hilltop town of Lunenburg, another New England beauty with the traditional white church and old wooden town hall facing each other across the road and a handsome, pillared library. You'll ride past Hickory Hills Lake and a picturesque dam about two miles ahead. The

1. Head west on Front Street, paralleling the railroad tracks on your right, for about 0.2 mile to fork (Lancaster Road bears left).

2. Bear right for less than 0.4 mile to another fork (Catacunemaug Road bears right).

3. Bear left on main road for 2.4 miles to Lancaster Avenue, which bears right (sign says TO LUNENBERG). You'll pass a small dam and millpond on your left at the beginning.

4. Bear right for 4.3 miles to traffic light (Route 2A) in the center of Lunenberg. You'll pass Massapoag Pond and a little dam on your left after 1.2 miles.

5. Right for 0.9 mile to Townsend Harbor Road on left at bottom of hill.

6. Left for 0.8 mile to fork (Mulpus Road bears right). Here the short ride bears right. You'll go along Hickory Hills Lake and pass an attractive dam on your left.

7. Bear left along lake for 0.4 mile to fork (South Row Road bears left).

8. Bear left for 1.5 miles to yield sign (merge right).

9. Bear right for 0.3 mile to Emery Road (unmarked) on left.

10. Left for 1.3 miles to end (Route 13).

11. Right for 1.3 miles to traffic light (Route 119) in the center of Townsend. You'll pass a handsome brick fire station on your right just before the light.

12. Go straight and stay on Route 13 for 2.2 miles to North End Road (unmarked) on right. A sign on your left at the intersection says BROOKLINE, N.H.

Route 13 bears right and just ahead bears left at the beginning of this section of the ride.

13. Right for 0.5 mile to Townsend Hill Road on right.

14. Turn right and stay on main road for 3.5 miles to diagonal crossroads and stop sign (Route 119). There's a long, steady hill at the beginning, but an even longer descent follows.

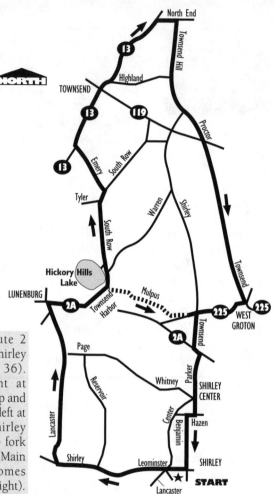

HOW TO GET THERE

From Route 2 take the Shirley exit (exit 36). Turn right at end of ramp and just ahead left at end on Shirley Road. Go 2 miles to fork just after stop sign (Main Street, which becomes Front Street, bears right). Center of town is just ahead.

From Roue 2 East take exit 36. Turn right at end of ramp on Shirley Road, go 2 miles to fork, and follow above directions.

15. Straight (**CAUTION** here) for 3.6 miles to stop sign (Route 225, unmarked) in West Groton. **CAUTION:** Bumpy spots. Notice the elegant stone church on your left, set back off the road on a hill, after 3.4 miles.

16. Turn right on Route 225 West. **CAUTION:** Bad railroad tracks as you turn—please walk across. Go 1.4 miles to crossroads and blinking light (Townsend Road). Most of this stretch is a steady climb, with a steep section near the beginning.

17. Left for 0.9 mile to end (Route 2A).

18. Left and just ahead right on Parker Road (it's unmarked; sign says TO SHIRLEY CENTER, CLINTON). Go 0.8 mile to fork in Shirley Center where the main road bears right and a smaller road goes straight. You'll climb for 0.3 mile at the beginning.

19. Straight for 0.5 mile to end (Hazen Road, unmarked).

20. Right for less than 0.2 mile to Benjamin Road (unmarked) on left.

21. Left for 1.3 miles to crossroads and stop sign.

22. Straight across railroad tracks and immediately right on Front Street. The starting point is just ahead.

Directions for shorter ride

1. Follow directions for the long ride through number 6.

2. Bear right for 2.1 miles to end (merge left on Route 225).

3. Bear left (**CAUTION** here) for 0.4 mile to crossroads and blinking light (Townsend Road).

4. Right for 0.9 mile to end (Route 2A).

5. Follow directions for the long ride from number 18 to end.

return leg to Shirley leads through woods and farmland, passing through Shirley Center about 2 miles before the end.

The long ride heads farther north to Townsend, yet another classic New England town. The handsome town green, highlighted by a bandstand in the center, is framed by the Victorian town hall and a magnificent church with a tall, ornate steeple, dated 1770. After leaving Townsend you'll climb a long, steady hill followed by an even longer descent. Several miles ahead you'll come to West Groton, a tiny village with an appealing country store, a lovely dam, and an old brick mill. You'll rejoin the short ride about 2 miles before Shirley Center.

West Boylston–
Sterling–Lancaster

Number of miles:	28 (14 without Lancaster extension)
Terrain:	Rolling, with several hills, one a real monster.
Food:	Groceries and snack bars in the towns.
Start:	Picnic area at the fork of Routes 12 and 140 in West Boylston, just north of the bridge over the Wachusett Reservoir. It's about 6 miles northwest of I–290 (take exit 23B). Park at side of road.

Just north of the Wachusett Reservoir, midway between Worcester and Fitchburg, superb biking abounds on narrow roads winding through woods and along broad, open hilltops with impressive views. The area is very rural except for the two classic New England towns of Sterling and Lancaster.

You start from the western edge of the Wachusett Reservoir, second largest lake in the state, and head north along its slender western arm to the fine valley town of Sterling, best known as the locale of "Mary Had a Little Lamb." The fabled schoolhouse was moved in 1926 by Henry Ford next to the Wayside Inn in Sudbury about 20 miles to the east. A small statue of a lamb on the green commemorates the nursery rhyme. From Sterling you'll return to the start, traversing a broad, open hillside through farms and orchards with fine views of the surrounding country-side. You'll pass Davis's Farmland, a petting zoo with a full lineup of barnyard animals who'll eat out of your hand.

The long ride heads farther north along country lanes and over an-

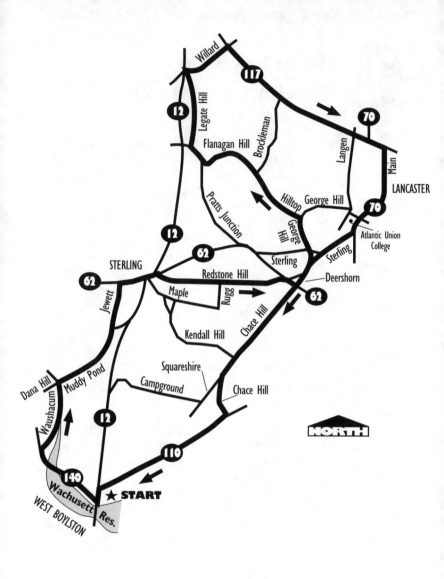

1. Head north on Route 140, paralleling the western arm of the reservoir on your left. Go 1.5 miles to Waushacum Street, which bears right. (A sign says TO STERLING.)

As soon as you start, notice the Old Stone Church, which was built in 1890, on your left. Only the stone exterior remains. You'll go through the village of Oakdale (part of West Boylston) shortly before the intersection.

2. Bear right for 1.4 miles to crossroads and stop sign (Dana Hill Road on left).

3. Right across a small metal-grate bridge for 1.1 miles to fork. (Jewett Road, a smaller road, bears left up a little hill.) **CAUTION:** Walk across the metal-grate bridge if the road is wet.

On your left you'll get a view of Mount Wachusett, 2,000 feet high. It's the tallest mountain in the state east of the Connecticut River.

4. Bear left for 0.9 mile to end (Route 62).

5. Right for 0.4 mile to stop sign (merge left on Route 12 in Sterling).

6. Bear left for 0.3 mile to fork where Route 12 bears left and Route 62 goes straight. Notice the brick Victorian library, built in 1885, on your left.

7. Go straight and just ahead bear right uphill on Redstone Hill Road. Go 2.2 miles to end (Route 62).

There's a tough climb to the top of the ridge, but you'll be rewarded with a long, lazy downhill through farms and orchards with views of distant hills. You'll pass Davis's Farmland on your right after 1.6 miles.

8. Right for 0.3 mile to crossroads (Chace Hill Road). There's an excellent farmstand on the right just before the intersection. At the crossroads the short ride turns right.

9. Left for 0.6 mile to unmarked road that bears left at a small green.

10. Bear left and just ahead turn right on George Hill Road. Go 1 mile to Hill Top Road on left at bottom of hill. (The main road bears right at the intersection.) The large, wrought-iron gate on the far side of the intersection leads into the Maharishi Ayurveda Health Center.

Wachusett Reservoir, West Boylston

11. Left for 2.4 miles to end (Pratts Junction Road).

12. Right for 0.5 mile to Legate Hill Road on right, just before Route 12.

13. Right for 1.5 miles to end (merge right on Route 12 at bottom of hill). **CAUTION:** Watch for bumps on the descent, which is very steep. You'll climb onto a ridge with fine views.

14. Bear right and then immediately turn right at blinking light on Willard Street (don't whiz past it). Go 1 mile to crossroads and stop sign (Route 117).

15. Right for 3.7 miles to Route 70 South (Main Street), which bears right shortly after Route 70 North on left. You'll climb a long steady hill, but you'll be rewarded by an even longer descent.

16. Bear right and stay on main road for 2.1 miles to Sterling Road, which bears right shortly after Atlantic Union College. You'll pass the Lancaster town green on your left after 0.9 mile.

17. Bear right for 0.8 mile to fork (Deershorn Road bears left).

18. Bear left and stay on main road for 0.5 mile to fork. (Chace Hill Road bears left).

19. Bear left and just ahead cross Route 62. Go 2.1 miles to fork at top of hill (Chace Hill Road bears left). This is a delightful ride through orchards and open fields.

20. Bear left for 0.7 mile to end (Route 110). Here the ride turns right, but if you turn left for 0.2 mile, you'll get a sweeping view of the Wachusett Reservoir.

21. Right for 2.7 miles to traffic light (Route 12).

22. Bear left, and picnic area is just ahead on right.

Directions for shorter ride

1. Follow directions for the long ride through number 8.

2. Right for 2.1 miles to fork at top of hill (Chace Hill Road bears left). This is a beautiful ride through orchards and broad fields.

3. Follow directions for the long ride from number 20 to the end.

other open hilltop to the elegant town of Lancaster, oldest in Worcester County. The town is on the Nashua River, surrounded by broad expanses of farmland. You'll pass the entrance to the Maharishi Ayurveda Health Center, a retreat for spiritual rejuvenation, meditation, and self-discovery. Ayurveda is a system of holistic health and medicine from ancient India. The town green is uniquely impressive, flanked by the graceful brick First Unitarian Church; an ornate, domed Victorian library dated 1867; and two fine old schools. The church, designed by Charles Bulfinch, was built in 1816. Just past the green you'll pass the handsome campus of Atlantic Union College, run by the Seventh-day Adventists. Shortly beyond Lancaster you'll join the short ride, traversing the hillside near the end.

36 Apple Country Adventure:
Northboro–Boylston–Berlin–Bolton

Number of miles:	29 (18 without Bolton extension)
Terrain:	Rolling, with a tough hill on the long ride.
Food:	Country store in Boylston. Country store in Berlin. Farm stand with snack bar in Berlin. Grocery and snack bar in Bolton. Coffee shop at end.
Start:	CVS Pharmacy, in a small shopping center at Routes 20 and 135 in the center of Northboro. It's on the north side of Route 20, at Church Street. From I–290, take exit 24 (Church Street) if you're heading east, or exit 25A (Hudson Street) if you're heading west. From either direction, turn right at the end of the exit ramp and go 2 miles into Northboro.

The rolling, refreshingly rural apple-orchard country along the western edge of I–495 provides delightful bicycling on an elaborate network of winding country roads with no traffic. This is a region of classic New England scenery, with old barns, rambling wooden farmhouses, and stone walls crisscrossing the rolling pastureland. Boylston, Berlin, and Bolton are unspoiled towns with elegant village centers. The best time to take this ride is in mid-May, when the apple blossoms cover the orchards with a pink canopy, or in September and early October, when the foliage is peaking and you can stuff your saddlebag full of apples for pennies.

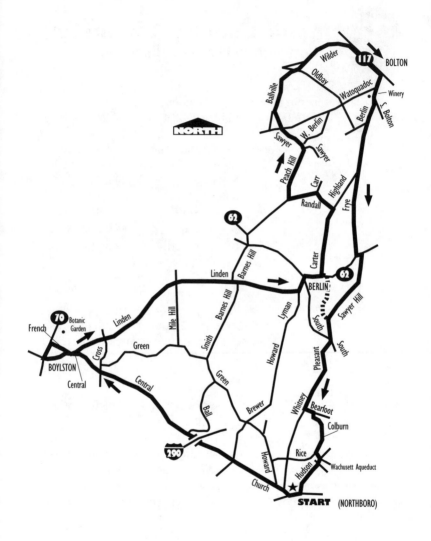

DIRECTIONS
FOR
THE RIDE

1. Turn right (west) onto Route 20 and immediately bear right on Church Street. (Don't get on Pierce Street.) Go 0.1 mile to fork where main road bears slightly left.

2. Bear left and stay on main road for 5.3 miles to end (Route 70, Main Street). You'll climb three short, fairly steep hills after you go under I–290. Tower Hill Botanic Garden is on your right just before the end.

3. Left for 0.3 mile to crossroads (Scar Hill Road on right, Central Street on left) in the center of Boylston. Notice the elegant stone library on the far right corner.

Here the ride turns left, but to see the Wachusett Reservoir, turn right for 0.6 mile to dead end, and walk on dirt road (sign says NO BICYCLES) for 0.2 mile to shore.

4. Left for 0.5 mile to end (merge right). You'll pass the green on your right and the stone former town hall on your left at the beginning.

5. Bear right and just ahead bear left on Linden Street. Go 5.6 miles to stop sign and blinking light (merge right on Route 62) in Berlin.

6. Bear right for 0.1 mile to second left (Carter Street). There's a country store on your right at the intersection. Here the short ride goes straight.

7. Left for 1.2 miles to Randall Road on left.

8. Left for 0.5 mile to fork at top of hill (Carr Road bears right).

9. Bear left (still Randall Road) for 0.8 mile to Peach Hill Road, which turns sharply right.

10. Sharp right for 1.2 miles to fork. (Sawyer Road, a small lane, bears right downhill.)

11. Bear left and immediately bear left again at another fork (also Sawyer Road, unmarked). Go 0.6 mile to crossroads and stop sign at bottom of steep hill (**CAUTION** here).

12. Straight for 0.4 mile to stop sign (merge right).

13. Bear right for 0.9 mile to fork (Oldbay Road bears right).

14. Bear left for 1 mile to stop sign (merge right on Route 117).

15. Bear right for 0.7 mile to Watoquadoc Road on right, at blinking light in the center of Bolton (sign may say TO BERLIN, CLINTON). Notice

Wachusett Aqueduct, Northboro

the fine stone library on your right just before the intersection.

16. Right for 0.25 mile to fork (Berlin Road bears left). Here the ride bears left, but if you bear slightly right up the hill, the Nashoba Valley Winery is just ahead on your left.

17. Bear left for 0.5 mile to fork where South Bolton Road goes straight and Berlin Road (unmarked) bears slightly right.

18. Bear right and stay on main road for 1.1 miles to fork where Frye Road bears left.

19. Bear left for 1.5 miles to end (Route 62). There's a combined farm stand, snack bar, and cider mill on your left at the end.

20. Jog left and immediately right onto Sawyer Hill Road, up a steep hill. Go 1.7 miles to end (Pleasant Street) at grassy traffic island. (Turn left at island.)

At the top of the hill you'll be rewarded with a panoramic view of Mount Wachusett and a relaxing descent.

21. Left for 0.4 mile to fork (South Street bears left).

22. Bear right (still Pleasant Street) for 0.6 mile to end (merge right on Whitney Avenue).

23. Bear right for 1 mile to Bearfoot Road on left just after going under I–295.

24. Left for 0.3 mile to Colburn Street on right just after railroad tracks.

25. Turn right and stay on main road for 0.9 mile to fork (Rice Avenue bears right uphill).

26. Bear left for 0.1 mile to crossroads and stop sign (Hudson Street, unmarked). There's a picturesque dam on the far left side of the intersection.

27. Right under Wachusett Aqueduct for 0.9 mile to end (Route 20).

28. Right for 100 yards to starting point on right.

Directions for shorter ride

1. Follow directions for the long ride through number 6.

2. Go straight and just ahead turn right on Pleasant Street. Go 1.5 miles to fork (South Street bears left).

3. Follow directions for the long ride from number 22 to the end.

The ride starts in Northboro, an attractive town with a graceful old church and a couple of Victorian mills on the Assabet River, a small stream here. You'll head to Boylston, an unspoiled gem of a town, with a triangular green framed by a stately white church, a stone former town hall built in 1830 (now the Boylston Historical Society), and a handsome fieldstone library constructed in 1904. As you come into the town, you'll pass the lovely Tower Hill Botanic Garden, a preserve that features a sweeping view of the Wachusett Reservoir from a hilltop.

From Boylston you'll head to Berlin (accented on the first syllable) on back roads winding through rolling hills crowned with orchards and open farmland. Berlin is a picture-postcard New England town with an exceptionally graceful church and green, a country store, and an old cemetery filled with weathered slate gravestones dating to 1800. From Berlin you'll head north through the same type of countryside to Bolton, another gracious little town with a handsome stone library and a cluster of antiques shops. The Nashoba Valley Winery, perched on a hillside with a glorious view and open for tours and tastings, is on the edge of town just off the route. The return leg to Northboro brings you along ridgetops with inspiring views and then down to the valley of the Assabet River through prosperous, well-landscaped farmland with grazing horses and cows. Just before the end, you'll go underneath the graceful stone arches of the Wachusett Aqueduct, which carries water from the Wachusett Reservoir to metropolitan Boston.

The short ride bypasses Bolton by taking a more direct route from Berlin back to Northboro.

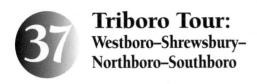

Triboro Tour:
Westboro–Shrewsbury–
Northboro–Southboro

Number of miles:	29 (21 without Shrewsbury extension)
Terrain:	Rolling. Several moderate hills, but nothing bad.
Food:	Groceries and snack bars in the towns. Friendly's and McDonald's on Route 9, 0.5 mile east of starting point.
Start:	Gold's Gym, on Lyman Street in Westboro, immediately north of Route 9. It's 2 miles west of I–495 and 0.5 mile west of Route 30.

On this ride you'll explore the rolling, well-groomed farm country and graceful small towns east of Worcester. The region is just far enough from both the Boston and Worcester metropolitan areas to be rural rather than suburban. Smooth, well-maintained back roads weave among the hillsides and rolling pastures, providing relaxed and scenic biking.

You start from Westboro, an attractive town with a compact, Victorian brick business block, several fine churches, and gracious Colonial-style homes on the outskirts of town. From Westboro it's a smooth ride to Northboro, with a spin along the Assabet Reservoir. The reservoir is one of the state's newest, formed in 1969 by damming the Assabet River. Northboro is another attractive community, with a graceful white church and a handsome stone Victorian library built in 1894. The stretch from Northboro to Southboro is a delight, heading across prosperous, open farmland with wooded hills rising in the background.

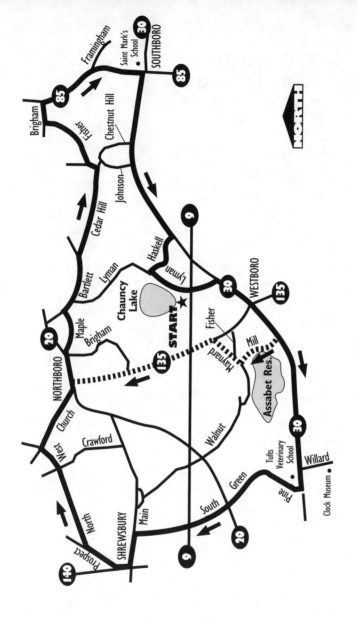

DIRECTIONS
FOR
THE RIDE

1. Turn right onto Lyman Street and immediately cross Route 9 at traffic light (**CAUTION** here). Go 0.4 mile to end (Route 30, East Main Street).

2. Right for 0.8 mile to center of Westboro, where you'll cross Route 135. **CAUTION** here—busy intersection.

3. Straight for 0.9 mile to Mill Road on right, just past top of hill. Here the short ride turns right.

4. Straight for 3.3 miles to Pine Street on right, shortly after the Tufts Veterinary School. To visit the clock museum, turn left after 2.9 miles on Willard Road, which leads into the grounds of the school, and go 0.6 mile to museum on right.

5. Right for 4.1 miles to third traffic light (Main Street, unmarked). **CAUTION** crossing Routes 20 and 9.

6. Left for 0.5 mile to traffic light (Route 140 in the center of Shrewsbury. Notice the handsome brick library on your right just before the intersection.

7. Turn right and just ahead bear right at fork on Prospect Street. Go 0.8 mile to North Street, which bears right.

8. Bear right for 2.5 miles to second crossroads and stop sign (Church Street, unmarked).

9. Right for 1.2 miles to end (Route 20) in Northboro. Shortly before the end, there's a graceful church on your left.

10. Left for 0.6 mile to Maple Street on right, immediately after Brigham Street on right.

You'll pass the Victorian library on your right and then a little dam at the bottom of the hill, also on the right. The White Cliffs, a restaurant in an elegant Victorian mansion, is on your left just before Maple Street.

11. Turn right and stay on main road for 0.7 mile to end, opposite the entrance to the high school.

12. Right for 1.2 miles to Cedar Hill Street (unmarked), which bears right at bottom of hill. You'll pass Bartlett Pond on your right near the beginning.

13. Bear right for 1.9 miles to Fisher Road (unmarked) on left, shortly after you go under I–495. You'll pass office buildings for a mile as you nick a corner of Marlboro, a town that promotes commercial development.

14. Turn left and just ahead bear right at fork (still Fisher Road). Go 1.3 miles to end (Brigham Street, unmarked).

15. Right for 0.4 mile to traffic light (Route 85, Maple Street).

16. Right for 0.9 mile to traffic light where Route 85 bears right.

17. Bear right for 1.1 miles to traffic light (Route 30) in Southboro. You'll pass Saint Mark's School on your left.

18. Right for 3.6 miles to Haskell Street on right, just as you start to go downhill. It's just after the Windsor Ridge apartments on left.

19. Right for 0.9 mile to end. **CAUTION:** Bumpy spots toward the end.

20. Left for 0.8 mile to parking lot on right, just before traffic light at Route 9. You'll pass the entrance to Westboro State Hospital and then Chauncy Lake on your right.

Directions for shorter ride

1. Follow directions for the long ride through number 3.

2. Right for 0.9 mile to end (Fisher Street). You'll pass the Assabet Reservoir on your left.

3. Turn right and just ahead bear left at fork on Maynard Street. Go 0.6 mile to crossroads at traffic island (Route 135, Milk Street).

4. Left for 3.3 miles to end (Route 20) in the center of Northboro.

5. Right for 0.6 mile to Maple Street on right, immediately after Brigham Street on right. Notice the Victorian library and then the little dam at bottom of hill, both on your right. Just before Maple Street on the left is the White Cliffs, a restaurant in an elegant Victorian mansion.

6. Follow directions for the long ride from number 11 to the end.

You'll cross the Wachusett Aqueduct, which carries water from the Wachusett Reservoir to the Boston metropolitan area, and pass Saint Mark's School, one of the numerous prestigious preparatory schools scattered across the state. Its main building is an elegant, rambling hall with English Tudor architecture surrounded by extensive lawns.

Saint Mark's is just outside the center of Southboro, the most classically New England of the three "boro" towns. The sloping, half-moon-shaped green is a beauty, framed by two fine old churches on a small rise. The return to Westboro heads along Route 30, a winner for biking among numbered routes, lightly traveled and passing through sweeping expanses of open farmland. At the end of the ride, you'll detour past unspoiled Chauncy Lake. The grounds of Westboro State Hospital, dominated by a massive, ornate Victorian building, crown a hilltop overlooking the lake in a hauntingly beautiful setting that seems more like an old, distinguished college campus than a psychiatric hospital.

The long ride heads farther west to Shrewsbury through magnificent rolling countryside with some sharp ups and downs. You'll pass the Veterinary School of Tufts University, built on the grounds of the former Grafton State Hospital, another psychiatric hospital. Massachusetts has dozens of state institutions for persons with mental and physical disabilities, most of them on gracious collegelike campuses in attractive rural surroundings. Adjacent to the veterinary school, just off the route, is the Willard House and Clockshop, an eighteenth-century saltbox house with an impressive collection of antique clocks.

Shrewsbury is another handsome old town on a hilltop, with a classic white church and a fine brick library. The community is a well-to-do suburb of both Worcester and Boston, with the look and feel of a smaller, rural town. Most people know Shrewsbury only from the ugly commercial strip along Route 9; the rest of the town is pleasant. From Shrewsbury you'll head through wooded hills and past an orchard to Northboro, where you'll pick up the route of the shorter ride.

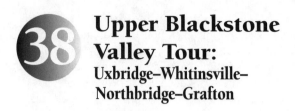

Upper Blackstone Valley Tour:
Uxbridge–Whitinsville–Northbridge–Grafton

Number of miles:	29 (17 without Grafton extension)
Terrain:	Rolling, with two tough hills. The long ride has an additional challenging climb.
Food:	Groceries and snack bars in the towns. Pizza shop at end.
Facilities:	Rest rooms at River Bend Farm.
Start:	Uxbridge Shopping Center, Route 122, Uxbridge, 0.6 mile north of Route 16.

Southeast of Worcester, between the city and Rhode Island, lies a fascinating and scenic area for bicycling dotted with ridges, wooded hills, and unspoiled little mill towns right out of the Industrial Revolution. Bisecting the region is the Blackstone River, among the first New England rivers to become industrialized. Traces of the old Blackstone Canal, which opened the valley to commerce during the 1830s, can still be seen in Uxbridge and Northbridge near Route 122. The river is being developed by both the state and the federal government into a linear historical park, called the Blackstone River and Canal Heritage State Park. Segments of the canal and its towpath have been restored, and in future years, the state plans to renovate some of the old mills into museums and visitors centers. Rhode Island has similar plans for its portion of the river. When the project is completed in both states, the Blackstone River will be a "heritage corridor" nearly 40 miles long.

The ride starts from Uxbridge, among the finest of the Blackstone Valley mill towns, with a compact old brick business block, a graceful brick library built in 1893, the Victorian Uxbridge Inn, and a distinctive Gothic-style church with a graceful turretlike steeple. Several of the mills have retail outlets where you can get bargains on clothing. Unlike many mill towns, Uxbridge has no congested tenements or even rows of identical mill housing, just old wooden homes that you'd expect to see in a more rural town.

From Uxbridge it's a short ride to Whitinsville, the largest village in the town of Northbridge. (The first syllable is pronounced "White.") Whitinsville is a fine example of a planned industrial community—a miniature Lowell. The formidable brick mill slants uphill for a quarter of a mile, and across the road just off the route are orderly rows of identical houses. As you climb the hill north of town, you pass gracious old wooden homes and then enter inspiring, rolling farm country. You'll fly downhill into Farnumsville, a mill village (part of Grafton) on the Blackstone River, and then climb onto a ridge through farms and orchards into the hilltop town of Grafton.

Grafton is among my favorite towns in the state. As you approach the center, you'll climb gradually past handsome Victorian homes. Suddenly the large oval green lies before you, complete with a bandstand in the middle and surrounded by several stately white churches, a handsome brick library, and the ornate brick Victorian town hall. From Grafton you'll return to Uxbridge along a succession of winding country lanes. Near the end you'll pass River Bend Farm, the main visitors center for the Massachusetts portion of the Blackstone corridor. Just ahead, a quarter-mile off the route, is the Stanley Woolen Mill, a handsome wooden building from the early 1850s on the Blackstone River and a good place to pick up bargains on woolen goods. It is the oldest operating textile mill in New England. Just ahead is the John Farnum House, built in 1715.

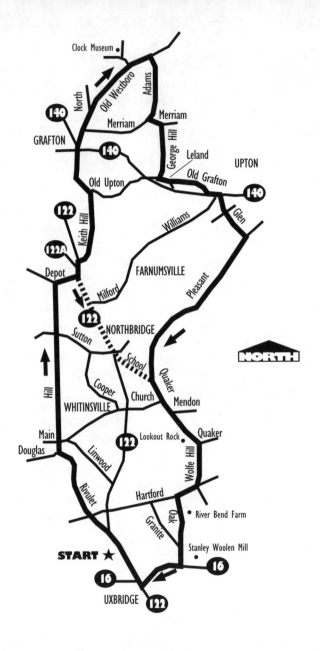

DIRECTIONS

FOR

THE RIDE

1. Left (north) on Route 122 for 0.4 mile to fork (Rivulet Street bears left).

2. Bear left and immediately bear left again on main road. Go 2.1 miles to end (Douglas Road) at yield sign. This is Whitinsville.

3. Right and just ahead straight at traffic light on well-named Hill Street (unmarked). Go 3.3 miles to crossroads and stop sign (Sutton Street).

At the very beginning, you'll cross the Mumford River. On the right there's a graceful, bell-towered mill that has been converted to apartments. On your left there's a fascinating view of the river flowing between massive mills and over a little dam.

Just ahead you'll climb steeply for 0.3 mile, passing a turreted Victorian mansion, currently a funeral home, on your right. The road levels off briefly and then ascends steeply again for 200 yards. Then the terrain is very rolling.

4. Straight for 1.2 miles to Depot Street, which turns right across railroad bridge just past bottom of long hill. The main road bears left at the intersection.

5. Right for 0.4 mile to end (Route 122). This is Farnumsville, a mill village that is part of Grafton. Here the short ride turns right.

You'll pass a fine dam across the Blackstone River on your left just before the end. It's hidden by the bridge abutment; dismount to take a look.

6. Left for 0.2 mile to fork where Route 122A bears left and Route 122 bears slightly right.

7. Bear right and then immediately turn right on Keith Hill Road. Go 1.7 miles to stop sign (merge left). The first mile is a steplike hill with some steep pitches.

8. Bear left and stay on main road for 1.1 miles to stop sign (Route 140) in the center of Grafton. The main road bears right uphill on South Street after 0.7 mile.

9. Go straight and then immediately bear right, passing the tall monu-

ment on your left. Go 0.8 mile to fork where North Street goes straight and the main road (Old Westboro Road) bears right.

10. Bear right for 2.4 miles to Adams Road on right.

You'll come within 0.5 mile of the Willard House and Clockshop, an eighteenth-century saltbox house with an impressive collection of antique clocks. To visit it, turn left after 1.6 miles on Wesson Street. Go 0.4 mile to Willard Street on right. Turn right for 0.1 mile to museum on left.

11. Right for 1.8 miles to traffic island where the main road bears right uphill and Merriam Road (unmarked) turns left.

12. Left for 0.3 mile to George Hill Road on right. You'll pass an excellent farm stand on your left at the beginning.

13. Right for 1.9 miles to end (Leland Street). This is a pleasant narrow lane along a hillside. **CAUTION:** The end comes up suddenly at bottom of hill.

14. Left for 0.3 mile to fork.

15. Bear left up short hill for 1 mile to end (Route 140). You'll see the dammed up West River on your right.

16. Left for 0.2 mile to second right (Glen Avenue).

17. Right for 1.4 miles to end (Pleasant Street, unmarked). **CAUTION:** Bumpy spots after crossroads.

18. Right for 2.5 miles to fork where Mendon Road bears left and Quaker Street goes straight downhill.

After 1.5 miles Riverdale Street on right leads 0.1 mile to the Blackstone River and an old mill that is part of the Blackstone Heritage State Park system. Church Street, the next right after Riverdale Street, also leads 0.1 mile to the river and the canal.

19. Straight for 1.3 miles to unmarked fork where Quaker Street bears left and Wolfe Hill Road bears right.

Just before the fork, a footpath on the right leads 0.25 mile to Lookout Rock, which offers a glorious view of the meandering river, 150 feet below.

20. Bear right for 1 mile to crossroads and stop sign (Hartford Avenue).

21. Bear right for 0.4 mile to Oak Street on left.

You'll cross the Blackstone River and Canal just before the intersection; you can see the remains of a lock on your left. Rice City Pond, a dammed-up portion of the river, is on your right.

22. Turn left and stay on main road for 1.3 miles to end (Route 16), at T-intersection.

After 0.2 mile you'll pass River Bend Farm, a visitors center for the Blackstone Heritage Corridor, on the left. At the end the ride turns right on Route 16, but to see the Stanley Woolen Mill, turn left and go 0.25 mile.

Behind the visitors center, the restored towpath follows the east bank of the canal to the woolen mill. If you wish, you may walk your bike (or ride, with caution) along the towpath to the mill, which is on Route 16. Turn right on Route 16.

23. Right for 0.3 mile (0.5 mile if you're coming from the woolen mill) to end (Route 122). Just before the end, there's a picturesque dam on your right.

24. Right for 0.6 mile to shopping center on left.

Directions for shorter ride

1. Follow directions for the long ride through number 5.

2. Right for 2 miles to School Street, which bears left uphill at blinking light. This is Northbridge, another mill town on the Blackstone River. Route 122 parallels the river on your right.

3. Bear left for 1.3 miles to stop sign (merge right on Quaker Street). You'll pass a magnificent brick church on your right at the beginning.

4. Bear right for 1.1 miles to fork where Mendon Road bears left and Quaker Street goes straight downhill.

At the beginning Riverdale Street on the right leads 0.1 mile to an old mill on the Blackstone River that is part of the Blackstone Heritage State Park system. Church Street, the next right after Riverdale Street, also leads 0.1 mile to the river and the canal.

5. Follow directions for the long ride from number 19 to the end.

Purgatory Chasm Ride:
Uxbridge–East Douglas–Sutton–Whitinsville

39

Number of miles:	27 (20 without Sutton extension)
Terrain:	Hilly.
Food:	Family restaurant and country store in Sutton. Refreshment stand at Purgatory Chasm, open during the summer in good weather. Grocery and snack bar in East Douglas. Pizza shop at end.
Start:	Uxbridge Shopping Center, Route 122, Uxbridge, 0.6 mile north of Route 16.

Southeast of Worcester, midway between the city and Rhode Island, is an area of ruggedly beautiful ridge-and-valley country dotted with picturesque small towns. Biking in this region is challenging but inspiring: There are several tough climbs, but each is balanced by a ridgetop run with sweeping views or a long, smooth downhill cruise. Highlighting this ride is a visit to Purgatory Chasm in Sutton, a deep, boulder-strewn gorge between towering rocky cliffs.

The ride starts in Uxbridge, a beautiful old mill town on the upper Blackstone River, which slices diagonally from Worcester to Providence. In the center of town is a compact brick business block, the graceful brick library built in 1893, the Victorian-style Uxbridge Inn, and a distinctive Gothic-style church with a graceful turretlike steeple. After a mile you'll tackle the first of three long hills (two on the short ride), which brings you onto an open ridge with superb views. A smooth descent leads to East Douglas, an attractive mill town with a pair of old churches and a handsome little red-brick library.

DIRECTIONS

FOR

THE RIDE

1. Left on Route 122 for 0.4 mile to fork (Rivulet Street bears left).

2. Bear left and immediately bear left again on main road. Go 0.3 mile to crossroads and stop sign (Hartford Avenue, unmarked).

3. Turn left and just ahead bear right on Sutton Street. Go 0.9 mile to William Street on left. This is a steady climb.

4. Left for 1.4 miles to end (Hartford Avenue, unmarked). You'll continue uphill for the first 0.4 mile.

5. Turn right and stay on main road for 1.9 miles to Mechanic Street on right, in East Douglas (signs say TO SUTTON, WORCESTER, MANCHAUG). There's a fine view to your right at the beginning. The road merges head-on into Route 16 after 1.4 miles.

6. Right for 0.3 mile to stop sign (merge left; Gilboa Street is on right).

7. Left for 4.9 miles to crossroads and stop sign (Central Turnpike). Here the short ride turns right. There's a good restaurant on your right at the intersection.

You'll pass a handsome brick church on your right at the beginning and ride through Manchaug after 2 miles. Tuckers Pond is on your left a half-mile beyond Manchaug. From here you'll climb gradually for 1.4 miles to the top of Putnam Hill.

8. Left for 1.4 miles to West Sutton Road on right, just after Manchaug Road on left.

9. Right for 4.3 miles to Harris Avenue on right, just after Singletary Lake on right. You'll pass the three small Stockwell Ponds on your right and then ride along Singletary Lake.

10. Right for 0.8 mile to end (merge right).

11. Bear right for 2.2 miles to second crossroads and stop sign (Central Turnpike, unmarked.

You'll see Singletary Lake again at the beginning and go through the center of Sutton at the first crossroads. There's a sharp descent out of Sutton followed by a steep 0.6-mile climb.

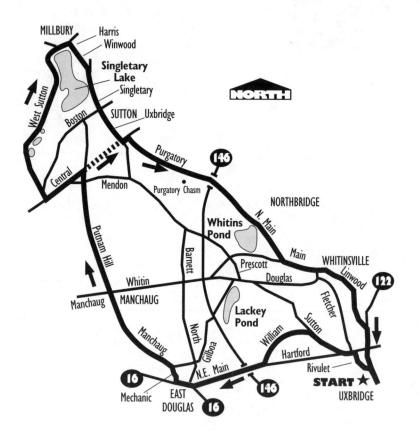

MILLBURY Harris
Winwood

**Singletary
Lake**
Singletary

West Sutton

Boston

SUTTON Uxbridge

Purgatory

146

Central

Mendon

Purgatory Chasm

NORTHBRIDGE

NORTH

Putnam Hill

Whitin

Manchaug

MANCHAUG

Barnett

**Whitins
Pond**

N. Main

Main

Prescott

Douglas

WHITINSVILLE

Linwood

122

Manchaug

North

Gilboa

**Lackey
Pond**

William

Fletcher

Sutton

Hartford

16

Mechanic

EAST
DOUGLAS

N.E. Main

16

146

Rivulet

START ★

UXBRIDGE

12. Left for 0.2 mile to Purgatory Road on right.

13. Right for 4.1 miles to stop sign (merge left on Main Street, unmarked) in Whitinsville. Most of this stretch is downhill. There's a good view to your left at the beginning, and you'll pass the trail to Purgatory Chasm on your right after 1.8 miles.

14. Bear left for 0.7 mile to traffic light. Notice the graceful stone mill, now apartments, on the far right corner.

15. Go straight and then immediately bear right on Linwood Avenue. Go 1.4 miles to end (Route 122, Providence Road). You'll pass a handsome stone church on your left at the beginning. Notice the elegant Victorian mansion on your left and the graceful brick mill on your right just before the end.

16. Right for 1.1 miles to shopping center on right.

Directions for shorter ride

1. Follow directions for the long ride through number 7.

2. Right for 1.7 miles to Purgatory Road on right, shortly after crossroads and blinking light (Uxbridge Road). You'll climb for 0.2 mile at the beginning and 0.5 mile farther on.

3. Follow directions for the long ride from number 13 to the end.

From East Douglas you'll ride along the valley of the Mumford River for about 2 miles to Manchaug, a mill village at a crossroads just over the Sutton town line that appears little changed since the Industrial Revolution. Beyond Manchaug you'll follow a chain of three small ponds, called Stockwell Ponds, and then larger Singletary Lake. A gradual rise brings you to the classic New England village of Sutton, with a graceful church, a green with a gazebo, and an old wooden town hall.

There's a screaming downhill plunge out of Sutton immediately followed by a steep half-mile climb. The rest of the ride is mostly downhill. A steplike descent called the Stairway to Heaven by local bicyclists leads to Purgatory Chasm, where a rocky trail leads half a mile along the bottom of a ravine between towering boulders. Two miles ahead you'll enter Whitinsville, the largest community in the town of Northbridge. Whitinsville is one of the state's best examples of a planned, orderly mill village—a miniature Lowell or Holyoke. Symmetrical rows of identical long, wooden mill houses with broad porches line the side streets, and just ahead a massive brick mill extends for nearly a quarter-mile along the Mumford River. An older mill with a graceful bell tower, recycled into apartments, stands in the center of town. A mile ahead you'll pass an elegant Victorian mansion built in 1871 and the strikingly beautiful Linwood Mill. From here it's a mile back to the starting point.

Chapter 5:
The South Shore

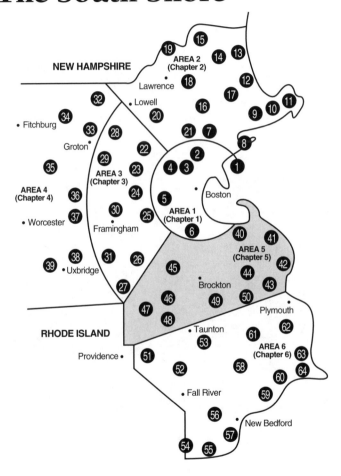

Massachusetts Bay, Hingham

40 Hingham

Number of miles:	22 (17 without World's End extension)
Terrain:	Gently rolling, with a few short, steep hills.
Food:	Several groceries and restaurants. Burger King at end.
Facilities:	Rest rooms at Wompatuck State Park.
Start:	Burger King on Route 228 at the Rockland-Norwell town line, immediately north of Route 3. Take exit 14.

This ride explores Hingham, the first town southeast of Boston that is spaciously and graciously suburban rather than congested. It is an affluent community graced with elegant wooden homes from the early 1800s, horse farms, country estates with gently rolling meadows, and a beautiful stretch of waterfront along Massachusetts Bay. Hingham is unique because it has two centers of town, Hingham and Hingham Center, a mile apart. Both are New England classics, with proud old churches and fine Colonial-style homes with peaked roofs and dormer windows.

Starting from the southern edge of the town, the ride heads north to the ocean at Crow Point, where you'll climb a short hill with a glorious view of Massachusetts Bay and the Boston skyline in the distance. You'll follow the waterfront and then head south for about 2 miles to the handsome center of town. Here you'll pass the Old Ship Church, built in 1681, the oldest church in America in continuous use.

The route now heads to World's End, as idyllic a spot as any on the Massachusetts coast. It is a small peninsula originally landscaped by

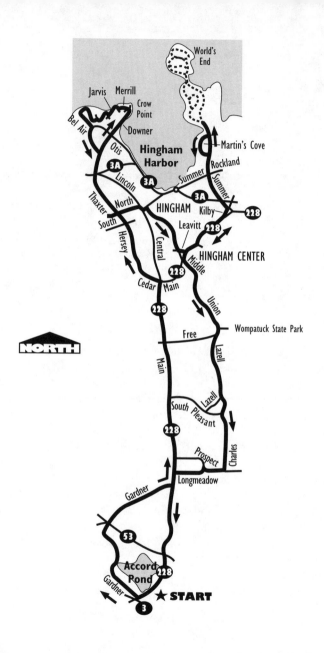

DIRECTIONS
FOR
THE RIDE

1. Left on Route 228 (**CAUTION** here) for less than 0.2 mile to Gardner Street on right. Accord Pond is on your right at the beginning.

2. Right for 1.3 miles to traffic light (Route 53). You'll see Accord Pond again after 0.6 mile.

3. Straight (**CAUTION:** busy intersection) for 1.1 miles to end (Route 228, Main Street).

4. Left for 2.7 miles to crossroads and stop sign where Route 228 (Main Street) turns right and Cedar Street (unmarked) turns left.

5. Turn left and stay on main road for 1.8 miles to traffic light (Route 3A). Cedar Street becomes Hersey Street and then Thaxter Street.

6. Straight (**CAUTION** here) for 1 mile to dead end at the Hingham Yacht Club. You'll follow Hingham Harbor on your right at the end. The yacht club is at the tip of Crow Point, a small peninsula.

7. Make a U-turn and immediately go straight up steep hill on Marion Street. Then just ahead turn right on Merrill Street (unmarked), which continues steeply uphill. Go 0.1 mile to end. Enjoy the view from the top of the hill!

8. Right down steep hill (**CAUTION** here) for 0.2 mile to crossroads (Jarvis Avenue). There's a small beach at the bottom of the hill.

9. Right for 0.2 mile to fork at top of hill (Bel Air Road bears left). You'll climb another short, steep hill.

10. Bear left and immediately curve right on the main road. Stay on main road for 1 mile to end at second stop sign. The road curves sharply right after 0.6 mile and becomes a divided parkway at the end.

11. Turn right and just ahead bear left at fork. (Don't go straight on Crow Point Lane.) Go 0.8 mile to crossroads and stop sign (North Street). **CAUTION** crossing Route 3A.

12. Turn left and stay on main road for 0.4 mile to fork in the center of Hingham. There's a handsome white church on the left just before the fork, and another one on the left just after it.

13. Bear left and immediately turn right on Main Street opposite Saint Paul's Church. Go 0.8 mile to diagonal crossroads (Garrison Road turns

right; Leavitt Street bears left). You'll pass the Old Ship Church on your left just past the business district.

14. Bear left for 1 block to end (Route 228). Here the ride turns left, but if you wish to omit the World's End section of the ride (4.2 miles round trip to the entrance and back), turn right. Go 0.1 mile to second left (Middle Street) at small traffic island. Resume with direction number 23.

15. Turn left and stay on Route 228 for 0.8 mile to Kilby Street (unmarked), which bears left. (Route 228 bears left after less than 0.2 mile.)

16. Bear left and just ahead turn left at crossroads (Summer Street, unmarked). Go 0.1 mile to diagonal crossroads and stop sign (Route 3A).

17. Straight (**CAUTION** here) for 1.1 miles to the entrance to World's End. **CAUTION:** Busy crossroads after 0.4 mile at traffic light. Also, if you bike onto the peninsula, some of the dirt roads have a soft or loose surface. Watch for pairs of wooden beams, with spaces wide enough to trap a bicycle tire between them, placed diagonally across the road to control erosion.

18. Leaving World's End, backtrack 0.2 mile to the first right (Martins Cove Road, unmarked), just past top of little hill.

19. Right for less than 0.5 mile to end (Martins Lane, unmarked).

20. Right for 0.6 mile to diagonal crossroads and stop sign (Route 3A). **CAUTION** again at traffic light.

21. Straight (**CAUTION** again) and just ahead left at crossroads (Kilby Street, unmarked). Go 0.1 mile to stop sign (merge right on Route 228).

22. Bear right and stay on main road for 0.9 mile to Middle Street on left at small traffic island. It's immediately after School Street on left. This is Hingham Center.

23. Left for 1.1 miles to fork where Free Street bears right and Lazell Street bears left up a little hill. Just before the fork, a road on your left leads to Wompatuck State Park, a massive, 3,000-acre expanse of woodland with campsites and 6 miles of bicycle paths.

24. Bear left for 0.8 mile to fork (Charles Street bears slightly left).

25. Bear left for 1 mile to end (Prospect Street).

26. Right for 0.3 mile to Longmeadow Road on left. The main road curves right at the intersection.

27. Left for 0.4 mile to end (Route 228, Main Street).

28. Left for 1.1 miles to Route 53, at traffic light.

29. Straight for 0.6 mile to Burger King on left. Accord Pond is on your right at the end. **CAUTION** crossing Route 53 and also turning left into Burger King.

Frederick Law Olmsted and now maintained by the Trustees of Reservations. It contains three drumlins, with a narrow neck between the first and second. Broad, grassy slopes lined with stately rows of trees slant gently down to the shore and give views of the Boston skyline. It's about a 3-mile loop on dirt roads to the far end of the peninsula; you may either ride or walk. The entrance fee is currently $4.00.

After leaving World's End, you'll ride through Hingham Center, the older and less commercial of the two centers of town. The last part of the ride, south of Hingham Center, leads into a pastoral landscape of meticulous gentleman farms with broad fields and gracious old farmhouses.

Atlantic surf, Scituate

Cohasset–Scituate

Number of miles:	26 (17 without Scituate extension)
Terrain:	Gently rolling, with a couple of short hills.
Food:	Groceries and restaurants in both Cohasset and Scituate.
Start:	Cohasset High School on Pond Street, Cohasset, just north of Route 3A. There's a traffic light at Route 3A and Pond Street.

On this ride you explore the shoulder of land southeast of Boston where the coastline curves primarily from an east–west to a north–south direction. It is the first really nice stretch of coast heading southeast from the city, and the Cohasset section, just east of Hull, is among the most scenic in the state. A network of smooth secondary roads connecting these two affluent communities provides bicycling at its best.

The ride starts in Cohasset, an unspoiled community that is one of the finest of the Boston suburbs. Its splendid rocky coastline, rimmed by large, impressive homes hovering above the waves with the Boston skyline in the distance, rivals Cape Ann and Newport for elegance. The center of town is a New England jewel, with a long, stately green framed by a pair of graceful white churches, the town hall, and fine Colonial-style wooden homes. The church at the head of the green was built in 1747. Cohasset received a burst of publicity in 1986 when much of the movie *The Witches of Eastwick* was filmed here.

The long ride heads farther southeast into Scituate, another handsome community with a large green, a small, boat-filled harbor, and a compact row of shops along its shore. Just outside of town is the Law-

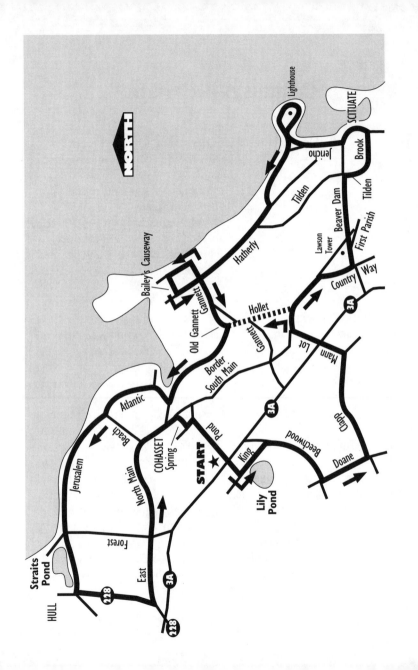

1. Right on Pond Street for 0.2 mile to Route 3A, at traffic light.

2. Straight for 0.2 mile to stop sign (King Street, unmarked).

3. Left for 0.6 mile to end (Beechwood Street). You'll pass Lily Pond on your right.

4. Right for 1 mile to crossroads (Doane Street).

5. Left and just ahead merge left at stop sign. Go 0.6 mile to crossroads (Clapp Road, unmarked).

6. Turn left. **CAUTION** making this turn—there are no stop signs for any of the four roads. Go 1.7 miles to a wide fork where Grove Street bears right and Mann Lot Road bears left.

7. Bear left for 1.1 miles to end (Country Way). **CAUTION** crossing Route 3A. A fine white church built in 1869 is opposite you at the end.

8. Right for 0.3 mile to Hollett Street, which turns left at a little traffic island. Here the short ride turns left.

9. Straight for 0.7 mile to fork where Branch Street goes straight and Country Way bears right.

10. Bear right for 0.5 mile to traffic light (First Parish Road). An old-fashioned variety store is on your right at the intersection.

11. Left for 0.3 mile to fork at the Scituate town green (Beaver Dam Road bears slightly left). There's a handsome Civil War monument on the green. Just before the green you'll pass the Lawson Tower on your left.

12. Bear left for 0.9 mile to traffic light (Tilden Road).

13. Right for 0.8 mile to crossroads and stop sign. Tilden Road becomes Brook Street.

14. Left for 0.4 mile to Jericho Road (unmarked) on right at traffic light. You'll go through downtown Scituate and then see the harbor on your right.

15. Turn right and stay on main road for 0.7 mile to traffic island (Lighthouse Road bears right). To your right is Cedar Point, a small peninsula with a lighthouse at the tip. You will now loop counterclockwise around the peninsula.

16. Bear right for 0.8 mile around Cedar Point back to this same traffic island.

17. Bear right, following the ocean on your right, for 1.2 miles to end. The road turns 90 degrees left shortly before the end.

18. Right for 1.8 miles to traffic light (Gannett Road).

19. Right for 0.6 mile to Bailey's Causeway on left. Here the ride turns left, but if you wish you can continue straight along the ocean for 0.5 mile until the road becomes a private driveway, and then backtrack to Bailey's Causeway.

20. Left for 0.3 mile to end (Hatherly Road). There's a golf course to the right.

21. Left for 0.4 mile to traffic light (Gannett Road).

22. Right for 0.4 mile to where the main road curves left and a smaller road, Old Gannett Road, goes straight.

23. Straight for 0.2 mile to Border Street (unmarked), which turns right up a short, steep hill.

24. Turn right and stay on main road for 1.6 miles to end (Elm Street on left, Margin Street on right).

The little bridge toward the end, with Cohasset Cove on your right, is worth a stop. Kimball's by the Sea, an elegant inn and restaurant overlooking the cove, is on your right at the end.

25. Right for 0.3 mile to fork (Howard Gleason Road bears right, Atlantic Avenue bears left).

26. Bear left for 0.7 mile to fork with a large flower pot in the middle (Beach Street turns left, the main road bears right).

27. Bear right for 1.9 miles to crossroads and stop sign (Forest Avenue). This is a magnificent ride along the coast.

28. Go straight (don't bear right along the ocean) for 1 mile to another crossroads and stop sign (Hull Street, Route 228 on left). You'll ride along Straits Pond and pass a handsome stone Greek Orthodox church on your right just before the crossroads.

29. Left for 1.1 miles to East Street, which turns sharply left at several small traffic islands (a sign may say TO COHASSET).

Just before the intersection, on your right, you'll pass Glastonbury Abbey, a Benedictine monastery open to visitors. It contains a bookstore, a chapel, a lovely stone bell tower, and an enclosure with barn-yard animals.

30. Sharp left (**CAUTION** here) for 2.7 miles to fork where Elm Street (unmarked) bears left and the main road bears slightly right in downtown Cohasset. You'll go past the lovely town green just before the fork.

31. Bear right for less than 0.2 mile to Spring Street (unmarked), a small road that bears right opposite the library.

32. Bear right for 0.1 mile to end (Cushing Road).

33. Left and just ahead right on Pond Street up a short, steep hill. Go 0.5 mile to school on right.

Directions for shorter ride

1. Follow directions for the long ride through number 8.

2. Left for 0.8 mile to stop sign (merge right at bottom of hill).

3. Bear right for 0.1 mile to fork.

4. Bear left and immediately bear left again on Border Street (unmarked). Go 1.6 miles to end (Elm Street on left, Margin Street on right).

The little bridge toward the end, with Cohasset Cove on your right, is worth a stop. Kimball's by the Sea, an elegant inn and restaurant overlooking the cove, is on your right at the end.

5. Follow directions for the long ride from number 25 to the end.

---

son Tower, a handsome wooden-shingled landmark with a water tower inside. It was built in 1902 and given to the town by Thomas Lawson, a copper magnate. At the top is a set of bells that are played on special town occasions. The Scituate coast, not as elegant as the Cohasset section, is bordered by smaller homes and cottages. It is spectacular, however, especially on a windy day when the surf crashes against the seawalls, which are necessary to protect the shore from the brunt of northeasters. There's a graceful white lighthouse at the tip of Cedar Point, and the bridge over the tidal inlet that forms the border of the two towns is a great spot.

Scituate–Marshfield

Number of miles:	27 (16 without Marshfield extension)
Terrain:	Gently rolling, with a couple of short hills and two long, gradual ones.
Food:	Groceries and restaurants in Scituate. Grocery and snack bar in Humarock.
Start:	Scituate High School, Route 3A, just north of First Parish Road, next to the police station and town offices.

This ride takes you exploring the midsection of the South Shore, midway between Boston and Plymouth. This area, bisected by the marshlined North River, is more rural than suburban, with gentle wooded hills and some prosperous farms sloping down to the river. Paralleling the shore, you'll pass extensive salt marshes at the river's mouth and loop around three headlands standing guard above the ocean.

The ride starts from Scituate, an affluent community that boasts a large green with a Civil War monument in the middle, a graceful white church, and one of the state's more striking landmarks, the 150-foot-high Lawson Tower. This is a water tower covered on the outside by wooden shingles and donated to the town in 1902 by Thomas Lawson, a copper magnate. Atop the tower is a set of bells that are played on special town occasions.

From Scituate you'll head south to Marshfield, inland from the coast. Marshfield is primarily a gracious rural community that unfortunately is becoming suburban because of its proximity to Route 3. The ride sticks to the unspoiled sections, heading through wooded hills and then along the salt marshes bordering the South and North rivers. A small detour brings you through the beach community of Humarock,

DIRECTIONS
FOR
THE RIDE

1. Left on Route 3A and just ahead right at traffic light on First Parish Road. Go 0.6 mile to crossroads (Grove Street, unmarked).

2. Left for 2.4 miles to end (Main Street, Route 123). You'll go straight at two crossroads and stop signs.

3. Left for 0.3 mile to Bridge Street on right.

4. Right for 1.1 mile to Highland Street, which bears left. You'll cross the North River and climb a long, gradual hill. **CAUTION:** The metal-grate bridge over the river is very slippery when wet. Walk across if the road is wet.

5. Bear left and just ahead turn left at end (still Highland Street). Go 0.5 mile to Spring Street on left, just past bottom of big hill. Here the short ride turns left.

6. Straight for 3 miles to fourth crossroads and stop sign (Furnace Street, unmarked). It's just after school on right.

7. Left for 0.4 mile to traffic light (Route 3A, Main Street).

8. Right for 1 mile to South River Street on left, immediately after the Marshfield Fairgrounds on left.

9. Left for 1.7 mile to fork at traffic island (Grove Street bears left). You'll pass the former Marshfield town hall, a handsome wooden Victorian building dated 1895, on your right at the beginning.

10. Bear right (still South River Street) for 1.2 miles to fork where the main road bears slightly right. You'll climb a short, steep hill.

11. Bear right and just ahead merge right at stop sign on Ferry Street (unmarked). Go 0.6 mile to Bayberry Road on right, just after Blueberry Road on right.

12. Turn right and stay on main road for 0.4 mile to crossroads and stop sign after bridge. This is Humarock. The ocean is 100 yards in front of you.

13. Left for 0.5 mile to another crossroads and stop sign (Marshfield Avenue). You'll follow the South River, a tidal inlet, on your left.

14. Left for less than 0.2 mile to crossroads immediately after bridge.

15. Turn right. Just ahead the main road turns 90 degrees left up a

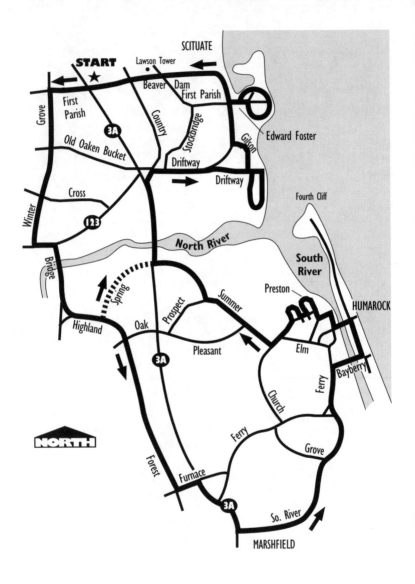

short, steep hill. Go 100 yards to Preston Terrace (unmarked), which turns sharply right at the top of the hill.

16. Sharp right for 0.3 mile to crossroads almost at top of hill (Pollard Street). Ignore another part of Pollard Street on left just before crossroads.

Enjoy the view of the South River and Humarock Beach to your right. 17. Right and just ahead right again at another crossroads. Go 0.4 mile to end, where you merge head-on into a larger road (Elm Street, unmarked). **CAUTION:** There is no stop sign here.

18. Straight for 0.3 mile to Summer Street, which bears right at traffic island.

19. Bear right for 1.6 miles to a large, grassy traffic island where Prospect Street goes straight and Summer Street bears right. A little pond is on your right at the intersection.

20. Bear right for 0.7 mile to Route 3A, at another large, grassy traffic island. You'll climb a long, gradual hill.

21. Bear right for 1.4 miles to a road that bears right just before traffic light (sign says SCITUATE, 2 MILES).

22. Bear right and then immediately turn right on Driftway. Go 1.3 miles to where Driftway bears right onto a smaller road just past pollution control facility on right.

23. Bear right for 1.4 miles to end. You'll loop around the headland of Rivermoor.

24. Jog left and immediately right on Gilson Road. Go 0.7 mile to end.

25. Right for 0.6 mile to crossroads and stop sign (Edward Foster Road).

26. Right for 0.3 mile to crossroads immediately after little bridge (Peggotty Beach Road on right). You will now loop around the Second Cliff headland.

27. Right for 0.7 mile to stop sign (the same bridge is to your right).

28. Bear right for 0.3 mile to crossroads and stop sign (Front Street on right).

29. Turn right and stay on main road for 2.7 miles to fourth traffic light (Route 3A).

You'll go through downtown Scituate at the beginning. About a mile ahead, you'll pass the town green on your left and the Lawson Tower on your right.

30. Turn right and high school is just ahead on right.

Directions for shorter ride

1. Follow directions for the long ride through number 5.

2. Left for 1.3 miles to wide crossroads and stop sign (Route 3A).

3. Left for 1.4 miles to a road that bears right just before traffic light (sign says SCITUATE, 2 MILES).

4. Follow directions for the long ride from number 22 to the end.

---

attractively located on a long, narrow peninsula with the open sea on one side and the South River, a tidal estuary, on the other. After crossing the North River back into Scituate, you'll pedal past broad salt marshes to the coast, where you'll go through two attractive oceanfront communities, Rivermoor and Second Cliff, both commanding headlands jutting into the ocean. From Second Cliff it's a short ride through the center of town back to your starting point.

Duxbury–Marshfield

Number of miles:	27 (20 without Marshfield extension)
Terrain:	Gently rolling.
Road Surface:	0.25 miles of sandy dirt road where you'll have to walk your bike.
Food:	Restaurant in South Duxbury. Country store in Green Harbor. Snack bar and ice-cream shop in Brant Rock. Pizza at junction of Routes 139 and 3A. McDonald's at end.
Start:	McDonald's, in the Kingsbury Square shopping center, at Routes 3A and 53 in Kingston. It's just west of Route 3; take exit 10. If you're heading south on Route 3, turn right at the end of the exit ramp. If you're heading north on Route 3, turn left at end of ramp.

The South Shore coast just north of Plymouth provides superb bicycling. The protected waters of Kingston and Duxbury Bays are lined with graceful old homes from the 1800s and even earlier. The coast itself, consisting mainly of slender peninsulas with the sea on one side and salt marshes on the other, is beautiful; inland lies a serene, rural landscape of cranberry bogs, small ponds, and snug, cedar-shingled homes.

The ride starts from Duxbury, one of the most affluent and thoroughly unspoiled of the Boston suburbs. The town green, graced by the handsome, pillared town hall and a classic white church, is one of the most dignified in the state. First you'll parallel the shore of Kingston Bay

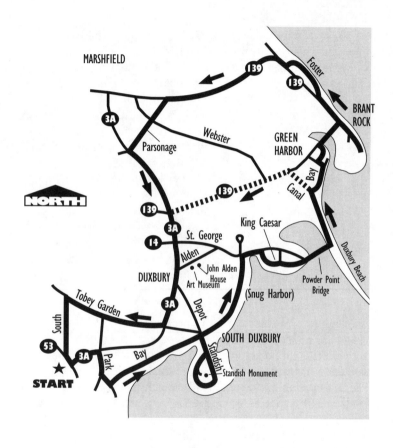

MARSHFIELD

3A

Parsonage

Webster

NORTH

139

3A

14   St. George

Alden

DUXBURY

Art Museum

John Alden
House

King Caesar

(Snug Harbor)

139

139

Foster

GREEN
HARBOR

BRANT
ROCK

Bay   Canal

Powder Point
Bridge

Duxbury Beach

Tobey Garden

South

53   3A   Park

Bay

Depot

3A

Standish

SOUTH DUXBURY

Standish Monument

START

1. Straight from shopping center at traffic light onto Route 3A (don't get on Route 53). Go 0.8 mile to crossroads (Oak Street on left, Park Street on right).

2. Right for 0.4 mile to fork (Loring Street bears left).

3. Bear left for 0.2 mile to stop sign (Bay Road).

4. Left for 2.1 miles to crossroads and stop sign (Standish Street on right) in South Duxbury.

The road follows Kingston Bay about 0.2 mile to your right. You will now make a loop and return to this crossroads after about 2 miles.

5. Right for almost 0.4 mile to Crescent Street, which bears right.

6. Bear right and stay on main road for 1.8 miles to crossroads and stop sign (Washington Street on right) back in South Duxbury. **CAUTION:** The road curves 90 degrees left at bottom of steep hill after 0.8 mile.

The road to the Myles Standish Monument bears left uphill after 0.4 mile. It's a steady 0.3-mile climb to the top.

7. Right for 1.9 miles to fork immediately after an intersection with a flagpole in the middle. (Powder Point Avenue, unmarked, bears right.)

You'll go through Snug Harbor after 1.3 miles. It's worth taking one of the little lanes on the right to the bay.

8. Bear right along harbor for 0.2 mile to King Caesar Road, which bears right.

9. Bear right for 0.5 mile to fork (Weston Road bears left). You'll pass the King Caesar House.

10. Bear right (still King Caesar Road) for 0.7 mile to the beginning of the Powder Point Bridge.

11. Cross the bridge. During the summer a police officer may be stationed at the bridge to make sure that only Duxbury residents drive across, but you're perfectly okay on a bike. At the far end of the bridge, the ocean is 100 yards in front of you.

12. Left at end of bridge into Duxbury Beach parking lot. At far end, continue 0.25 mile along a dirt road. Walk your bike; most of this

Myles Standish Monument

stretch is soft sand. At the end of the dirt section, you'll enter another beach parking lot.

13. Straight for 1.2 miles to Bay Street on right, immediately after the Marshfield town line. Here the short ride goes straight.

14. Right for 0.7 mile to dead end, where you have a fine view of Green Harbor.

15. Make a U-turn and just ahead turn right at stop sign on Beach Street (unmarked). Go less than 0.2 mile to Marginal Street (unmarked) on right.

16. Right for 0.3 mile to end (Route 139). You'll pass an old-fashioned country store on your right after 0.1 mile.

17. Right for 0.6 mile to end at a wide intersection.

This is the village of Brant Rock, which is part of Marshfield. At the end, notice the fine stone church on the left. You will now head out to the Brant Rock peninsula.

18. Right onto a wide divided road for 0.2 mile to fork (Island Street, unmarked, bears right).

19. Bear left along ocean for 0.5 mile to the dead end.

20. Make a U-turn and go 1.3 miles to Foster Avenue (unmarked), which bears right along the coast. You'll pass Brant Rock jutting into the ocean.

21. Bear right and stay on main road for 0.8 mile to end (Route 139 again).

22. Turn right and stay on Route 139 for 1.9 miles to Parsonage Street on left, immediately after police station on left.

23. Left for 1.1 miles to Route 3A at traffic island (bear left at island).

24. Left for 2.4 miles to traffic light (Route 14 on right).

25. Straight for 1.8 miles to crossroads and blinking light (Tobey Garden Street on right). You'll go by the Duxbury town green on your right after 1 mile.

To visit the Duxbury Art Complex Museum, turn left after 0.4 mile on Alden Street. The museum is just ahead on your right. The John Alden House, built in 1653, is 0.2 mile beyond the museum, set back from the road on your right.

26. Right for 1.9 miles to South Street (unmarked), which turns left at a little green. It's 0.4 mile after bridge over Route 3. This is the Tree of Knowledge Corner. A tablet on the green explains the origin of the name.

27. Left for 1.2 miles to end (Route 53).

28. Turn left, and shopping center is just ahead on right.

Directions for shorter ride

1. Follow directions for the long ride through number 13.

2. Straight for 0.7 mile to Route 139 at stop sign.

3. Left for 2 miles to Route 3A (Enterprise Street) at stop sign. You'll pass the Governor Winslow House on your right after 0.6 mile.

4. Left for 0.8 mile to traffic light (Route 14 on right).

5. Follow directions for the long ride from number 25 to the end.

---

to the Myles Standish monument, a graceful stone tower 100 feet high on top of a hill that rises 200 feet from the shore. The view from the top is as dramatic as any in the state. Unfortunately, like so many of the most interesting places in Massachusetts, it's open only during the summer. From here you'll follow Duxbury Bay to the picturesque Currier-and-Ives village of Snug Harbor, with a rambling wooden block of stores and gracious old homes just inland from the harbor full of boats. Just ahead is Powder Point, a peninsula lined with mansions and estates. One of them, the King Caesar House, is a Federal-era beauty open to the public on summer afternoons. It was built in 1807 by Ezra Weston, nicknamed King Caesar, one of the many post-Revolutionary merchant princes who made millions in shipbuilding and the China trade and then flaunted their success by constructing mansions on the Massachusetts coast.

From Powder Point you'll cross the bay over the Powder Point Bridge, a narrow wooden span nearly half a mile long. On the far side is Duxbury Beach, the South Shore's finest. Completely undeveloped, it extends southward 4 miles along a fragile sandy spit of land only a tenth of a mile wide. You'll head north along the ocean to Brant Rock, another peninsula with a road hugging the rocky coastline. Beyond Brant Rock you'll enter an area of beach cottages across the town line in Marshfield, which is more built-up and not as well-to-do as Duxbury. You'll now head a short distance inland and then return south into Duxbury along Route 3A, a smooth, quiet road lined with handsome houses and small farms. At the end of the ride, you can visit the Duxbury Art Complex Museum, a striking modern building opened in 1971. From here it's a short trip back to the start past the town green.

The short ride takes a more direct route back to the start after crossing the Powder Point Bridge. You'll pass the Governor Winslow House, built in 1699 and one of the finer historic houses on the South Shore, with a full complement of period furnishings. On the grounds are Daniel Webster's law office and a blacksmith shop. Across the street is a schoolhouse built in 1857, now headquarters of the Marshfield Historical Society.

44 South Shore Scenic Circuit:
Norwell–Pembroke–Hanson–Hanover

Number of miles:	25 (15 without Pembroke–Hanson extension)
Terrain:	Gently rolling, with some gradual hills.
Food:	Groceries and restaurants in the towns. Restaurant at end.
Start:	Merchants Row Marketplace, Routes 53 and 123 in Hanover.

The pond-studded landscape just inland from the shoulder of land jutting east between Boston and Plymouth offers delightful bicycling. The region is fairly affluent, with spacious homes nestled among pine groves; gentleman farms with rustic barns and rambling farmhouses; and cedar-shingled houses with peaked roofs. The area is generally rural, although development has occurred near Route 3 in Pembroke. The North River, a tidal stream meandering through salt marshes, flows through the area.

The ride starts through Norwell, a gracious town with many homes built around 1800. At the beginning you'll pass Jacobs Pond and an environmental education center with nature trails. From Norwell you'll proceed to Hanover, another fine town with a beautiful town hall topped by a cupola, built in 1863, and a handsome brick library next to it. Most people know Hanover by its congested commercial strip on Route 53, but when you get away from this road, the rest of the town is appealing.

The long ride heads farther south into a more rural area of pines and ponds. In Pembroke you'll skirt the edge of the cranberry-growing region farther south and see the Pembroke Herring Run, a small cascading

1. Right on Route 123 for 0.25 mile to Jacobs Lane on left, just after Jacobs Pond.

2. Left for 0.6 mile to end (merge left on Prospect Street).

3. Bear left for 0.8 mile to crossroads and stop sign (Grove Street).

4. Right for 1.1 miles to fork (School Street bears left).

5. Left for 0.5 mile to end (Mount Blue Street).

6. Right for 0.6 mile to fork (Lincoln Street bears right).

7. Bear left for 1.2 miles to end, at traffic island (Old Oaken Bucket Road, unmarked).

8. Right for 0.3 mile to end (Norwell Avenue on right, Central Street on left).

9. Left for 0.9 mile to crossroads and stop sign (Route 123, Main Street). On the far side of the intersection is a little green and a fine, traditional white church. This is the center of Norwell.

10. Straight for 3.6 miles to crossroads and stop sign (Washington Street). Here the short ride turns right.

11. Left for 0.8 mile to end (Routes 53 and 139). You'll cross the North River.

12. Turn left (**CAUTION** here) and just ahead go straight at traffic light onto Route 53. Go 1.3 miles to Route 14 West (Barker Street), which bears right.

13. Bear right for 1.5 miles to where Route 14 curves left and Oldham Street goes straight, as you come into the center of Pembroke. You'll pass the Pembroke Herring Run on your right after a mile.

14. Straight for 0.7 mile to fork where West Elm Street bears right.

15. Bear left (still Oldham Street) for 0.2 mile to Wampatuck Street on left.

16. Left for 0.9 mile to end (Route 14, Mattakeesett Street). You'll follow Oldham Pond on the right and pass a beach near the end. At the end, Furnace Pond is in front of you.

17. Turn right and stay on Route 14 for 1.7 miles to stop sign (merge

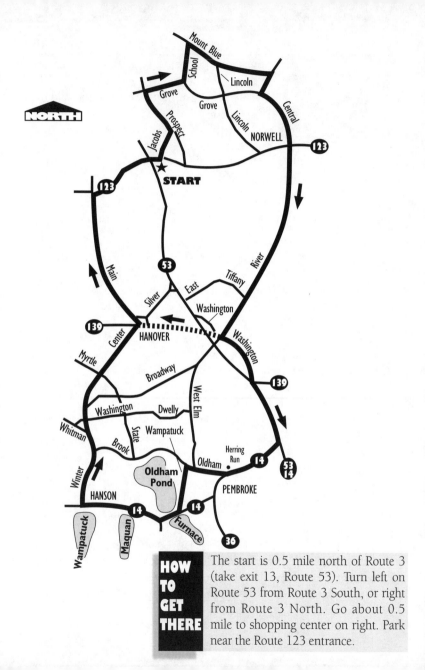

NORTH

Mount Blue

Schools

Lincoln

Grove

Grove

Prospect

Lincoln

Central

Jacobs

NORWELL

123

123

★ START

Main

53

River

Silver

East

Tiffany

139

Washington

Center

HANOVER

Washington

Myrtle

Broadway

West Elm

139

Washington

Dwelly

Whitman

Wampatuck

State

Brook

Herring
Run

Oldham

14

53
14

Winter

Oldham
Pond

PEMBROKE

HANSON

14

14

Wampatuck

Maquan

Furnace

36

HOW TO GET THERE

The start is 0.5 mile north of Route 3 (take exit 13, Route 53). Turn left on Route 53 from Route 3 South, or right from Route 3 North. Go about 0.5 mile to shopping center on right. Park near the Route 123 entrance.

right on Route 58). You'll pass Maquan Pond on your left.

18. Bear right for 0.3 mile to Winter Street on right at traffic light. The striking Hanson town hall is on your left immediately after the intersection, overlooking Wampatuck Pond.

19. Turn right and stay on main road for 2.1 miles to fork (Broadway bears right, Center Street bears left).

20. Bear left for 1.8 miles to end (Route 139) in the center of Hanover.

21. Jog right and immediately left on Center Street. Go 50 yards to stop sign (Main Street). Notice the town hall and library across from the church.

22. Bear left for 2.4 miles to traffic light (Webster Street, Route 123).

23. Right for 1.2 miles to shopping center on right, just past traffic light at Route 53.

Directions for shorter ride

1. Follow directions for the long ride through number 10.

2. Right for 0.1 mile to fork (Rockland Street bears left).

3. Bear left for 0.25 mile to traffic light (Route 53).

4. Straight onto Route 139 West. **CAUTION:** Busy intersection. Go 1.3 miles to Center Street on right immediately after old white church on right. This is the center of Hanover. Notice the town hall opposite the church and the brick library next to the town hall.

5. Right for 50 yards to stop sign (Main Street).

6. Follow directions 22 and 23 for the long ride.

---

stream and picnic area. Every spring, millions of herring swim upstream to spawn. The migration, which lasts about a week, occurs around April 19, although the actual dates vary each year depending on the temperature of the water. The center of Pembroke, with an attractive library, old school building, and white church is just ahead.

From Pembroke you'll weave past a pleasing cluster of ponds into Hanson, an attractive town with a Victorian town hall built in 1872 overlooking Wampatuck Pond. From Hanson it's 4 miles to Hanover, where you'll pick up the route of the short ride.

Stoughton Water Works

45 Canton–Stoughton–North Easton–Sharon

Number of miles:	26 (16 without North Easton extension)
Terrain:	Gently rolling.
Food:	Groceries and snack bars in the towns. Restaurant at end.
Start:	Ground Round, a restaurant on the southeast corner of junction of Routes 1 and 27 in Walpole.

This ride explores four pleasant suburban communities about 20 miles south of Boston. The landscape is semirural and semisuburban. The long ride visits North Easton, a nineteenth-century planned industrial community with magnificent stone buildings.

The ride heads first into Canton, passing the Canton Viaduct, a graceful stone-arched railroad abutment above a small valley. It was built in 1834 and is a landmark of early railroad engineering. Built to accommodate the small, slow-moving early trains, it now supports continual Amtrack and commuter rail traffic. Then you'll bike past Reservoir Pond and head into Stoughton, a middle-class residential community.

Soon you'll come to North Easton, a village of impressive elegance bearing the stamp of Oliver Ames, a nineteenth-century industrialist who amassed his fortune by manufacturing most of the shovels used to build the railroads and mine the earth of the developing West. After making his millions, he donated money to construct a village that his workers could be proud of, hiring the foremost architect of the day, H. H. Richardson, and the foremost landscape designer, Frederick Law

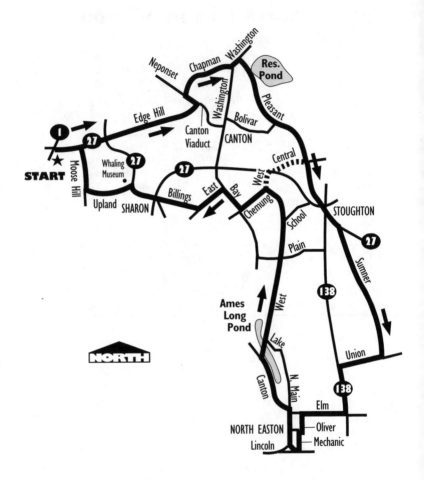

DIRECTIONS
FOR
THE RIDE

1. Right (east) on Route 27 for 1 mile to crossroads and stop sign where Route 27 turns right.

2. Straight for 2.7 miles to end. The first half mile is downhill. At the end, the Canton Viaduct is on your right.

3. Left for 0.4 mile to fork where Chapman Street bears right. As soon as you turn, there's a little dam on the right.

4. Bear right for 1.2 miles to end (Washington Street). If you make a hairpin right turn just after the railroad bridge and go 0.2 mile, you'll come to the old stone Canton Junction railroad station.

5. Left for 0.3 mile to Pleasant Street on right. Here the ride turns right, but if you go straight for 200 yards you'll come to a beautiful old church and school on the left.

6. Right for 3.3 miles to Central Street, at the second of two traffic lights about 0.2 mile apart. Here the short ride turns right.

Just after you turn onto Pleasant Street, you'll see Pequitside Farm, a small recreation area owned by the town of Canton, on your right. A short distance ahead, you'll see Reservoir Pond on your left.

7. Straight for 0.8 mile to fork where Route 138 bears right and Route 27 bears left in the center of Stoughton.

8. Bear left (**CAUTION** here) for 0.3 mile to Sumner Street, which bears right.

9. Bear right for 2.6 miles to end (Pleasant Street on left).

10. Right for 0.8 mile to end (Route 138), passing French Pond on right.

11. Left for 0.7 mile to small crossroads (Elm Street). There's a cemetery on the far right corner.

12. Right for 0.8 mile to Oliver Street on left. You'll pass an arched stone gatehouse designed by H. H. Richardson on your left.

13. Left for almost 0.2 mile to Mechanic Street on left. The road turns 90 degrees right immediately before the intersection.

14. Left for 0.3 mile to end passing old train station on right.

The station, built in 1881, now maintained by the Easton Historical

Society. Behind it are the long stone buildings of the Ames shovel factory, recently recycled into offices. A children's museum, formerly an old fire station, is on the left just before the end.

15. Turn right and just ahead bear right at fork. Go 0.4 mile to Canton Street, which bears left.

The little terraced park in the middle of the fork is the Rockery. Then you'll pass the Memorial Hall, the library, and the stone church on the left. The library is worth visiting if it's open.

16. Bear left for 1.3 miles to West Street, which bears right at stop sign. You'll go along Ames Long Pond.

17. Bear right across pond for 1.7 miles to crossroads and stop sign (Plain Street).

18. Go straight and stay on main road for 1.5 miles to Chemung Street, which bears left uphill at a wooded traffic island. (Don't bear right on School Street after 0.7 mile.)

19. Bear left for 0.6 mile to crossroads and stop sign (Bay Road).

20. Right for 0.4 mile to East Street on left. There's an excellent ice-cream shop at the intersection.

21. Left for 0.7 mile to Billings Street, which bears right at bottom of hill.

22. Bear right for 1 mile to traffic light in the center of Sharon (Route 27 goes straight and right).

After 0.3 mile you'll see Manns Pond on your left. If you follow the shore for 100 feet with the pond on your right, you'll cross a footbridge above a picturesque little dam. When you get to Route 27, notice the fine white church on the far side of the intersection.

23. Straight for 0.5 mile to where the road curves sharply right at large traffic island with a house on it.

24. At the far end of the traffic island, make a U-turn to the left, then immediately bear right downhill on Upland Road (sign says KENDALL WHALING MUSEUM). Go 0.2 mile to where Upland Road curves sharply left and Everett Street turns right. Here the ride bears left, but if you turn right for 200 yards, you'll come to the Whaling Museum.

25. Curve left and stay on main road for 1 mile to end (Moose Hill

Street) at T-intersection. The information center for the Moose Hill Wildlife Sanctuary is on your right at the end.

26. Right for 1.4 miles to end (Route 27).

27. Left for 0.4 mile to Ground Round on left. **CAUTION** turning left into parking lot.

Directions for shorter ride

1. Follow directions for the long ride through number 6.

2. Right for 0.8 mile to stop sign (merge right on Route 27).

3. Bear right for 0.2 mile to West Street on left. It's immediately after the Stoughton Water Works, an ornate building dated 1892, on your left.

4. Left for 0.3 mile to fork (Chemung Street bears right uphill).

5. Bear right for 0.6 mile to crossroads and stop sign (Bay Road).

6. Follow directions for the long ride from number 20 to the end.

Olmsted, to do the job. Coming into town, you'll pass the handsome stone railroad station with its graceful arched entryway and then imposing the Ames Memorial Hall. Next to this is the beautiful Ames Free Library, with a clock tower and an ornate, wood-paneled interior. It was built in 1883. Just ahead is a stone church with a tall, slender spire. In the middle of the town's main intersection is a small terraced park, complete with a stone archway, called the Rockery, designed by Olmsted in 1879.

Leaving North Easton, you'll follow lovely Ames Long Pond and ride into the center of Sharon, a pleasant upper-middle-class community with lots of rural land. The Kendall Whaling Museum, a collection of whaling objects and art, is just outside town. Near the end, you'll pass the Moose Hill Wildlife Sanctuary, run by the Massachusetts Audubon Society, and skirt the base of 530-foot Moose Hill, the highest point in southeastern Massachusetts outside of the Blue Hills.

Sharon–Easton–Norton–Mansfield–Foxboro

Number of miles:	30 (15 without Easton–Norton–Foxboro extension)
Terrain:	Flat, with 3 little hills near the end.
Food:	None on the short ride. Restaurant on Bay Street, Norton. Restaurant and pub in the Holiday Inn, Taunton. Grocery and pizza shop in Mansfield. Snack bar at end.
Facilities:	Restrooms at Borderlands State Park.
Start:	Shaw's Plaza, South Main Street, Sharon, just east of I–95 at the South Main Street–Mechanic Street exit (exit 8).

On this ride you'll explore a delightfully rural, lake-dotted area midway between Boston and Providence. Flat terrain, smooth secondary roads, and a spin along the shore of Massapoag Lake in Sharon make for relaxed pedaling. The longer ride heads farther south through the lovely rural town of Norton and along the shore of Winnecunnet Pond.

The ride starts from Sharon, an attractive, upper-middle-class community. It has a few housing developments, but most of the town is still rural. The focal point of the community is refreshingly unspoiled Massapoag Lake, most of its shoreline graced by handsome older homes. You'll follow the lakeshore for half its perimeter and then head through woods and farmlands into Easton. At the town line you'll pass Borderlands State Park, an idyllic expanse of meadows and woodland surrounding Leach Pond, with paths looping around its shore. A magnificent stone mansion that formerly belonged to the Ames family,

1. Right (northeast) on South Main Street for 0.6 mile to Wolomolopoag Street on right.

2. Right for 1.5 miles to end (East Foxboro Street).

3. Left for 1.5 miles to fork where the main road curves left and Beach Street bears right.

4. Bear right for 0.9 mile to end (Pond Street). You'll follow Massapoag Lake on your right.

5. Right for 4.6 miles to crossroads and stop sign (Rockland Street). Here the short ride turns right. **CAUTION:** Bumps and potholes on the last mile.

You'll ride along the eastern shore of Massapoag Lake at the beginning. The entrance to Borderlands State Park is on your left after about 3.5 miles.

6. Straight for 1.3 miles to stop sign (Poquanticut Avenue). **CAUTION:** Watch for potholes.

7. Right for 1.2 miles to South Street on left. The main road curves sharply right at the intersection.

8. Left for 0.5 mile to end (Highland Street, unmarked). **CAUTION** crossing Route 106.

9. Left for 0.3 mile to end (Bay Road, unmarked).

10. Right for 4.4 miles to Industrial Park Road on right at traffic light, just after bridge over I–495. You'll pass Winnecunnet Pond on your right about a mile before the intersection.

11. Right for 0.3 mile to first right, North Boundary Road.

12. Right for 2.7 miles to second crossroads and stop sign (Route 123). Here the ride goes straight, but to see Wheaton College turn left for 1.2 miles to campus on left.

13. Straight for 1.8 miles to fork shortly after bridge over I–495 (Essex Street, unmarked, bears slightly right).

14. Bear right for 1.4 miles to end (Mill Street).

15. Left for 0.5 mile to fork at the East Mansfield green (Cherry Street, unmarked, bears right).

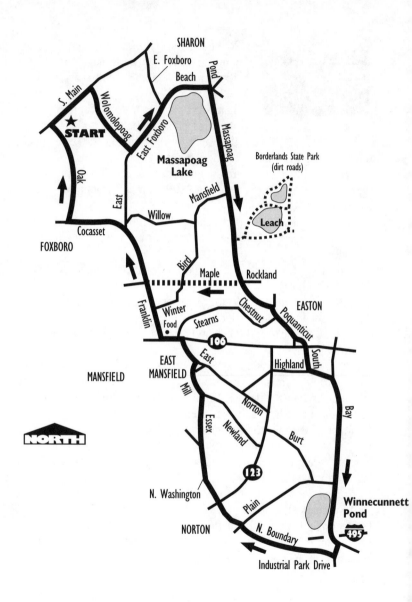

16. Bear left and just ahead merge left at stop sign. Go 0.5 mile to end (Route 106, Eastman Street).

17. Left for 0.4 mile to Franklin Street on right, at traffic light. There's a grocery and pizza shop on the right just before the corner.

18. Right for 2.1 miles to fork where East Street bears right and Cocasset Street (unmarked) bears left.

19. Bear left for 1 mile to Oak Street on right, at blinking light.

20. Right for 2.1 miles to end (Mechanic Street).

21. Right for 0.5 mile to shopping center on right.

Directions for shorter ride

1. Follow the directions for the long ride through number 5.

2. Right for 1.6 miles to crossroads and stop sign (Franklin Street).

3. Right for 0.9 mile to fork where East Street bears right and Cocasset Street (unmarked) bears left.

4. Follow directions for the long ride from number 19 to the end.

---

whose legacy is concentrated in nearby North Easton, is on the grounds of the park.

The long ride heads farther south through prosperous farmlands into Norton, one of the most pleasantly rural towns within commuting distance of Boston. In the center of town (about a mile off the route) is Wheaton College, a small, high-quality school with a traditional, tree-shaded campus of stately ivy-covered buildings. The return to Sharon passes through the rural eastern edges of Mansfield and Foxboro.

Foxboro–Mansfield–North Attleboro–Plainville

Number of miles:	23 (14 without Mansfield–North Attleboro extension)
Terrain:	Gently rolling, with a few short hills.
Food:	McDonald's and Burger King in Plainville. Country store in West Mansfield. Snack bar in North Attleboro. Friendly's at end, 0.1 mile south of starting point on Route 140.
Start:	Foxboro town green, Route 140. There are no time restrictions on Route 140 South, facing the green on the left side of the road.

On this ride we explore the rural, lake-dotted countryside just south of the midpoint between Boston and Providence. You start from Foxboro, an attractive town with two fine churches and a green forming a central square. A landmark in the town is a small, ornate building that was constructed as a Civil War memorial and for many years served as the town library. From Foxboro you'll head through tidy residential areas to Plainville, a pleasant rural town consisting mainly of woods, farmland, and orchards. You'll bicycle along two unspoiled ponds, Turnpike Lake and Lake Mirimichi, and return to Foxboro along forested narrow lanes.

The long ride heads south into Mansfield, a compact mill town surrounded by countryside. The route stays in the rural western part of Mansfield, avoiding the center of town. You'll pass Greenwood Lake and then the North Attleboro National Fish Hatchery, a fascinating spot to visit if open (its hours are limited). You'll descend steeply into Plainville and rejoin the short ride near Turnpike Lake.

DIRECTIONS
FOR
THE RIDE

1. Head south on Route 140 and just ahead turn right on South Street at end of green. As you approach South Street, notice the stone, churchlike Civil War memorial in front of you. Go 2.3 miles to crossroads (West Street on right, North Grove Street on left).

2. Left for 0.6 mile to end (Route 106). There's a steep hill at the beginning.

3. Right for 0.1 mile to South Grove Street on left immediately after the bridge over I–495. Here the short ride goes straight.

4. Left for 1.5 miles to end (Williams Street, unmarked).

5. Left for 0.4 mile to stop sign where the main road bears right.

6. Bear right for 0.3 mile to end.

7. Right and just ahead right at crossroads on Otis Street. Go 1.2 miles to end. A country store is on your left at the beginning of Otis Street in West Mansfield, Sweets Pond is on your right at the end.

8. Turn right and stay on main road for 1.1 miles to end. (Don't bear left on Bungay Road after 0.9 mile.)

9. Left for 0.7 mile to Bungay Road on right. (There are two Bungay Roads, one in Mansfield and one in North Attleboro.) You'll see Greenwood Lake on the right.

10. Right for 0.5 mile to end (Route 152).

You'll pass the North Attleboro National Fish Hatchery on your right, worth visiting if it's open. Just ahead there's a little red schoolhouse built in 1810, currently used as an office, also on the right.

11. Left for 1.3 miles to Robert F. Toner Boulevard (unmarked) on right, at traffic light (sign says TO I–95).

12. Right for 0.4 mile to John Dietsch Boulevard on right, immediately before shopping center on right. **CAUTION:** Watch for traffic entering and exiting I–95.

13. Right for 0.6 mile to small crossroads (Towne Street, unmarked). Bliss Ice Cream, on your left in the shopping center, is a good halfway stop. (The back of the snack bar is next to the road.)

14. Left for 0.8 mile to crossroads and stop sign (Commonwealth Avenue, unmarked).

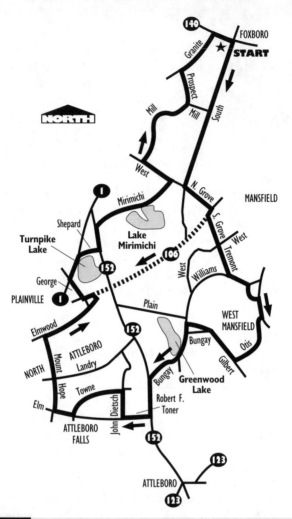

HOW TO GET THERE

If you're heading south on I–95, take the South Main Street–Mechanic Street exit (exit 8). Turn right at end of ramp and go about 2.5 miles to the Foxboro green. Park on the far side of the green. If you're heading north on I–95, exit north onto Route 140 and go about 1.5 miles to the Foxboro green. Park on the opposite side of the green.

15. Turn right and stay on main road for less than 0.4 mile to traffic light (Mount Hope Street, unmarked). The round brick building on the far right corner was built as a gasworks in 1855. This area is Attleboro Falls, a section of North Attleboro.

16. Right for 1.6 mile to end (Elmwood Street, unmarked). Shift into low gear at end.

17. Right for 1.2 miles to end (Route 106).

After 0.5 mile you'll pass World War I Memorial Park on the right; there's a small zoo here and a good view from the base of a fire tower. Then you'll descend steeply. At the end the ride turns left, but if you turn right, a Burger King is on your right just before traffic light, set back from the road.

18. Left for less than 0.2 mile to crossroads (George Street).

19. Right for 0.5 mile to Route 1, at stop sign.

20. Right for 0.4 mile to Shepard Street, which bears right. You'll pass Turnpike Lake on your right.

21. Bear right for 0.4 mile to end (Route 152).

22. Left for 0.4 mile to Mirimichi Street on right.

23. Right for 2.3 miles to end at traffic island. The main road bears right after 0.4 mile and crosses Lake Mirimichi.

24. Left for 0.3 mile to Mill Street on right (sign says TO STATE FOREST).

25. Right for 1.3 miles to fork (Prospect Street, unmarked, bears left).

26. Bear left for 0.8 mile to end (Granite Street, unmarked).

27. Right for 0.9 mile to end (Route 140). You'll pass Sunset Lake on your left at the beginning.

28. Turn right on Route 140. The Foxboro green is just ahead.

Directions for shorter ride

1. Follow directions for the long ride through number 3.

2. Straight for 2.5 miles to Route 152 at traffic light.

3. Straight for 0.4 mile to crossroads (George Street).

4. Follow directions for the long ride from number 19 to the end.

Norton–Taunton

Number of miles:	28 (13 without Taunton extension)
Terrain:	Flat to gently rolling.
Food:	McDonald's on Route 140 near beginning of ride. Restaurant on Bay Street, Norton.
Start:	Wheaton College visitors parking lot, on the north side of Route 123 in Norton, just east of Route 140.

Midway between Taunton and Attleboro, about 30 miles south of Boston, is a very enjoyable area for biking. The terrain is nearly level, with an extensive network of little-traveled country roads looping past ponds and prosperous farmland. The region is far enough from Boston to be fairly rural, without much infiltration of suburban development.

The ride starts from Norton, one of the most pleasantly rural towns within commuting distance of Boston and a graceful New England classic. The centerpiece of the community is Wheaton College, a high-quality school with a lovely campus graced by elegant, ivy-covered wood and brick buildings. A small pond with a footbridge across it adds to the beauty of the setting. Adjacent to the campus are a stately white church and a handsome brick turn-of-the-century former library.

Near the beginning of the ride, you'll ride along the Norton Reservoir and pass the Great Woods Performing Arts Center, the scene of many popular concerts. Just ahead you'll follow the north shore of the reservoir and go through the small lakeside community of Norton Grove. After a few miles of woods and farmland, you pass Winnecunnet Pond, Watson Pond, and Lake Sabbatia in quick succession. Across from the latter pond is the Paul A. Dever School, an institution for chil-

1. Right for less than 0.2 mile to fork where Route 123 bears left, and then straight (don't bear left) for 100 yards to end (Route 140).

Notice the handsome brick former library on the far side of the intersection.

2. Right for 2.7 miles to Reservoir Street (unmarked) on right, just before bridge over I–495. You'll follow the Norton Reservoir on your right and then pass the Great Woods Performing Arts Center on your left just before the intersection.

3. Right for 1.9 miles to Elm Street on left. It's 0.5 mile after a laundromat and Cobb Street on left. You'll follow the Norton Reservoir on your right.

4. Left for 0.4 mile to Cross Street on left, immediately after a factory on left.

5. Left for 0.7 mile to end. A little dam is on the left just past the factory.

6. Left for 0.4 mile to Newcomb Street on right.

7. Right for 1.1 miles to crossroads and stop sign (dirt road if you go straight).

8. Right for 0.6 mile to end (Route 123).

9. Right for 0.6 mile to Leonard Street on left, just before bridge over I–495.

10. Left for 1 mile to end. Here the short ride turns right.

11. Turn left and stay on main road for 0.7 mile to end (Bay Road).

12. Right for 1.4 miles to traffic light (Myles Standish Industrial Park on right). You'll pass Winnecunnet Pond on your right.

13. Straight for 2.1 miles to Whittenton Street, which bears right at the far end of Sabbatia Lake on your left. The main road curves sharply left at the intersection.

You'll pass Watson Pond on your right and then Sabbatia Lake. There's a small state park with a beach at Watson Pond. The Paul A. Dever State School is on your right across from Sabbatia Lake.

14. Bear right for 0.8 mile to fork at a traffic island (Warren Street bears right).

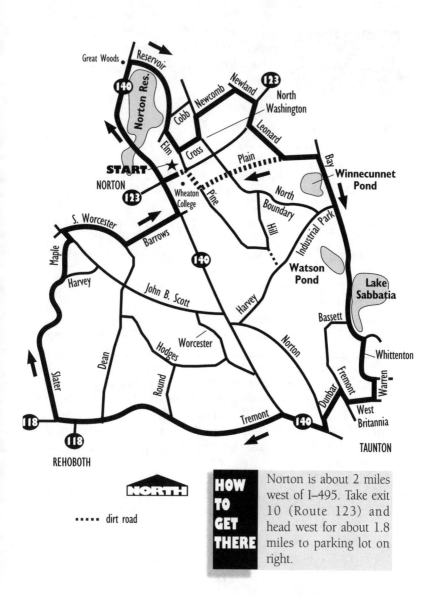

Great Woods
Reservoir
Norton Res.
140
Newcomb
Newland
123
North
Washington
Cobb
Leonard
Elm
Cross
Plain
Bay
START
Winnecunnet
Pond
NORTON
123
North
Boundary
Wheaton
College
Pine
Hill
S. Worcester
Industrial Park
Maple
Barrows
140
Watson
Pond
Lake
Sabbatia
Harvey
John B. Scott
Harvey
Bassett
Worcester
Whittenton
Dean
Hodges
Norton
Fremont
Warren
Slater
Round
Dunbar
118
Tremont
140
West
Britannia
118
TAUNTON
REHOBOTH

NORTH

····· dirt road

HOW TO GET THERE

Norton is about 2 miles west of I–495. Take exit 10 (Route 123) and head west for about 1.8 miles to parking lot on right.

15. Bear right for 0.3 mile to end (West Britannia Street, unmarked).

16. Right for 0.6 mile to end (Fremont Street). You'll pass an attractive brick school built in 1888 on your left at the beginning.

17. Right and just ahead left on Dunbar Street. Go 0.5 mile to stop sign (merge left on Norton Avenue).

18. Bear left and just ahead turn right at end (Route 140). Go 0.7 mile to Tremont Street, which bears left (sign says LA SALLETTE). It's several streets after Glebe Street, which also bears left.

19. Bear left for 0.3 mile to fork (Worcester Street bears right).

20. Bear left (still Tremont Street) for 4.5 miles to Slater Street on right, shortly after Route 118 South on left.

21. Turn right and stay on main road for 2.3 miles to fork where Harvey Street bears right and Maple Street bears left.

22. Bear left and stay on main road for almost 0.8 mile to end (John B. Scott Boulevard). Don't go straight on dead-end road just before end.

23. Left and just ahead right at crossroads on South Worcester Street. **CAUTION:** Diagonal railroad tracks just before crossroads. Go 0.9 mile to Barrows Street on left, just before railroad tracks.

24. Left for 1.2 miles to wide crossroads and stop sign (Route 140).

25. Left for 0.7 mile to end (Route 123, East Main Street) in the center of Norton. The town green is in front of you at the intersection.

26. Right for 0.2 mile to parking lot on left.

Directions for shorter ride

1. Follow directions for the long ride through number 10.

2. Right for 1.2 miles to crossroads and stop sign (South Washington Street).

3. Straight for 0.8 mile to end (Pine Street).

4. Right for 0.5 mile to crossroads and stop sign (Route 123).

5. Left for 0.1 mile to parking lot on right.

dren who have mental disabilities and a port of embarkation for troops during World War II. Watson Pond and Lake Sabbatia are just over the town line in Taunton, a city of 40,000 covering a wide area in the southeastern part of the state. The city, best known for the manufacture of fine silver products, is rural around its outer edges. You'll bike through a pleasant, tree-shaded residential area and then quickly get back into the undeveloped western edge of the city. The return run to Norton brings you through a fine mixture of woods, farmland, and old wooden houses.

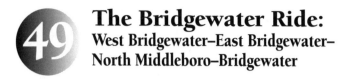

The Bridgewater Ride:
West Bridgewater–East Bridgewater–North Middleboro–Bridgewater

Number of miles:	28 (20 without North Middleboro extension)
Terrain:	Gently rolling, with one hill.
Food:	Groceries and restaurants in the towns. Restaurant at Plymouth Street and Route 18 in North Middleboro (good halfway stop). Pizza shop at end.
Start:	Center Shopping Plaza, junction of Routes 28 and 106, West Bridgewater. It's 2 miles east of Route 24.

The three Bridgewaters, just south of Brockton and about 30 miles south of Boston, mark the transition between suburbia to the north and an extensive rural area to the southeast, encompassing nearly all the land down to the Cape Cod Canal and New Bedford. As you head south and southeast from Brockton, the landscape acquires characteristics unique to the southeastern portion of the state—sandy soil, scrub pine, cranberry bogs, generally flat and often swampy terrain, and cedar-shingled houses with peaked roofs. This landscape provides some of the easiest and most scenic bicycling in the state on a superb network of well-maintained country lanes and secondary roads. Most of southeastern Massachusetts has a tidy, prosperous look that is subtly pleasing. This ride is the closest to Boston that offers some of the ambience of this section of the state.

The ride starts from West Bridgewater, a pleasant community with some tract housing (which you won't go through) toward the Brockton line and lots of undeveloped land. You'll quickly cross into East Bridge-

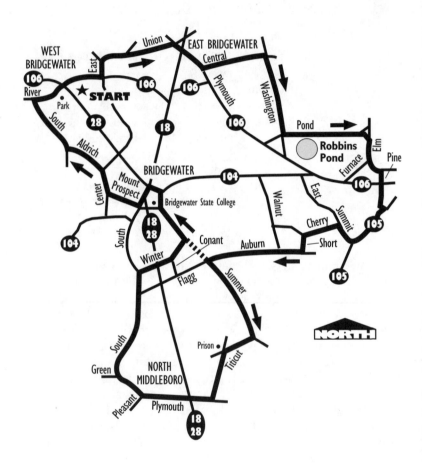

DIRECTIONS
FOR
THE RIDE

1. Right (east) on Route 106 for 0.9 mile to crossroads and blinking light (East Street).

2. Left (**CAUTION** here) for 0.4 mile to fork (Union Street bears right).

3. Bear right and stay on main road for 1.6 miles to crossroads and stop sign (North Central Street) in East Bridgewater.

4. Turn right and just ahead cross Route 18 diagonally at traffic light. Go 0.3 mile to fork at the East Bridgewater town green (Plymouth Street bears right).

5. Bear left (still Central Street) and stay on main road for 1.8 miles to traffic light (Washington Street).

6. Right for 1.9 miles to second crossroads (Pond Street). There's a convenience store on the left at the intersection.

7. Turn left (it's a somewhat sharp left) and stay on main road for 1.8 miles to end at large traffic island (Elm Street, unmarked). It's 0.6 mile after Hudson Street on left. You'll pass Robbins Pond on your right.

8. Curve right and stay on main road for 1 mile to Pine Street, which bears right. (Don't bear right on Furnace Street after 0.5 mile.)

9. Bear right and just ahead cross Route 106. Go 0.5 mile to end (Route 105). You'll pass a cranberry bog on the right.

10. Right for 1.2 miles to fork (Summit Street bears right).

11. Bear right for 0.4 mile to end (merge right on Walnut Street). There is no stop sign at the intersection.

12. Bear right for 0.2 mile to Cherry Street (unmarked) on left.

13. Left for 0.9 mile to fork where Cherry Street bears right and Short Street bears left.

14. Bear left for 0.3 mile to end (Auburn Street) at large traffic island.

15. Bear right and stay on main road for 1.7 miles to crossroads and stop sign (Summer Street, unmarked). Here the short ride turns right.

16. Left for 1.8 miles to Titicut Street on right. You'll see the prison on your right in the distance.

17. Right for 0.6 mile to crossroads and stop sign immediately before the prison.

18. Left for 1 mile to end (Plymouth Street, unmarked). **CAUTION:** Watch for bumps and cracks while going down the hill. You'll cross the Taunton River shortly before the end.

19. Right for 0.3 mile to traffic light (Routes 28 and 18, Bedford Street). There's a good restaurant on your left at the intersection.

20. Straight for 0.8 mile to fork at the North Middleboro green (main road bears right). Notice the fine old buildings in the graceful village.

21. Bear right for 0.6 mile to fork just after you cross the Taunton River (Green Street bears left, South Street bears right).

22. Bear right for 2.3 miles to fork where South Street bears left and Winter Street bears right.

23. Bear right for 0.8 mile to end (Conant Street, unmarked). **CAUTION** crossing Route 18.

24. Left for 0.5 mile to stop sign at bottom of hill (merge left on Summer Street, unmarked).

25. Bear left and stay on main road for 1 mile to end (Route 104). You'll go through the campus of Bridgewater State College at the end.

26. Left for less than 0.2 mile to traffic light in center of Bridgewater.

27. Left (still Route 104) for 0.2 mile to crossroads (Grove Street on left, Mount Prospect Street on right). Notice the old library on your right immediately after the new one.

28. Right for 0.5 mile to end.

29. Right for 0.4 mile to Aldrich Road on left, just before a large brick church on left.

30. Turn left and stay on main road for 0.8 mile to end (South Street, unmarked).

31. Right for 1 mile to end (River Street, unmarked), immediately after a little bridge.

32. Right for 0.4 mile to Route 28 (South Main Street). Shopping center is on far right side of intersection.

You'll pass a delightful riverfront park on your right after 0.2 mile.

Directions for shorter ride

1. Follow directions for the long ride through number 15.

2. Turn right and stay on main road for 1.7 miles to end (Route 104). You'll go through the campus of Bridgewater State College at the end.
3. Follow directions for the long ride from number 26 to the end.

water, which is somewhat more rural. The center of town is beautiful, if you can somehow ignore the broad slash of Route 18 that bisects it. The large green is framed by an unusually graceful white church and a handsome old schoolhouse. Heading east of town, you'll go through broad farms and past unspoiled Robbins Pond. You'll now start seeing cranberry bogs as you pass through the eastern edge of Halifax, one of the most thoroughly rural towns within commuting distance of Boston, and then into Bridgewater itself, which lies south of its East and West companions. The town center is a New England classic, with a small green smack in the middle of Route 18, framed by a compact row of old business buildings, a fine church, and an ornate brick former library built in 1881. Adjoining the center of town is the campus of Bridgewater State College, the earliest state college in Massachusetts, with attractive red-brick buildings. From Bridgewater it's not far back to West Bridgewater on back roads. Just before the end, you'll pass a beautiful park along the Town River, originally the site of a factory during the 1800s.

The long ride heads farther south through broad sweeps of farmland bordered by stately rows of shade trees. Looming in the distance on a hilltop is the Bridgewater Correctional Institution, a grim, turreted monstrosity resembling a medieval fortress, strangely out of place in this pastoral setting. You'll go right by the prison and then follow the Taunton River into North Middleboro, a charming, unspoiled village. Its small green is framed by a graceful yellow wooden church with a clock tower; a white, pillared mansion; and a classic old schoolhouse. From here you'll have a fine run past farms and meadows to Bridgewater, where you'll pick up the route of the short ride.

Middleboro–Halifax

Number of miles:	25 (16 without Halifax loop)
Terrain:	Flat.
Food:	None on short ride. Grocery and restaurant in Halifax.
Start:	Oliver Mill Park, Route 44 and Nemasket Street in Middleboro, 3 miles east of I–495. Entrance is on Nemasket Street.

On this ride you explore the lakes and broad expanses of farmland midway between Boston and the Cape Cod Canal and about 10 miles inland from the coast. The area is far enough from Boston, about 35 miles, to be completely rural. Very flat terrain, good secondary roads without much traffic, and fine countryside make bicycling in this region a pleasure. A section of the ride parallels Great Cedar Swamp, an extensive wetland bordered by large, prosperous farms.

The ride starts from the outskirts of Middleboro at Oliver Mill Park, site of an industrial enterprise dating to the 1700s. It included a gristmill, a sawmill, a forge, and other operations. The area has recently been landscaped and the old stone channel for the Nemasket River restored. In the early spring, this is a prime spot to watch the annual herring run, when millions of the fish swim up the rivers to their spawning grounds. Shortly after you leave the park, you'll head toward Halifax along Route 105, one of the best numbered routes in the state for biking. This section is narrow, well-surfaced, and almost traffic-free, and passes through magnificent open farmland.

Halifax is one of the most rural communities within commuting distance of Boston, consisting primarily of woods, cranberry bogs, swamp-

DIRECTIONS

FOR

THE RIDE

1. Turn left out of parking lot and immediately cross Route 44 at traffic light. Go 0.2 mile to Precinct Street on right.

2. Right for 2 miles to end (Route 105).

3. Turn left and stay on Route 105 for 5 miles to end (Route 106).

4. Right for 0.2 mile to Carver Street on right. Here the short ride turns right.

5. Straight for 1.4 mile to traffic light (Route 58, Monponsett Street).

You'll go through the center of Halifax. Notice the pillared town hall on your left after 0.4 mile, immediately after church on left.

6. Left for 2.7 miles to South Street on right, immediately before the modern Calvary Baptist Church on right. **CAUTION** turning left, and at diagonal railroad tracks after 2.1 miles. You'll cross Monponsett Pond at the beginning.

7. Turn right and stay on main road for 1.7 miles to crossroads and stop sign (Route 36). You'll pass Stetson Pond on your left.

8. Right for 1.7 miles to end (Route 106, Plymouth Street). You'll pass the other side of Monponsett Pond near the end.

9. Right for 0.7 mile to traffic light (Route 58, Monponsett Street).

10. Straight for 1 mile to South Street on left, opposite church.

11. Left for 0.3 mile to end (Carver Street on right).

12. Turn left (still South Street) and stay on main road for 1 mile to fork where River Street bears right. (Don't bear left on Franklin Street after 0.3 mile.)

13. Bear left (still South Street). Stay on main road for 1.3 miles to fork where Wood Street goes straight and Fuller Street bears left.

14. Bear left for 3.1 miles to end (merge left on Route 105, Thompson Street).

15. Bear left and stay on Route 105 for 0.9 mile to traffic light (Route 44).

16. Straight for 0.2 mile to crossroads (Plymouth Street) just after church. Notice the one-room schoolhouse on far left side of intersection.

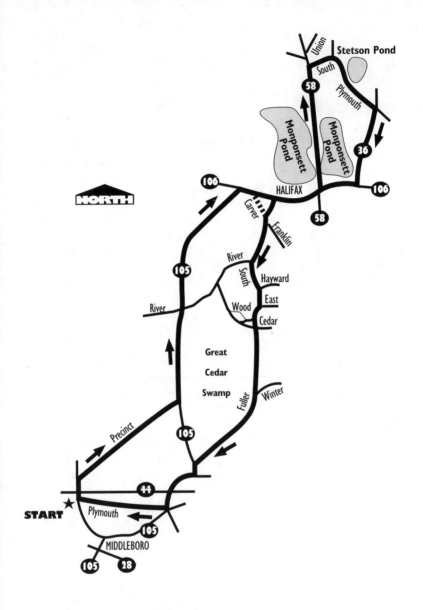

17. Right for 1.4 mile to end. The park is in front of you.

Directions for shorter ride

1. Follow directions for the long ride through number 4.
2. Turn right and stay on main road for 1.4 miles to fork where River Street bears right. (Don't bear left on Franklin Street after 0.7 mile.)
3. Follow directions for the long ride from number 13 to the end.

---

land, and Monponsett Pond. The town center is beautiful, with a fine, white-pillared town hall and old schoolhouse. Just north of town, you'll thread across Monponsett Pond along a causeway that splits the lake in two. From here you'll make a loop, passing unspoiled Stetson Pond, going along the far side of Monponsett Pond, and arriving back in Halifax. The return trip to Middleboro goes along narrow lanes, passing a couple of cranberry bogs and skirting the eastern edge of the Great Cedar Swamp. Shortly before the end, you'll pass a magnificent white church on a splendid green in the middle of nowhere.

Chapter 6:
Southeastern Massachusetts

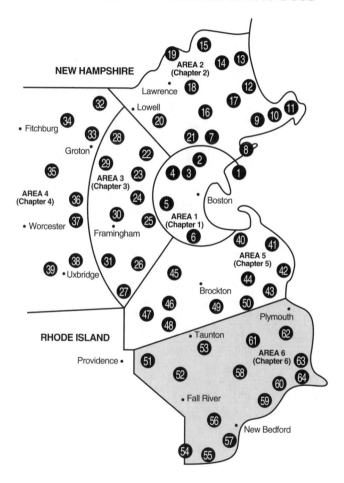

Seekonk–Rehoboth

Number of miles:	28 (15 without southern extension)
Terrain:	Gently rolling, with one hill. The long ride has an additional hill.
Food:	Country store in Rehoboth.
Start:	Seekonk High School, Arcade Avenue and Ledge Road in Seekonk, 0.7 mile north of Route 44.

Just east of Providence is a very rural, gently rolling area that provides superb bicycling. Narrow country lanes wind past large farms, a couple of ponds, and weathered barns. The center of Rehoboth is a beauty, with a little dam and millpond, a fine small church, and a library in a graceful brick building. The Carpenter Museum, with exhibits of local history and rural artifacts, is next to the church.

The ride begins in Seekonk, a residential suburb of Providence that quickly becomes rural toward its eastern edge. You'll bike through a pastoral landscape of gentleman farms and gracious homes to Rehoboth Village, the center of Rehoboth. The return to Seekonk leads through similar scenery. The long ride heads farther east and south through a more rural area, following the Warren Upper Reservoir and then the beautiful valley of the Palmer River, which is lined with large farms. Just ahead you'll pass Shad Factory Pond, a small millpond with a sloping dam. From here it's a short ride back to the start.

1. Left onto Ledge Road, (not Arcade Avenue). **CAUTION:** Speed bump as you leave the parking lot. Just ahead cross Arcade Avenue and go 0.3 mile to fork (Greenwood Avenue bears left, Ledge Road bears right).

2. Bear right and stay on main road for 0.9 mile to end (Jacob Street, unmarked). Don't bear right on Hope Street after 0.2 mile.

3. Left (it's a somewhat sharp left) for 0.4 mile to Prospect Street on left.

4. Turn left and stay on main road for 2.9 miles to end (Pine Street, unmarked). The main road bears right after 1.4 miles. There's a gradual hill at the end.

5. Right for 2.2 miles to end (Broad Street).

6. Left for 0.3 mile to fork where the main road bears slightly left.

7. Bear left for 0.3 mile to crossroads and stop sign (River Street).

8. Bear left for 0.7 mile to end (Danforth Street).

9. Right for 0.3 mile to wide crossroads and stop sign (Route 44).

10. Straight onto Bay State Road, jogging 20 feet to right as you go through the intersection. Go 0.8 mile to fork (Bay State Road bears left, County Street bears right). Rehoboth Village is just before the fork.

11. Bear right for 0.3 mile to crossroads and blinking light (Route 118).

12. Right for 0.2 mile to crossroads (Summer Street on right, Elm Street on left). Here the short ride turns right.

13. Left for 0.7 mile to end (merge right; no stop sign). County Street (unmarked) is at the end.

14. Bear right for 1.6 miles to crossroads and stop sign at top of hill. There's a country store on the far right corner.

15. Right for 2 miles to end (Gorham Street). You'll enjoy a descent to the Warren Upper Reservoir on your right.

16. Left for 0.2 mile to end (Cedar Street on left, Plain Street on right).

17. Right for 0.6 mile to stop sign (Route 118). At the intersection, Route 118 turns right and also goes straight.

18. Turn right on Route 118 North. Just ahead it turns right, but go straight for 0.7 mile to Brook Street, a smaller road that bears right.

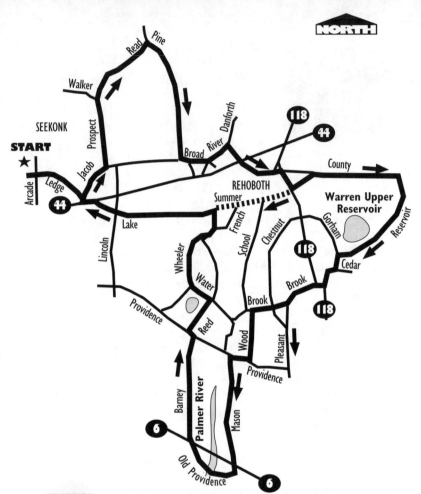

NORTH

HOW TO GET THERE

From I–95 South, exit south onto Route 1A, Newport Avenue (exit 2A). Go 1 mile to third traffic light (Central Avenue). Turn left for 1 mile to end (Route 152). Turn right for 3.4 miles to Arcade Avenue on left at blinking light, and left for 0.6 mile to school on right.

From I–195, exit north onto Route 114A (exit 1). After 1 mile, Route 114A bears left, but go straight onto Arcade Avenue for 0.8 mile to traffic light (Route 44), and straight for 0.7 mile to school on left.

19. Bear right for 0.9 mile to Wood Street on left, just before short hill.

20. Left for 0.8 mile to end (Providence Street, unmarked).

21. Right for almost 0.4 mile to Mason Street, which turns sharply left at traffic island.

22. Sharp left for 1.9 miles to Route 6 at stop sign.

At this point the ride goes straight and then right to a bridge that is under construction and impassable. If a sign indicates that the road is closed, turn right (west) on Route 6 for 0.8 mile to Barney Avenue, which bears right. Bear right for 1.9 miles to end. Resume with direction 26.

23. Cross Route 6 diagonally (**CAUTION** here) and just ahead turn right at end (Old Providence Road). Go 1 mile to Route 6 again at stop sign. The bridge over the Palmer River is a delightful spot.

24. Cross Route 6 diagonally (**CAUTION** again). Go 1.9 miles to end.

25. Left and just ahead right on Reed Street. Go 0.6 mile to crossroads and stop sign (Water Street, unmarked). You'll pass Shad Factory Pond and the dam on your left.

26. Left for 0.3 mile to yield sign at bottom of hill (Wheeler Street bears right).

27. Bear right for 1.1 miles to fork (French Street bears right).

28. Bear left for 0.3 mile to end (Summer Street, unmarked).

29. Turn left and stay on main road for 2 miles to end (merge left onto Route 44).

30. Bear left and immediately turn right on Jacob Street. Go 100 yards to Ledge Road on left.

31. Left for 1.3 miles to school entrance on right just after crossing Arcade Avenue. **CAUTION:** Speed bump at entrance.

Directions for shorter ride

1. Follow directions for the long ride through number 12.

2. Turn right and stay on main road for 1.5 miles to fork where French Street bears left and the main road bears slightly right. It's shortly after you climb a steep little hill.

3. Bear right and stay on main road for 2.4 miles to end (merge left on Route 44).
4. Follow directions 30 and 31 for the long ride.

Swansea–Somerset–Dighton–Rehoboth

Number of miles:	30 (19 without Rehoboth extension, 15 with shortcut)
Terrain:	Gently rolling, with one moderate hill and one steep one. The 15-mile ride avoids the steep hill.
Food:	None on 15-mile ride. Country store in Dighton. Restaurant in Swansea. Restaurant at end.
Start:	Quality Inn, Route 103 in Somerset, just south of I–195 at the Swansea town line.

This ride takes you exploring the gently rolling countryside along the west bank of the lower Taunton River, the major river in the southeastern part of the state. The route parallels the river for several miles and then returns along the ridge rising just inland from the west bank. The long ride heads farther west into farm country and then finishes with a relaxing spin along Mount Hope Bay, the broad estuary at the mouth of the river.

You'll start by crossing the Lees River (a tidal inlet of Mount Hope Bay) into Swansea, a pleasant rural community midway between Fall River and Providence. Swansea is just far enough from both cities to have avoided much suburban development. The center of town boasts a handsome stone town hall with a clock tower, built in 1890, and a fine stone library next door.

From Swansea you'll traverse a low ridge into Somerset, which lies along the Taunton River across from Fall River. Most of Somerset is suburban, but you'll bike through the older and less-developed northern

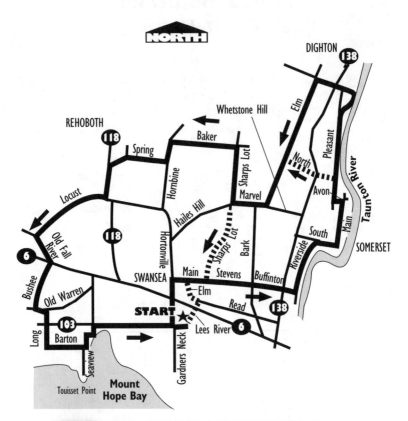

NORTH

DIGHTON

REHOBOTH

Whetstone Hill

SOMERSET

SWANSEA

START

Lees River

Bushee

Old Warren

Long

Barton

Seaview

Touisset Point

Mount Hope Bay

Gardners Neck

Old Fall River

Locust

Spring

Baker

Hornbine

Hailes Hill

Hortonville

Main

Elm

Read

Stevens

Bark

Sharps Lot

Sharps Lot

Marvel

North

Avon

Pleasant

Elm

Main

South

Riverside

Buffinton

Taunton River

HOW TO GET THERE

If you're heading west on I–195, take exit 4A (Route 103 West). Bear right at end of ramp for 0.3 mile to motel on right. If you're heading east on I–195, take exit 4 (Lees River Avenue). The motel is on your right as you're getting off the highway.

1. Right (west) on Route 103 for 0.4 mile to crossroads and blinking light at top of hill (Gardners Neck Road). You'll cross the Lees River into Swansea at the beginning.

2. Right for 1.4 miles to Main Street on right at second traffic light. **CAUTION** crossing Route 6. An attractive brick school, now an administration building, is on your left at the intersection.

3. Right for 2.8 miles to traffic light at bottom of hill (County Street, Route 138).

There's a little dam on your left as you turn right. Then, just ahead, you'll pass the handsome stone Swansea town hall and library.

4. Straight for 0.3 mile to end (Riverside Avenue). The Taunton River is in front of you.

5. Turn left and stay on main road along river for 1.5 miles to South Street, which bears right uphill.

6. Bear right for 0.4 mile to end (Main Street, unmarked).

7. Left for 0.5 mile to Avon Street on left. Notice the pillared mansion on your left at the beginning.

8. Left and just ahead right at grassy traffic island onto Pleasant Street (unmarked). Go 0.7 mile to crossroads (North Street). Here the 15-mile ride turns left and the two longer rides go straight.

9. Straight for 1.8 miles to Water Street, a little lane on right just after a small bridge with concrete abutments. You'll pass Broad Cove, an inlet of the river, on your left.

10. Right for 0.6 mile to Route 138 (County Street) at stop sign and blinking light. This is the center of Dighton.

11. Straight for 0.4 mile to crossroads (Elm Street). Notice the graceful church a little to the right at the crossroads.

12. Left for 3 miles to end (Whetstone Hill Road on left).

As soon as you turn left, a lovely dam is on your right. Then you'll climb a steep hill. Farther on you'll go along a ridge with fine views of the river to your left.

13. Right for 1 mile to crossroads and blinking light (Sharps Lot Road,

unmarked). Here the 19-mile ride turns left.

14. Right for 1.7 miles to crossroads (Williams Street on right, Baker Road on left).

15. Left for 1.6 miles to end (Hornbine Road). Opposite the intersection is the Hornbine School, a one-room wooden schoolhouse. It was built during the 1830s and used until 1934.

16. Left for 0.5 mile to Spring Street on right.

17. Turn right and stay on main road for 1.3 miles to end (Route 118). The main road bears left after 1 mile.

18. Left for 0.8 mile to end (Locust Street), where a big water tower stands on the right.

19. Right for 1.8 miles to end (Old Fall River Road).

20. Left for 0.8 mile to stop sign (merge left on Route 6).

21. Bear left and then immediately turn right on Bushee Road, unmarked. (**CAUTION** here.) Go 1.4 miles to end (Schoolhouse Road). You'll enter Warren, Rhode Island, just before the end.

22. Left for 0.2 mile to Long Lane on right.

23. Right for 0.2 mile to crossroads and stop sign (Route 103).

24. Go straight and stay on main road for 2.6 miles to traffic light (Route 103 again, Wilbur Avenue). You'll cross back into Swansea after 1.3 miles and then ride along Mount Hope Bay.

If you wish you can turn right immediately before the bay onto Seaview Avenue, which parallels the water for 1 mile to a dead end. The massive building across the bay is the coal-fueled Brayton Point power plant.

25. Right for 1.7 mile to Quality Inn on left, immediately after crossing Lees River.

Directions for shorter ride: 19 miles

1. Follow directions for the long ride through number 13.

2. Left for 1.7 miles to end (Stevens Road, unmarked).

3. Right for 0.5 mile to Elm Street on left at bottom of hill.

4. Left for 0.7 mile to Lees River Avenue on right, just after you go under power lines.

5. Turn right and just ahead cross Route 6 at traffic light. **CAUTION:** Bumps and potholes on this short stretch. Go 0.8 mile to end (Route 103). Quality Inn is on right at end.

Directions for shorter ride: 15 miles

1. Follow directions for the 30-mile ride through number 8.
2. Left for 1 mile to end (Elm Street, unmarked). You'll cross Route 138 and then pass the Somerset Reservoir hidden behind an embankment on your left.
3. Left for 1 mile to end (Whetstone Hill Road on left).
4. Right for 1 mile to crossroads and blinking light (Sharps Lot Road, unmarked).
5. Follow directions for the 19-mile ride from number 2 to the end.

---

portion of town. You'll follow the river on a narrow street lined with fascinating old wooden buildings in a wide variety of architectural styles and then continue along the water into an increasingly rural landscape to the center of Dighton, another attractive riverfront town extending westward into gently rolling farm country.

In Dighton you'll head back toward Swansea along a ridge a short distance inland from the riverbank, with impressive views of the river and the surrounding landscape. The long ride heads farther inland to Rehoboth, a beautiful rural town of broad farms and winding, wooded roads. You'll cross briefly into a little strip of Warren, Rhode Island, to the shore of Mount Hope Bay, just back over the Massachusetts line. After a scenic, curving ride along the shore, it's a short distance back to the start.

Profile Rock, Assonet

Profile Rock and Dighton Rock:
Taunton–Berkley–Assonet–North Dighton

Number of miles:	24 (13 without Profile Rock–Dighton Rock extension)
Terrain:	Gently rolling, with one moderate hill.
Food:	Country store in Berkley. Restaurant and farm stand in Assonet. Burger King and Papa Gino's at end.
Start:	Burger King or Papa Gino's at Route 44 and Joseph E. Warner Boulevard in Taunton, about 1.5 miles west of the center of town.

The region just south of Taunton, along the east bank of the Taunton River, is ideal for bicycling. Country lanes wind through a fairly flat landscape, with some stretches along the river. You'll go through the gracious New England town centers of Berkley and Assonet and then through the attractive mill village of North Dighton. You can visit two unique landmarks—Profile Rock, a large boulder with a striking resemblance to an Indian's profile, and Dighton Rock, on which are inscriptions of disputed origin.

The ride starts from the western edge of Taunton, a city of 40,000 best known for the manufacture of fine silver products, and avoids the downtown area. Near the beginning, you'll pass the massive nineteenth-century plant of the F. B. Rogers Silver Company stretching along the riverbank. You cross the river into gently rolling countryside and ride to Berkley, a pretty village with a large green. From here you'll proceed to Profile Rock, where a short path leads to a spot from which the profile is

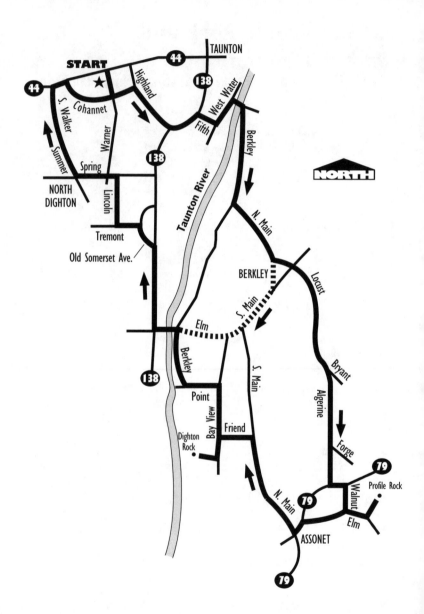

DIRECTIONS
FOR
THE RIDE

1. Right on Warner Boulevard (not Route 44) for 0.2 mile to crossroads and blinking light (Cohannet Street).

2. Turn left and stay straight on main road for 0.5 mile to crossroads and stop sign (Highland Street).

3. Right for 0.9 mile to end (Route 138, Somerset Avenue). **CAUTION:** Bumpy sections.

4. Left for 0.3 mile to Fifth Street, which bears right under railroad bridge.

5. Bear right for 0.2 mile to end (West Water Street).

6. Left past Rogers Silver Company for 0.3 mile to your first right (Plain Street), which crosses the Taunton River.

7. Turn right. Immediately after the bridge, turn right again and then immediately bear left on main road (Berkley Street). Go 1.7 miles to North Main Street on left.

8. Left for 1.2 miles to fork at the Berkley town green. Here the short ride bears slightly right. A small brick library is in the middle of the fork.

9. Bear left for less than 0.2 mile to crossroads and stop sign (Porter Street).

10. Straight on Locust Street for 1.8 miles to fork shortly beyond the bridge over Route 24 (Bryant Street bears left, Algerine Street bears right).

11. Bear right and stay on the main road for 1.9 miles to end (Mill Street, Route 79). There's a nice dam and an old mill on your left just before the end.

12. Left and just ahead right on Walnut Street. Go 0.3 mile to end (Elm Street, unmarked).

13. Left for 0.25 mile to entrance to Profile Rock on left, at a long, grassy traffic island.

14. Left for 0.2 mile to dead end. From here a gravel path leads about 100 yards to the viewpoint for the rock. Backtrack to main road.

15. Right for 0.6 mile to stop sign (merge left onto Route 79, Mill Street).

16. Bear left for 0.1 mile to crossroads and yield sign in the center of Assonet.

Notice the small dam on your right as you bear left. At the crossroads the ride turns right, but if you go straight, the Assonet Inn will be on your right after less than 0.2 mile.

17. Right for 1.5 miles to Friend Street on left (sign says STATE PARK). Notice the attractive old buildings at the beginning.

18. Left for 0.8 mile to end (Bay View Avenue).

19. Left for 0.3 mile to the entrance to Dighton Rock on your right. It's about 0.6 mile to the museum and picnic area on the bank of the river. Backtrack to main road.

20. Left for 1 mile to the second left, Point Street.

21. Left for 0.7 mile to Berkley Street on right (dead end if you go straight).

22. Right for 0.9 mile to crossroads and stop sign (Elm Street).

23. Left for 0.7 mile to traffic light (Route 138, Somerset Avenue). You'll cross the narrow bridge over the Taunton River at the beginning.

24. Right for 1 mile to Old Somerset Avenue, which bears left.

25. Bear left for 0.2 mile to Tremont Street on left.

26. Left for 0.3 mile to Lincoln Avenue on right.

27. Right for 0.7 mile to end (Spring Street). A picturesque little dam is on the right just before the end.

28. Turn left and stay straight on main road for 0.5 mile to crossroads and stop sign at end of long brick mill (Summer Street). This is North Dighton.

29. Right for 1.4 miles to end (Route 44, Winthrop Street). **CAUTION:** Bumpy spots.

30. Right for less than 0.2 mile to Cohannet Street (unmarked) on right. A bridge at the beginning of this street is blocked off to cars but is passable by bike.

31. Right for 0.8 mile to crossroads and stop sign (Joseph E. Warner Boulevard). **CAUTION:** Bumpy spots. (If the bridge at the beginning be-

comes impassable or is torn down, simply stay on Route 44 for 0.8 mile to starting point on right.) You'll pass an attractive park and bird sanctuary on the right.

32. Left for 0.2 mile to parking lot on left, just before traffic light.

Directions for shorter ride

1. Follow the directions for the long ride through number 8.

2. Bear right and stay on main road for 2.6 miles to traffic light (Route 138, Somerset Avenue). The main road bears right after 1.2 miles. Then you'll cross a narrow bridge over the Taunton River.

3. Follow directions for the long ride from number 24 to the end.

---

best seen. Nearby is the lovely old village of Assonet, the main community in the town of Freetown. The turreted town hall, an old wooden school, an inviting little library, and a bell-towered church built in 1809, all in traditional New England white, grace the hillside that slopes upward from the village crossroads. Just off the route is the Assonet Inn, a Victorian building with wide porches. It looks elegant, but inside is an informal, old-fashioned restaurant serving good food at reasonable prices.

From Assonet it's about 3 miles to Dighton Rock State Park, a grassy area along the Taunton River, which widens into an estuary as it flows between Taunton and Fall River. The rock is enclosed in a small museum open during the summer. Its strange pictographs are clearly visible; their origins have been attributed to a Portuguese explorer (the most generally accepted theory), Vikings, Phoenicians, and Indians.

After you leave Dighton Rock, you'll follow the river on a narrow lane and then cross it over the picturesque, one-lane, Berkley Bridge. It's not far to the unique village of North Dighton, which is completely surrounded by farmland. A massively grim brick mill on one side of the road contrasts with a large, well-kept green and fine old homes on the other. From here, it's a couple of miles to the end.

Westport–Tiverton, Rhode Island–Little Compton, Rhode Island

Number of miles:	33 (19 without Tiverton–Little Compton extension)
Terrain:	Gently rolling, with one tough hill.
Food:	Country store and restaurant in both Adamsville and Little Compton.
Start:	Westport Community Center Playground on Main Road, Westport, just south of the town hall.

The southwestern corner of coastline directly south of Fall River, extending into Rhode Island along the broad Sakonnet River, has some of the most ideal and idyllic bicycling in the state. The region is a pedaler's paradise of untraveled country lanes winding past salt marshes and snug, cedar-shingled homes with immaculately tended lawns, trim picket fences, and broad meadows sloping down to the bay.

The ride starts from Westport, a slender town stretching from east of Fall River all the way down to the coast. The Westport River, a broad tidal estuary, bisects the town, and you'll be exploring the thin strip of land between the river and Rhode Island. You'll ride across sweeping expanses of farmland to the tiny village of Adamsville, which lies in Little Compton, Rhode Island, 100 yards over the state line. In the town are a country store in a rambling old wooden building, a little millpond, and a monument to the Rhode Island Red breed of poultry. From Adamsville you'll head south to the most southwesterly bit of coast in Massachusetts, an unspoiled strand framed by salt ponds and stately homes. At its eastern tip, guarding the mouth of the Westport River, is the exclusive summer colony of Acoaxet. From here you have a beauti-

DIRECTIONS

FOR

THE RIDE

1. Turn left (south) on Main Road for 0.25 mile to Adamsville Road on right.

2. Right for 0.8 mile to Sodom Road on right (sign visible from opposite direction).

3. Right for 2.1 miles to traffic island where the main road curves sharply right.

4. Straight and then immediately left at end on Narrow Avenue (unmarked). Go 0.7 mile to fork (Amory Petty Road bears right).

5. Bear left (still Narrow Avenue) for 0.9 mile to end (Route 81). Here the short ride turns left. Shortly before the end, you'll cross the state line into Tiverton, Rhode Island.

6. Right for 0.4 mile to crossroads (East King Road on right, King Road on left).

7. Left for 1 mile to second right, Brayton Road (unmarked).

8. Right for 1.8 miles to crossroads and blinking light (Bulgarmarsh Road, Route 177).

9. Left for 1.8 miles to end (Route 77). There's a great descent at the end. **CAUTION** at end at bottom of hill.

10. Right for 0.5 mile to Nannaquaket Road on left.

11. Left for 1.6 miles to yield sign (merge right on Route 77).

12. Bear right for 0.5 mile to small crossroads at top of hill (Seapowet Avenue on right).

13. Turn right and stay on main road for 3.4 miles to Pond Bridge Road on left, just past top of hill. The main road bears right after 2.2 miles.

You'll pass an Audubon sanctuary near the beginning and then cross a rustic bridge over an inlet of the Sakonnet River.

14. Left for 0.5 mile to end (Route 77). You'll pass a curved wooden dam and a fish ladder on your left.

15. Left for 3.6 miles to Meetinghouse Lane (unmarked) on left at traffic island (a sign says TO THE COMMONS). You'll pass the Sakonnet Vineyards on your left after 1.5 miles.

16. Left for 0.6 mile to fork, at the Little Compton green.

17. Bear right for 0.2 mile to end.

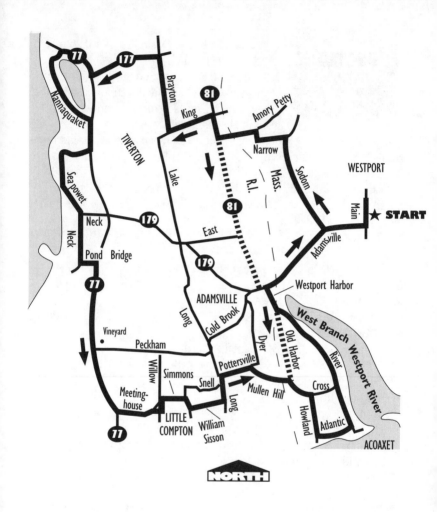

NORTH

18. Left and just ahead right on Simmons Road. Go 0.6 mile to traffic island where the main road curves sharply left and a smaller road turns right.

19. Right for 0.3 mile to William Sisson Road on left.

20. Left for 0.6 mile to end (Long Highway, unmarked).

21. Left for 0.6 mile to fork immediately after stop sign (Pottersville Road, unmarked, bears right).

22. Bear right for 0.9 mile to fork where the main road bears right at a traffic island.

23. Bear right for 0.8 mile to end. You cross back into Massachusetts just before the end.

24. Right for 0.5 mile to Howland Road on right.

25. Right for 1.1 miles to Atlantic Avenue on left, just before the ocean.

26. Left for 0.7 mile to end (River Road, unmarked), in the village of Acoaxet, which is part of Westport.

Here the ride turns left, but if you turn right, a dirt road leads 0.5 mile through the dunes to a high boulder at the tip of the point between the Westport River and the ocean. There's a great view from the boulder.

27. Left for 3.3 miles to end (merge right at stop sign).

28. Bear right for 0.5 mile to end in the village of Adamsville.

At the end, notice the unique, three-story white tower on the right. It covers a well. On the left-hand corner is a plaque commemorating the Rhode Island Red breed of poultry. Abraham Manchester's, opposite you, is a good lunch spot.

29. Right for 2.5 miles to end (Main Road).

30. Left for 0.25 mile to playground on right.

Directions for shorter ride

1. Follow directions for the long ride through number 5.

2. Left for 3.3 miles to end in the village of Adamsville.

3. Left for 100 yards to Westport Harbor Road on right.

A plaque commemorating the Rhode Island Red breed of poultry is on the near corner, and an unusual three-story wooden tower, covering a well, is on the far corner. Abraham Manchester's, on your left, is a good lunch spot.

4. Right for 0.5 mile to fork where River Road bears left and Old Harbor Road goes straight up a steep hill.

5. Straight for 2.2 miles to Howland Road on right. It's 0.5 mile after Mullen Hill Road on right.

6. Follow directions for the long ride from number 25 to the end.

---

ful ride back to Adamsville along the West Branch of the Westport River and a short spin through farms to the starting point.

The long ride heads west into the little strip of Rhode Island south of Fall River lying along the mile-wide Sakonnet River, which is the easternmost section of Narragansett Bay. The landscape is beautiful as you hug the river on narrow country lanes and then climb onto a ridge with dramatic views of broad meadows sloping down to the shore. You'll pass Sakonnet Vineyards, which is open for wine-tastings. Just ahead is the center of Little Compton, the finest traditional New England village in Rhode Island. The long green is framed by a classic white church, a delightful country store, and an old cemetery where Elizabeth Pabodie, daughter of John and Priscilla Alden and the first white girl born in New England, is buried. From here you'll wind through gently rolling, open farmland to Adamsville, where you'll pick up the short ride heading toward Acoaxet.

Westport–Horseneck Beach

Number of miles:	22 (9 without Horseneck Beach extension)
Terrain:	Gently rolling, with one tough hill.
Food:	Snack bar just before Horseneck Beach. Country store just before end.
Start:	Tennis courts behind Westport Middle School, Old County Road. From Route 24, head east on I–195 for 2 miles to Route 88 South. Go 3.5 miles to Old County Road at second traffic light. Turn left for 0.6 mile to school on left.

If you draw a line from Fall River to New Bedford and chip away the urban areas, everything south of that line is an absolute paradise for biking. This is a gently rolling landscape of little-traveled country roads winding past snug, cedar-shingled homes with trim picket fences, flawless lawns, and broad meadows sloping gently down to wide tidal rivers and salt marshes. This ride takes you exploring the heart of this area, heading along the east bank of the East Branch of the Westport River, a broad tidal estuary, and returning along the west bank. You'll stay within the borders of Westport, a slender town stretching from I–195 to the ocean at Horseneck Beach, among the most unspoiled in the state. With its splendid harbor and the broad reaches of both the east and west branches of the river, Westport is an active boating center.

The ride starts from the broad, gradual hillside stretching along the river and descends to its narrow northern end. You'll go by the Westport Vineyard and Winery, open most afternoons for tours and tastings. The

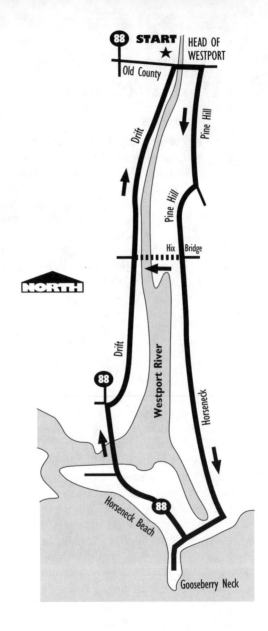

DIRECTIONS
FOR
THE RIDE

1. Left on Old County Road for 0.7 mile to Pine Hill Road on right. You'll go through the small village of Head of Westport at the bottom of the hill and then climb steadily for 0.4 mile.

2. Right for 2.1 miles to where Pine Hill Road (unmarked) bears right and Old Pine Hill Road goes straight. It's 0.3 mile after Riverview Drive on right.

3. Bear right for 1.4 miles to crossroads and stop sign (Hix Bridge Road, unmarked). Here the short ride turns right. If you turn right, you'll come to the Westport Vineyard and Winery after 0.2 mile.

4. Straight for 6.3 miles to dead end at entrance to dirt parking lot.

The Bayside Restaurant, a good lunch spot, is on your right after 4.8 miles. Just ahead the road curves sharply right and follows the ocean to Gooseberry Neck. A foot trail leads from the parking lot about 0.5 mile to the tip of the peninsula.

5. Backtrack 0.5 mile to Route 88 on left at grassy traffic island (road sign visible after you turn left).

6. Left for 2.9 miles to traffic light (Drift Road). **CAUTION:** The metal-grate bridge after 2.1 miles is very slippery when wet. If the road is wet, walk across.

You'll pass the main part of Horseneck Beach, set back from the road on your left. For a side trip, you can turn left just before the bridge and go 0.5 mile along the harbor to the Westport Yacht Club.

7. Right for 3.3 miles to crossroads and stop sign (Hix Bridge Road).

8. Straight for 3.7 miles to end (Old County Road). You're now back in Head of Westport. The little square building on your left at the end is a powder house built in 1812. There's a country store on the far side of the intersection 50 yards to your right.

9. Left for 0.25 mile to school on right. It's uphill—the same hill that you went down at the beginning.

Directions for shorter ride

1. Follow directions for the long ride through number 3.

2. Right for 1 mile to crossroads and stop sign (Drift Road). You'll pass the Westport Vineyard and Winery on the left after 0.2 mile. The bridge over the river is a pretty spot. There's a short, steep hill after the bridge.
3. Follow directions 8 and 9 for the long ride, turning right at crossroads instead of going straight.

---

ride down to Horseneck is delightful, and when you reach the ocean, the road hugs the shoreline for nearly a mile. Just before the main portion of the beach, you'll ride along a causeway to Gooseberry Neck, a small sliver of land that extends into Buzzards Bay. At the far end of the beach, you'll enjoy superb views of the harbor from the bridge across the mouth of the river. Near the end you'll go along the top of the ridge that runs along the west bank of the river, enjoying splendid views of the river below and the neighboring ridge on the other side.

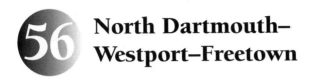

56 North Dartmouth– Westport–Freetown

Number of miles:	29 (13 without Freetown extension)
Terrain:	Gently rolling, with two long, gradual hills and one short, steep one.
Food:	Country store in Westport. Grocery in North Dartmouth. Fast-food places on Route 6 near starting point.
Start:	North Dartmouth Mall at the junction of Faunce Corner Road and Route 6 in North Dartmouth. From I–195 take the Faunce Corner–North Dartmouth exit (exit 12) and turn south at end of exit ramp. Go almost 1 mile to mall on right. Park near Faunce Corner Road.

This ride takes you exploring the surprisingly rural area midway between Fall River and New Bedford. The region is an attractive mixture of forest and farmland crisscrossed by smooth secondary roads. The architectural highlight of the ride is the bold, strikingly modern campus of the University of Massachusetts at Dartmouth, the major educational facility for this part of the state.

The ride starts from North Dartmouth, the section of town near the university and along the Route 6 commercial strip (which you won't ride along). Within a mile and a half, you'll pass the university campus, which crowns a broad hill. The main road looping around the perimeter of the campus is worth following. The route descends into the lovely small village of Head of Westport, where a stream flows between grassy banks and some graceful old Colonial-style homes. From here you'll

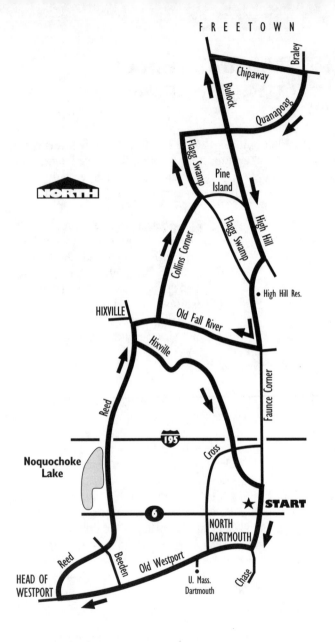

1. Right on Faunce Corner Road for 0.2 mile to Route 6 at traffic light.

2. Straight (**CAUTION:** busy intersection) for 0.4 mile to Old Westport Road on right. The main road bears left at the intersection.

3. Right for 3.8 miles to Reed Road on right at bottom of hill.

You'll pass the entrance to the University of Massachusetts at Dartmouth on your left after 0.8 mile. The ride turns right on Reed Road, but immediately after the intersection is the attractive village of Head of Westport and a country store.

4. Right for 1.8 miles to traffic light (Route 6). An old wooden school, now a senior center, is on your right after 0.3 mile. You'll see the Lincoln Park roller-coaster on your left a mile ahead, just after a crossroads.

5. Straight (**CAUTION** here) for 3 miles to Hixville Road on right. Here the short ride turns right. You'll pass Noquochoke Lake on your left.

6. Straight for 0.2 mile to Old Fall River Road (unmarked) on right in the tiny village of Hixville (part of Dartmouth). Notice the fine church on your left just past the intersection.

7. Right for 0.3 mile to Collins Corner Road on left.

8. Left for 2.2 miles to crossroads and stop sign (Flagg Swamp Road). Pine Island Road continues on the far side of the intersection.

9. Left for 1.8 miles to crossroads and stop sign (Bullock Road, unmarked). After 1 mile the road curves sharply right, nicking the eastern border of Fall River for 100 yards.

At the crossroads the ride turns left, but you can cut 5.2 miles off the route by turning right for 2.1 miles to Faunce Corner Road on right and resuming with direction 14.

10. Left for 1.3 miles to Chipaway Road on right. It's a somewhat sharp right.

11. Right for 1.9 miles to crossroads and stop sign (Braley Road on left, Quanapoag Road on right).

12. Right for 2 miles to another crossroads and stop sign (Bullock Road

again, unmarked). You'll pass a cranberry bog on your right shortly before the crossroads.

13. Left for 2.1 miles to fork where High Hill Road bears slightly left and Faunce Corner Road turns right.

14. Right for 1.5 miles to crossroads and stop sign (Old Fall River Road). There's a small grocery on the far left corner. You'll pass the High Hill Reservoir on your left, hidden behind a tall embankment.

15. Right for 2.3 miles to end back in Hixville. There's a great downhill run halfway along this stretch.

16. Left for 0.2 mile to Hixville Road on left.

17. Left for 2.9 miles to crossroads and stop sign (Cross Road, unmarked).

18. Straight for 0.8 mile to end (Faunce Corner Road, unmarked).

19. Right for 0.1 mile to mall on right, at traffic light.

Directions for shorter ride

1. Follow directions for the long ride through number 5.

2. Right for 2.9 miles to crossroads and stop sign (Cross Road, unmarked).

3. Follow directions 18 and 19 for the long ride.

---

head north, passing the back of Lincoln Park, a former amusement park (now sometimes used for flea markets) with a big roller-coaster. Just ahead you'll enjoy riding along Noquochoke Lake. As you continue north, the landscape becomes more rural and wooded. After turning south back toward the starting point, you'll climb gradually to a small hilltop reservoir within an embankment and then be rewarded with a fast downhill run toward the tiny village of Hixville. A quiet secondary road brings you past small farms back to the starting point.

Dartmouth

Number of miles:	27 (29 if you visit Demarest Lloyd Memorial State Park; 18 without southwestern loop; 13 with shortcut)
Terrain:	Flat, with a couple of gradual, easy hills.
Food:	Grocery and restaurant in Padanaram. Ponderosa and Burger King at end.
Start:	Ponderosa Steak House, Route 6 and Tucker Road in North Dartmouth. From I–195 take exit 12 (the Faunce Corner– North Dartmouth exit), and turn south at the end of the ramp. Go 1 mile to Route 6. Turn left on Route 6; Ponderosa is just ahead on the right.

Dartmouth, an extensive oceanfront town south and west of New Bedford, offers ideal biking on numerous back roads. The landscape is flat, with broad stretches of farmland and salt marshes. The ride starts in North Dartmouth, the commercial center of the town and home of the University of Massachusetts at Dartmouth. The bold, modern campus is about 1 mile off the route. You'll head down to the picturesque village of Padanaram on Apponagansett Bay, with antiques shops and fine old homes. From here you'll cross the bridge over the bay and enjoy bicycling along its shore. The marvelous Children's Museum, one of the best in New England, is on the 13-mile ride. From Padanaram you'll work your way to the southern coast and the tiny village of Russells Mills on winding, wooded roads. The focal point of Russells Mills is Davoll's

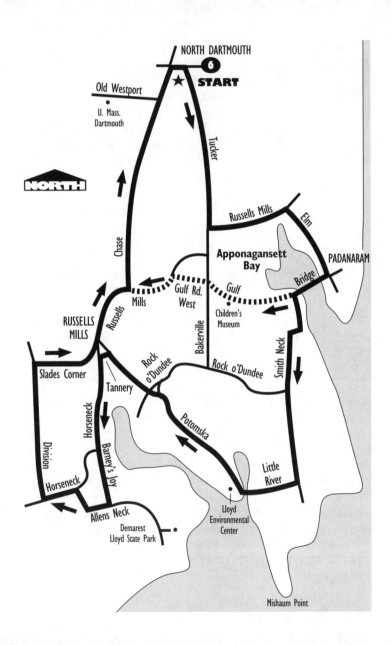

1. Right on Route 6 and then immediately right at traffic light on Tucker Road. Go 3 miles to Russells Mills Road on left at the bottom of a long, very gradual hill. A snack bar is on the far left corner.

2. Left for 1.2 miles to Elm Street on right, immediately before the brick police station on left.

3. Right for 1.3 miles to the second crossroads and stop sign (Bridge Street) at bottom of hill. This is the center of Padanaram, also called South Dartmouth. Notice the handsome stone former library, built in 1889, on your right at the first crossroads.

4. Right for 0.4 mile to Smith Neck Road on left. Here the 13-mile ride goes straight. You'll cross Apponagansett Bay.

5. Turn left and stay on main road for 3.2 miles to Little River Road (unmarked) on right (it's a dead end if you go straight).

You'll follow the bay at the beginning and pass an ice cream stand shaped like a milk bottle on your right after about 2 miles. Shortly before the intersection, you'll see a grand mansion in the distance on your left. This is Round Hill, a former estate divided into multimillion-dollar condominiums.

6. Right for 3.3 miles to stop sign at bottom of hill, at traffic island (Rock o'Dundee Road on right). **CAUTION:** Watch for sand at the intersection. After 1.6 miles, you'll pass the Lloyd Center for Environmental Studies on your left. The main building is 0.1 mile down the dirt entrance road.

7. Bear left and then immediately bear right on main road. Go 0.8 mile to Tannery Lane (unmarked), which bears left. Here the 18-mile ride goes straight and the 27-mile ride bears left. There's a small dam on your right immediately before the intersection.

8. Bear left and then immediately turn left at end (Horseneck Road, unmarked). Go 1.9 miles to fork where Horseneck Road bears right and the main road curves left (becoming Barney's Joy Road). This is a nice stretch past broad farms with views of the river to your left.

9. Curve left for 0.8 mile to end (Barney's Joy Road on left, Allens Neck Road on right). Here the ride turns right, but if you turn left, you'll come to Demarest Lloyd Memorial State Park after 1.1 miles.

10. Right for 0.7 mile to end (Horseneck Road, unmarked).

11. Left for 0.7 mile to Division Road on right.

12. Right for 2.7 miles to Slades Corner Road on right. Division Road runs along the town line of Dartmouth on your right and Westport on your left.

13. Right for 1.5 miles to end, at stop sign. This is the tiny village of Russells Mills. Davoll's General Store is in front of you at the intersection. You'll pass a windmill built in 1888 on your left.

14. Left for 1 mile to Chase Road (unmarked) on left, shortly after Woodcock Road on left.

15. Left for 4 miles to traffic light (Route 6). To visit the University of Massachusetts at Dartmouth, turn left after 3.5 miles on Old Westport Road for 0.8 mile to the strikingly modern campus on your left.

16. Turn right on Route 6. Ponderosa is just ahead on right.

Directions for shorter ride: 18 miles

1. Follow the directions for the 27-mile ride through number 7.

2. Straight up short hill for 100 yards to end (Russells Mills Road). This is the tiny village of Russells Mills. Davoll's General Store is on your left at the intersection.

3. Right for 0.9 mile to Chase Road (unmarked) on left, shortly after Woodcock Road on left.

4. Follow directions 15 and 16 for the 27-mile ride.

Directions for shorter ride: 13 miles

1. Follow the directions for the 27-mile ride through number 4.

2. Straight for 1.5 miles to crossroads and stop sign (Bakerville Road). You'll pass the Children's Museum on your left after 1 mile.

3. Straight for 0.6 mile to end (Russells Mills Road).

4. Left for 0.7 mile to Chase Road on right.

5. Follow directions 15 and 16 for the 27-mile ride, turning right on Chase Road instead of left.

General Store, a wonderful country store built in 1793. You'll pass the Lloyd Center for Environmental Studies, dramatically located on Buzzards Bay at the mouth of the Slocum River. Nature trails wind through the grounds, and there's a spectacular view from the top of the main building.

The long ride heads farther into Dartmouth to the Westport town line, passing broad, well-tended farms. Demarest Lloyd Memorial State Park is about 1 mile from the route and worth visiting. It's a lovely expanse of woods and shoreline, with a good beach that doesn't get as crowded as nearby Horseneck Beach.

58 Land o' Lakes:
Lakeville–Freetown–Acushnet–Rochester

Number of miles:	28 (16 without Freetown–Acushnet–Rochester extension).
Terrain:	Gently rolling, with two short hills.
Food:	Ice-cream shop in Acushnet. Grocery in Rochester. Grocery and deli at end.
Start:	Savas Plaza, a small shopping center on Routes 18 and 105 in Lakeville, 4 miles south of Route 44. From I–495, exit south on Route 18 and go 4 miles to shopping center on right. It's just south of the traffic light where Route 105 North turns left.

Ten miles north of New Bedford is a cluster of large, unspoiled lakes surrounded by woods, prosperous farms, and a few cranberry bogs. Lightly traveled roads threading among the lakes make this one of the nicest regions for biking in southeastern Massachusetts.

The ride starts from the rural town of Lakeville, which is accurately named. Most of Assawompset Pond and adjacent Long Pond, two of the larger lakes in the state, lie within its borders. Lakeville is unusual in that it has no distinct town center; the closest approximation is where the ride starts. The combination town hall and fire station, housed in a handsome brick building with a bell tower, is close to the starting point. A little beyond is a fine church overlooking the water. You start off by going along the shore of Assawompset Pond, which, along with most of the other lakes in the area, supplies Taunton and New Bedford with water. Shortly you'll weave between Great Quittacas and Little Quittacas

DIRECTIONS
FOR
THE RIDE

1. Turn right (south) out of parking lot for 2.6 miles to where Route 18 turns right and Route 105 goes straight. You'll ride along Assawompset Pond on your left. Notice the brick town hall on the right near the beginning.

2. Straight for 2.1 miles to Negus Way, which bears right at the bottom of a little hill. **CAUTION:** Watch for bumps and potholes for the last 0.5 mile. You'll pass Little Quittacas Pond on your right.

3. Bear right along pond for 1.1 miles to end (Route 18). **CAUTION:** Several speed bumps. You'll pass the New Bedford Water Works.

4. Left for 0.5 mile to where Route 18 curves sharply right and a smaller road goes straight. You'll see Long Pond on the right.

5. Straight and then immediately left at end (Morton Road, unmarked). Go 1.1 miles to crossroads and stop sign (Route 105, Braley Hill Road). Here the short ride goes straight.

6. Right for 0.5 mile to first right, Doctor Braley Road.

7. Right for 1 mile to fork where Rounsevell Drive bears right and the main road curves sharply left.

8. Curve left and stay on main road for 3.4 miles to end (Peckham Road, unmarked). The main road turns 90 degrees left after 1.6 miles.

9. Left for 0.25 mile to Lake Street on left.

10. Left for 1 mile to end (Route 105). You'll cross the New Bedford Reservoir.

11. Right for 0.2 mile to Robinson Road (still Route 105) on left. You'll pass the Long Plain Museum on your right. An ice-cream shop is on the right immediately after the intersection.

12. Turn left and stay on Route 105 for 3.1 miles to crossroads (Vaughan Hill Road). Route 105 turns right after 1.5 miles and then left 0.5 mile farther on.

13. Left for 0.8 mile to fork.

14. Bear right for 0.6 mile to another fork (Neck Road, unmarked, bears left).

15. Bear left for 3.1 miles to crossroads and stop sign (North Avenue). You'll go along Snipatuit Pond on your left.

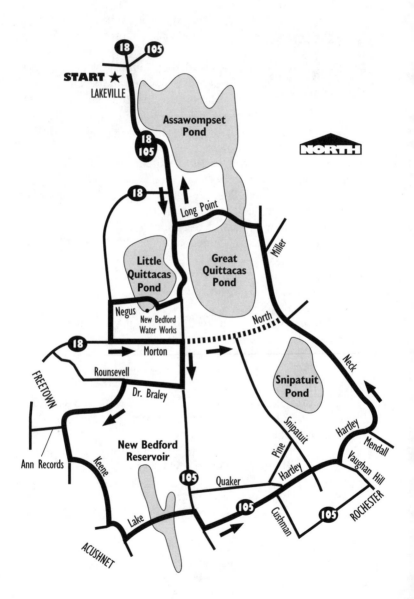

16. Go straight and stay on main road for 1.7 miles to Long Point Road on left. (Don't bear right on Miller Street after 1.4 miles.)

17. Left for 2 miles to end (Route 105).

18. Right for 3.1 miles to shopping center on left, just before Route 105 bears right at traffic light.

Directions for shorter ride

1. Follow directions for the long ride through number 5.

2. Go straight and stay on main road for 2.1 miles to crossroads (Neck Road).

3. Follow directions for the long ride from number 16 to the end, turning left at crossroads instead of going straight.

Ponds, both surrounded by pine groves. On the south shore of Little Quittacas Pond is the graceful stone New Bedford Waterworks building; just ahead the lane carves through a perfectly groomed, symmetrical row of trees.

For a few miles you'll ride past small farms and a couple of cranberry bogs on narrow lanes. Then you'll cross the New Bedford Reservoir to the little village of Long Plain (part of the town of Acushnet), which is surrounded by broad farms. It contains a museum of local history housed in a fine Victorian building dated 1875. A little farther along, you'll pass Snipatuit Pond and bike across the gracefully curving causeway between Great Quittacas Pond and Assawompset Pond. At the end you'll go along the latter pond back to the start.

Mattapoisett–Rochester

Number of miles:	30 (18 without northern loop)
Terrain:	Flat or gently rolling.
Food:	Great country store in Rochester.
Start:	Commuter parking lot on North Street, Mattapoisett, just south of I–195 (exit 19A).

The cranberry bog country of southeastern Massachusetts provides some of the finest biking in the state. On this ride you explore a sample of that country just inland from Buzzards Bay, midway between New Bedford and the Cape Cod Canal. The area is very rural but there's a tidiness about it—in the cozy, cedar-shingled homes behind picket fences and stone walls; the broad fields bordered by rustic wooden fences; and the close-cropped, reddish-hued cranberry bogs surrounded by pine groves. Smooth, lightly traveled narrow lanes and back roads spin their web across the landscape, connecting a bog here, a pond there, and a gracious old farmhouse around the bend.

The ride starts from Mattapoisett, an elegant, well-preserved harborfront town on Buzzards Bay. At one time a shipbuilding center, the waterfront is now lined with attractive wooden homes, a few tastefully designed shops, and a fine park complete with a bandstand overlooking the harbor. As you leave town, you'll head into a peaceful landscape of woods and prosperous farms to Rochester, an unspoiled rural village. The center consists of a good country store and a large green framed by a stately Gothic-style church and the old wooden town hall. Beyond Rochester you enter the cranberry bog country, with runs along Blackmore Pond and Mary's Pond for variety. The return trip to Mattapoisett is a smooth run passing small farms and fine old wooden homes.

DIRECTIONS

FOR
THE RIDE

1. Right on North Street for 0.6 mile to traffic light (Route 6).

2. Left for 0.6 mile to an unmarked road that bears right. Notice the tall sculpture of a sea-horse on your left immediately after turning left.

3. Bear right for less than 0.2 mile to crossroads and stop sign. **CAUTION:** Bumpy road.

4. Turn right for 1.3 miles to Route 6, at traffic light. The main road curves sharply right onto Beacon Street after 0.25 mile.

You'll follow Mattapoisett Harbor on your left. When you come to Route 6, notice the graceful white grange hall on the far left corner.

5. Straight and just ahead left on main road (Acushnet Road). Go 0.4 mile to end.

6. Left (still Acushnet Road) for 0.7 mile to where Acushnet Road turns left, just after bridge over I–195. At the beginning the main road curves sharply right and then sharply left in quick succession.

7. Left for 1.6 miles to Long Plain Road on right, just after the main road turns 90 degrees left. This is a beautiful stretch, and the rest of the ride is just like it! You'll pass a cranberry bog on your left.

8. Turn right for 2.3 miles to end (merge right; there is no stop sign here). You'll pass through a wooded area where the trees arch across the road in a vaulted green canopy.

9. Bear right for 3.4 miles to stop sign (merge right on Route 105) in the center of Rochester. Here the short ride turns sharply left. After 2.4 miles, look for a sculpture of a family of horses on the left, set back from the road.

10. Bear right and stay on Route 105 for 2.3 miles to crossroads just before the bridge over I–195 (Pumping Station Road on right, County Road on left).

The country store is on your right at the beginning. If you don't want to stop there now, you'll go by it again toward the end of the ride.

11. Turn left and stay on main road for 0.8 mile to Blackmore Pond Road on right.

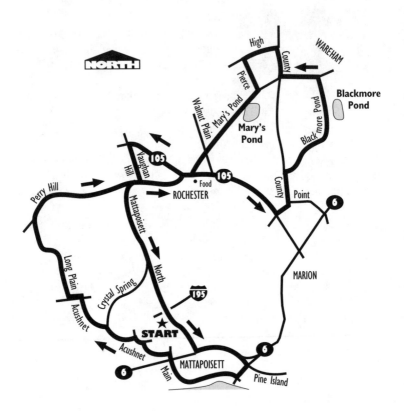

12. Right for 2.6 miles to end (Fearing Hill Road, unmarked). You'll pass Blackmore Pond on your right.

13. Left for 0.8 mile to crossroads and stop sign (County Road, unmarked).

14. Right for 0.9 mile to High Street on left (sign says TO OUTDOOR WORLD).

15. Left for 0.9 mile to Pierce Street on left.

16. Left for 1 mile to end (Mary's Pond Road).

17. Right for 2.7 miles to stop sign (merge right on Route 105) back in Rochester.

You'll pass Mary's Pond on your left; then you'll go by a picturesque old wooden mill on the left, opposite a smaller pond. When you come to Route 105, the country store is 100 yards to your left.

18. Bear right and stay on Route 105 to crossroads (Vaughan Hill Road). You'll pass a distinctive Gothic-style church overlooking the Rochester town green on your left at the beginning.

19. Left for 1 mile to end (New Bedford Road). **CAUTION:** Potholes and cracks.

20. Right for less than 0.2 mile to Mattapoisett Road on left.

21. Left for 4 miles to parking lot on right.

Directions for shorter ride

1. Follow directions for the long ride through number 9. Here the short ride turns sharply left on Route 105, but if you bear right, a great country store is just ahead on your right.

2. Make a sharp left on Route 105 (bear right if you're coming from the store), passing a distinctive Gothic-style church and the Rochester town green on your left. Go 1.5 miles to crossroads (Vaughan Hill Road).

3. Follow directions for the long ride from number 19 to the end.

Marion Ride

Number of miles:	17
Terrain:	Flat.
Food:	Grocery and restaurant at the center of town.
Start:	Corner of Spring and Main Streets in the center of Marion, about a mile south of Route 6. Park where legal on Spring Street, facing north, across from either the town hall or the elementary school.

This is a one-town ride on which you explore Marion, one of the series of waterfront communities along Buzzards Bay between the Rhode Island border and the Cape Cod Canal. Midway between New Bedford and the canal along both sides of Sippican Harbor, Marion is a yachting center and the site of Tabor Academy, a prestigious private school. The expansive harbor divides the town into two portions, with the center of town on the western shore. On the eastern shore of the harbor is Sippican Neck, a peninsula rimmed with estates and large, gracious homes. One of the estates, Great Hill, matches anything to be found along the Massachusetts coast. It makes up its own 300-acre subpeninsula, with a majestic mansion overlooking the bay, narrow lanes hugging the shore, and a hill 125 feet high with spectacular views. Unfortunately the estate is open only on weekdays from 9:00 A.M. to 3:00 P.M. It's worth doing this ride during the week just to see the estate.

The ride starts off by going through the unspoiled, untouristed center of town, with a white Victorian town hall, several churches, and cedar-shingled homes and shops. You'll bike along the shoreline, pass-

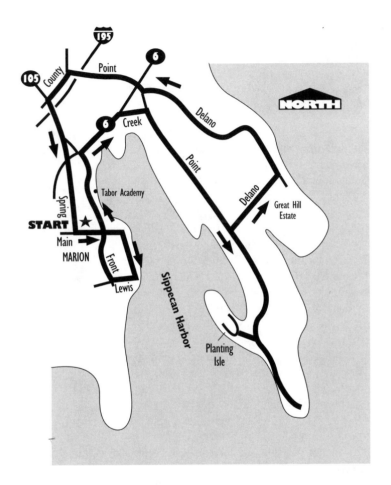

HOW TO GET THERE

From I–95 South, take exit 20 (Route 105, Marion). Turn right (south) at end of ramp and go about 0.5 mile to fork where Front Street bears left and Spring Street bears right. Bear right for 0.2 mile to Route 6. Go straight for 0.9 mile to end (Main Street).

1. From the end of Spring Street, turn left on Main Street for 0.2 mile to crossroads and stop sign (Front Street).

2. Straight for 0.8 mile to another crossroads and stop sign (Front Street again, unmarked). The road turns 90 degrees right twice on this stretch, bringing you back to Front Street. Here the ride turns right, but if you turn left for 0.2 mile you'll come to the town beach.

3. Right for 1.4 miles to traffic light (Route 6).

4. Right for 0.7 mile to Creek Road, which bears right.

5. Bear right for 0.4 mile to end (Point Road).

6. Right for 2.9 miles to Planting Isle Road, a narrow lane on the right. It's 0.3 mile after the main road curves sharply right.

7. Right for 0.4 mile to far end of causeway, where the road becomes private. Backtrack to main road. **CAUTION:** Bumps and potholes at the beginning.

8. Right for 1 mile to end, at the tip of Sippican Neck. At the very end is a country club where the road becomes private; turn around at this point.

9. Backtrack 2.6 miles to Delano Road on right.

10. Right for 3.1 miles to end (Point Road). After 1 mile the road curves sharply left along the ocean. (At this point the entrance to the Great Hill estate is on your right; explore it if it's open.)

11. Turn right and immediately cross Route 6 at traffic light. Go 1 mile to end (County Road). You'll pass a cranberry bog on the left.

12. Left for 0.3 mile to crossroads and stop sign (Route 105, Front Street).

13. Left for 0.7 mile to fork where Route 105 bears left and Spring Street bears right.

14. Bear right for 0.2 mile to Route 6, at stop sign. (Don't bear right on Mill Street after 0.1 mile.)

15. Straight (**CAUTION** here) for 0.9 mile to end (Main Street). At the end notice the town hall with a bell tower on the right.

ing Tabor Academy with its Tudor-style main building directly on the water. From here you'll swing over to Sippican Neck, bike to its tip along traffic-free roads, and return along its opposite shore, passing the Great Hill estate.

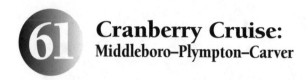

Cranberry Cruise:
Middleboro–Plympton–Carver

Number of miles:	28 (18 without Carver extension)
Terrain:	Flat, with a couple of short hills.
Food:	Country store and pizza shop in Plympton. Grocery in Carver. Mc-Donald's across from starting point.
Start:	Osco Drug, junction of Routes 105 and 28 in Middleboro, just north of I–495.

This is a tour of the heart of the cranberry-growing country, midway between Taunton and Plymouth. Biking through the bogs, which are crosshatched by narrow, straight channels and have rustic little wooden sheds next to them, is a true pleasure. Narrow, untraveled lanes wind past peaked-roof, cedar-shingled homes and scrub pine from one bog to another across one of the most appealing rural landscapes in Massachusetts. The nicest time to do this ride is during the harvest season in October, when the berries form a deep red carpet across the land, or during the spring, when the bogs are flooded ponds.

The ride starts from Middleboro, a handsome town with large old wooden homes along the main street leading into the center, a dignified white town hall with a graceful dome, and a stately white church across from it. A fascinating place to visit is the Middleboro Historical Museum, with a display relating to the lives of Tom and Lavinia Thumb, the most famous midgets in history. Lavinia was born in Middleboro. Across the street is the Robbins Museum of Archaeology, which offers exhibits of Indian artifacts from southeastern Massachusetts. Two miles out of town, you'll pass a large green with a magnificent white church standing over it, unusual because it stands in splendid isolation. A little

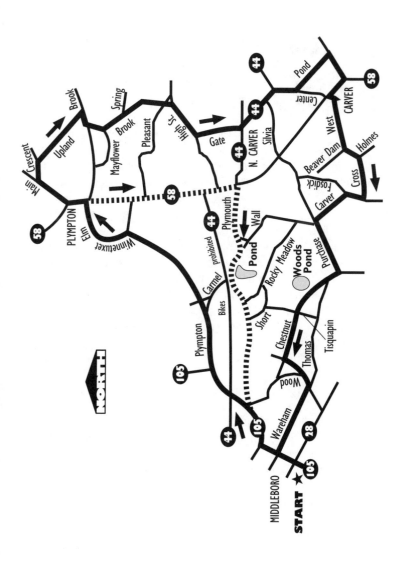

DIRECTIONS

FOR

THE RIDE

1. Turn left (north) on Route 105 and stay on it for 3.3 miles to where it turns left on Thompson Street. It's 0.7 mile after you cross Route 44.

You'll pass the handsome town hall on your left after 0.5 mile and a one-room schoolhouse 1.9 miles farther on at a five-way intersection. Just ahead there's a beautiful church and green on your left.

To visit the museums, turn right on Jackson Street in the center of town a block after traffic light. The Robbins Museum is just ahead on your right, and the historical museum is just beyond it on your left.

2. Straight for 1.4 miles to fork (Eddy Street bears right, Plympton Street bears left).

3. Bear left for 2.2 miles to blinking light where the main road curves sharply right and a smaller road turns left. The Eddy Homestead is on your left after 0.2 mile, immediately after a crossroads.

4. Left for 1.2 miles to end (Route 58) in the center of Plympton. Here the short ride turns right. There's a pizza shop 0.1 mile to your right.

5. Left for 0.25 mile to Main Street (unmarked) on right immediately after cemetery.

6. Right for 0.7 mile to Crescent Street, which bears right up a short hill.

7. Bear right for 0.3 mile to Upland Road, which bears right up another short hill.

8. Bear right for 1.2 miles to end.

9. Right and just ahead left on Brook Street. Stay on main road for 0.6 mile to fork where Spring Street bears left.

10. Bear right (still Brook Street) for 0.8 mile to yield sign (merge right on High Street).

11. Bear right for 0.7 mile to second paved left (Gate Street) at traffic island.

12. Left for 0.5 mile to end (Route 44).

13. Left for 1.3 miles to Center Street (unmarked) on right at blinking

light. Notice the unusual wooden church on your right at the beginning.

14. Right for 0.5 mile to Pond Street on left.

15. Left for 1.1 miles to end (South Meadow Road).

16. Right for 1 mile to end (Route 58).

17. Right for 0.5 mile to West Street on left immediately before traffic light. This is the center of Carver. A convenience store is on the far side of the intersection, and a park with a Civil War monument is on the near side.

18. Left for 1.1 miles to end (Holmes Street on left).

19. Left for 0.3 mile to Cross Street on right.

20. Right for 0.8 mile to end.

21. Right for 0.3 mile to fork where Carver Street (unmarked) bears left.

22. Bear left for 0.9 mile to end (Purchase Street, unmarked).

23. Left for 1.7 miles to end (Chestnut Street).

24. Right for 0.3 mile to where the main road curves left and a narrow lane goes straight.

25. Go straight onto the lane (still Chestnut Street) for 2.2 miles to end (Wood Street, unmarked). You'll pass Woods Pond on your right after 0.7 mile.

26. Left for 1.2 miles to diagonal crossroads and stop sign (Wareham Street, unmarked).

27. Right for 1.2 miles to traffic light (Route 105) back in the center of Middleboro.

28. Left for 0.6 mile to Route 28 at traffic light. Osco Drug is on far side of intersection on right.

Directions for shorter ride

1. Follow directions for the long ride through number 4. Here the ride turns right, but it's worth turning left to see Plympton.

2. Right for 2.3 miles to traffic light (Route 44 East on left, Plymouth Road on right). Here the ride turns right, but if you turn left for 0.25 mile you'll pass through North Carver, another delightful village with a handsome white church.

3. Turn right and stay on main road for 4.8 miles to stop sign where you merge left on Route 105 at a five-way intersection. Notice the one-room schoolhouse on the left at the intersection.

4. Bear slightly left and stay on Route 105 for 2.4 miles to Route 28 at second traffic light. Osco Drug is on the far side of the intersection on the right.

---

farther on is the Eddy Homestead, a Federal-style mansion built by Zachariah Eddy, a prominent local lawyer. From here you'll head along inviting narrow lanes to Plympton, an unspoiled gem of a town. The long green, with a monument in the middle, is framed by a fine old church and country store. The rest of the ride brings you past dozens of bogs on country lanes, passing through Carver, the number-one cranberry town in the state. The tiny center of town has a little park with a handsome Civil War monument.

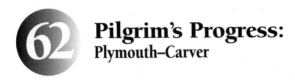

Pilgrim's Progress:
Plymouth–Carver

Number of miles:	28 (9 without extension to Myles Standish State Forest and South Carver)
Terrain:	Gently rolling, with a few short hills.
Food:	Country store in South Carver. Grocery on South Meadow Road.
Start:	Shaw's Supermarket, just south of Route 44, in Plymouth. It's 0.4 mile west of Route 3 (take exit 6B and turn left at traffic light on Pilgrim Hill Road).
Facilities:	Rest rooms just before Plymouth Rock, near rotary, and at the headquarters of Myles Standish State Forest.

This is a tour of Plymouth and the scrub-pine and cranberry-bog country surrounding it. You'll go past or near many of the town's historic landmarks. Outside of town you'll go through the Myles Standish State Forest, a large, unspoiled area of pines and ponds.

The cranberry-growing area is a uniquely beautiful part of the state to explore by bicycle, especially during the harvest season in October when the berries turn the bogs into a crimson carpet. Surrounded by pines and sandy banks, with little wooden sheds next to them, the bogs have a trim, rustic appeal. Narrow roads guide the bicyclist from bog to bog past cedar-shingled, cozy-looking homes.

You'll start the ride by visiting the Pilgrim Monument, a soaring, Victorian granite statue built in 1889. From here it's just a couple of blocks to the waterfront, where you'll go by Cranberry World, a mu-

1. Left on Pilgrim Hill Road for 0.2 mile to end at traffic light (Summer Street, unmarked).

2. Left for 0.7 mile to Oak Street on left, just after cemetery on left.

3. Left for 0.4 mile to end (Samoset Street, Route 44). You'll pass an old wooden school on left after 100 yards.

4. Right for 1 block to crossroads (Allerton Street). Shift into low gear as you approach it.

5. Left (**CAUTION** here) up a short, steep hill. Go 0.3 mile to end (Route 3A), passing the Pilgrim Monument on left at top of hill.

6. Jog right and immediately left on Lothrop Street. Go 0.2 mile to end (Water Street, unmarked). Here the ride turns right, but if you turn left for 100 yards, you'll come to Cranberry World, which is free and fascinating.

7. Right for 0.25 mile to rotary. You'll pass the Plymouth Bay Winery on your right.

8. Straight for 0.4 mile to Leyden Street (unmarked), which bears right uphill. You'll pass the *Mayflower II* and then Plymouth Rock on your left. Pilgrim Hall Museum is opposite Plymouth Rock.

9. Bear right for 0.1 mile to traffic light (Route 3A, Main Street). Notice the fine old homes along this street.

10. Straight and then immediately left for 1 block to Summer Street on right. **CAUTION:** There's a sewer grate with dangerous slots at the intersection.

If you go straight instead of left, you'll go up Old Burial Hill, a well-landscaped cemetery with most of its gravestones dating to the 1700s. The view from the top of the hill is impressive.

11. Right (**CAUTION:** Sewer grate) for 0.4 mile to Billington Street, which bears left downhill. You'll pass a beautifully landscaped park on your left with the restored Jenney Gristmill; the original was built in 1636.

12. Bear left for 0.5 mile to fork.

13. Bear left under Route 3 for 1.4 miles to Black Cat Road on right opposite cranberry bog. Here the short ride turns right. You'll pass Lout Pond on your right.

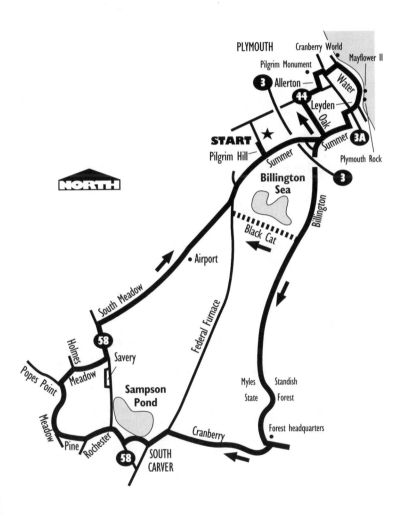

PLYMOUTH   Cranberry World

Pilgrim Monument   Mayflower II

3   Allerton

44

Leyden

START

Pilgrim Hill

Summer   **3A**

Plymouth Rock

3

Water

Oak

Summer

NORTH

Billington Sea

Black Cat

Billington

• Airport

South Meadow

Federal Furnace

58

Holmes

Savery

Popes Point

Meadow

Sampson Pond

Meadow

Pine

Rochester

58

SOUTH CARVER

Cranberry

Myles   Standish

State   Forest

Forest headquarters

14. Straight for 6 miles to fork where the main road goes straight and another road bears left at the top of a tiny hill. **CAUTION:** Watch out for sandy spots on the second mile of this long stretch.

15. Straight for 1 mile to a traffic island on right, opposite the headquarters of the Myles Standish State Forest on your left.

16. Sharp right for 1.5 miles to fork where Federal Road (unmarked) bears left and the main road curves right.

17. Curve right for 1.2 miles to end (Federal Furnace Road, unmarked). Here the ride turns left, but you can shorten the distance to 23 miles by turning right for 7.9 miles to Pilgrim Hill Road on left at traffic light at top of hill. Turn left for 0.2 mile to supermarket on right.

18. Left for 0.4 mile to fork where Tremont Street bears left and Lakeview Street bears right. This is South Carver. A small grocery is at the intersection.

19. Bear right for 0.6 mile to end (Route 58, South Main Street), passing Sampson Pond on your right.

20. Right for 0.25 mile to Rochester Road on left.

21. Left for 0.6 mile to Pine Street, which bears right. It's the second right.

22. Bear right for 0.8 mile to end (merge right on Meadow Street, unmarked). You'll pass the former Edaville Railroad, a narrow-gauge railway through cranberry bogs, on your right.

23. Bear right for 1.3 miles to large traffic island where Meadow Street bears right.

24. Bear right for 1.8 miles to end (Route 58). Here the ride goes left, but if you turn right for 0.2 mile, you'll come to Savery Avenue on the right.

25. Left for 0.7 mile to South Meadow Road on right. There may be signs pointing to the airport and Carver High School.

26. Right for 5.2 miles to end (Federal Furnace Road). You'll pass the Plymouth Airport on your right.

27. Left for 1.4 miles to Pilgrim Hill Road on left at traffic light at top of hill.

28. Left for 0.2 mile to supermarket on right.

Directions for shorter ride

1. Follow directions for the long ride through number 13.
2. Right for 1.7 miles to end (Federal Furnace Road). **CAUTION:** Sandy spots. You'll go past Billington Sea, a freshwater lake, and up and down several short, sharp hills.
3. Right for 1.6 miles to Pilgrim Hill Road on left at traffic light at top of hill.
4. Left for 0.2 mile to supermarket on right.

---

seum of the cranberry and the cranberry industry. It's free and worth seeing. Just ahead is Plymouth Bay Winery, which manufactures and sells wine from locally grown grapes and cranberries. Stop in for a taste of cranberry wine. A little farther along the waterfront are the *Mayflower II* and Plymouth Rock. When you see the *Mayflower II,* you'll be surprised at how small it is. Plymouth Rock is just a plain old rock covered by an ornate pillared portico. Within a couple of blocks are numerous other attractions and historic buildings, including a wax museum depicting Pilgrim life; the Federal-era Antiquarian House; and the outstanding Pilgrim Hall Museum, one of the oldest in the country, founded in 1824. It contains extensive displays of Pilgrim possessions and artifacts.

Leaving Plymouth you'll head to the Myles Standish State Forest, an extensive wilderness area of scrub pine spreading up and over an endless succession of bubblelike little hills and hollows. Biking through this terrain is a lot of fun if you use your gears properly, roller-coastering down one little hill and over the next one. Several small ponds lie nestled in the pines. Beyond the forest you abruptly enter cranberry-bog country. You'll go through a long string of bogs and pass near Savery Avenue, the first divided highway in America, built in 1861. The road consists of two narrow lanes with pine trees between them and on each side, extending a half-mile alongside Route 58.

Southeastern Shore:
Manomet–Cedarville–Cape Cod Canal

Number of miles:	34 (16 without Cedarville–Cape Cod Canal extension)
Terrain:	Gently rolling, with some sharp ups and downs.
Road surface:	0.8 mile of dirt road, which can be avoided.
Food:	Grocery and snack bars in Manomet and Cedarville. Friendly's and McDonald's near the canal. Cafeteria at Plimoth Plantation.
Facilities:	Rest rooms at Cape Cod Canal in Bournedale.
Start:	Plimoth Plantation, Route 3A in Plymouth. From Route 3, take the Plimoth Plantation Highway exit (exit 4) and follow the signs. Finish the ride before the plantation closes (currently at 5:00 P.M.); the gates may be locked later. I recommend getting an early start and visiting the Plantation after the ride.
	Another good starting point is the Herring Run Recreation Area on Route 6 in Bourne (see Ride 64). If you start here, begin with direction 13.

The southeastern shoulder of Massachusetts between Plymouth and the

Cape Cod Canal provides ideal bicycling through a rural, unspoiled area of scrub pine, lots of lakes, cranberry bogs, a few farms, and refreshingly undeveloped coastline, with the exception of White Horse Beach. The long ride goes along a section of the bicycle path hugging the Cape Cod Canal, which is one of the nicest places in the state to bike. The ride has both a cultural highlight and a cultural low point—Plimoth Plantation, a superb reconstruction of the original Pilgrim colony, and Pilgrim I, a nuclear power plant.

You'll start from Plimoth Plantation, a successful attempt to portray as accurately as possible the village and the style in which the Pilgrims lived in 1627. Employees dress in period costume, imitate the Pilgrims' speech as well as it has been determined, raise farm animals, and reenact episodes from the daily life of the colony such as court sessions, trade with the Indians, and military drills.

Leaving the Plantation you immediately enter the delightful landscape of scrub pine and cozy, cedar-shingled homes characteristic of southeastern Massachusetts. The terrain is rolling but in miniature, with little ups and downs that are fun to bike through if you time your gear-shifting properly. You'll pass Little Long Pond and then enjoy a smooth, straight run past cranberry bogs to Manomet (part of Plymouth), the community where the shoulder of land protrudes farthest out to sea. You'll follow the shore along a steep bluff nearly 100 feet high, and then descend past the access road to the public shorefront behind the Pilgrim I nuclear power plant. It's worth visiting this spot to see what a nuke looks like—a monolithic concrete slab jutting up starkly from the otherwise-unspoiled coastline, with the effluent gushing from beneath the building to the ocean along a concrete channel lined with people fishing. An information booth displays booklets extolling the benefits and safety of nuclear energy, and you can decorate your bike with free bumper stickers saying "Know Nukes" and "Build Pilgrim II." From here it's not far along the bay back to the starting point.

The longer ride heads south all the way to the canal through more of this beautiful woods-and-lakes landscape, passing weathered, cedar-shingled homes nestled in pine groves, a country church, and two old

Cape Cod Canal

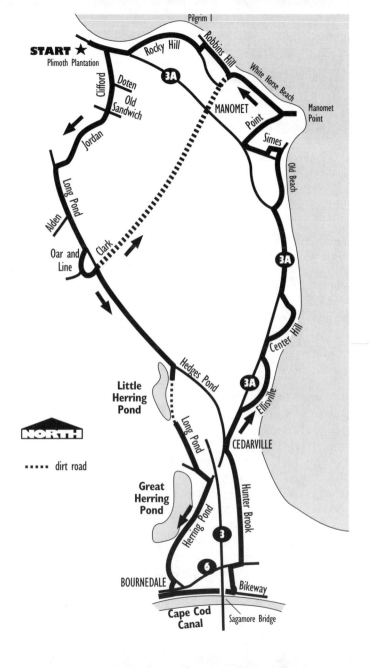

START ★
Plimoth Plantation

Pilgrim I

Rocky Hill

3A

Robbins Hill

White Horse Beach

Clifford

Doten

Old
Sandwich

Jordan

MANOMET

Point

Manomet
Point

Simes

Long Pond

Alden

Clark

Oar and
Line

Old Beach

3A

Center Hill

Hedges Pond

Little
Herring
Pond

3A

Ellisville

Long Pond

CEDARVILLE

Great
Herring
Pond

NORTH

••••• dirt road

Herring Pond

Hunter Brook

3

6

BOURNEDALE

Bikeway

Cape Cod
Canal

Sagamore Bridge

1. Follow the entrance road at the back of the parking lot, climbing a short, steep hill. Go 0.3 mile to end (Route 3A).

2. Right (south) for 0.5 mile to Clifford Road, which bears right midway up the hill.

3. Bear right for 0.8 mile to fork (Doten Road bears left).

4. Bear right (still Clifford Road) and stay on main road for 2.1 miles to end (Long Pond Road, unmarked). Clifford Road becomes Jordan Road.

5. Turn left and stay on main road for 2.6 miles to Oar and Line Road, which bears right.

6. Bear right for 0.4 mile to fork, passing Little Long Pond on right. At the fork the ride bears left, but if you bear right for 50 yards, you'll come to a captivating little beach on Long Pond.

7. Bear left for 0.4 mile to crossroads and stop sign (Long Pond Road, unmarked). Here the short ride goes straight.

8. Right for 3.1 miles to unmarked fork where the main road curves left (becoming Hedges Pond Road) and Long Pond Road bears right onto a smaller road.

Here the ride bears right and soon reaches an 0.8-mile stretch of dirt. If you wish to avoid this section, curve left on main road for 1.8 miles to end (Route 3A, in Cedarville). Turn right and just ahead bear right at fork (sign says TO ROUTE 3). Bear right for 3.1 miles to unmarked road on right opposite country store (sign says TO ROUTE 6). Resume with direction number 12.

9. Bear right on Long Pond Road for 1.6 miles to stop sign (merge left; Carter's Bridge Road is on right). The road becomes dirt after 0.25 mile. You'll see Little Herring Pond below on your right.

10. Bear left (still Long Pond Road) for 0.4 mile to crossroads and stop sign (Herring Pond Road, unmarked). There's an old schoolhouse with a bell tower on your left at the intersection.

11. Right for 2.6 miles to unmarked road on right opposite country store (sign says TO ROUTE 6). You'll go along Great Herring Pond and

pass the Bournedale Village Hall, a picturesque red building with a cupola, on your right just before the intersection.

12. Turn right and just ahead cross Route 6 at traffic light (**CAUTION** here). The Cape Cod Canal is in front of you. Carry your bike down the stairs to the bicycle path running along the canal.

13. Left on bicycle path, following the canal on your right, for 0.9 mile to fork just before the Sagamore Bridge where the left-hand road bears up a steep hill. (**CAUTION:** The bikeway is heavily used by both cyclists and noncyclists, including people fishing.

14. Bear left under bridge and into the parking lot of the Sagamore Recreation Area. Turn sharply left out of the lot and go up a moderate hill, paralleling the bridge on your left. Just ahead is a Friendly's on your left and a rotary.

15. Turn right at rotary, passing McDonald's on left. Immediately after McDonald's, turn left (sign says TO ROUTES 3 AND 3A). Go 3.1 miles to Ellisville Road, a smaller road that bears right. It's 0.5 mile beyond Cedarville (part of Plymouth).

16. Bear right for 1.5 miles to Route 3A again at stop sign.

17. Right for 0.25 mile to Center Hill Road, a smaller road that bears right. At the beginning you'll pass Ellisville Harbor State Park on the right. From here a footpath leads about 0.3 mile to a bluff overlooking a tidal inlet and salt marsh.

18. Bear right for 1.8 miles to stop sign (merge right on Route 3A).

19. Bear right for 2.5 miles to Old Beach Road on right. It's a small road immediately before a snack bar on right. If you come to a large pond on your left, you've gone 0.2 mile too far.

20. Right for 1.2 miles to Simes Road on left. The main road bears right at the intersection. You'll bob up and down several short, sharp hills.

21. Left for less than 0.2 mile to end.

22. Right for 0.25 mile to end (Manomet Point Road, unmarked). A sign points right to WHITE HORSE BEACH, PRISCILLA BEACH.

23. Right for 1.2 miles to the tip of Manomet Point.

24. Backtrack 0.3 mile to Taylor Avenue on right.

25. Right for 1.1 miles to Robbins Hill Road (unmarked) on right. It's

your first right after the road curves sharply inland. You'll ride along White Horse Beach.

26. Right for 0.6 mile to Warrendale Road (unmarked) on left, immediately after a large rock in the middle of the road.

27. Left and just ahead right at end, at bottom of steep hill. (**CAUTION** here.) Go 2.4 miles to end at yield sign (merge right on Route 3A).

After 0.8 mile you'll pass the access road to the public shorefront behind the nuclear power plant. It's the third driveway on the right (a sign points to shorefront and nature trail). All three access roads bristle with forbidding signs that say "exclusion area" and other dire warnings, but the third road is public and you won't be shot on sight if you venture down it. The shorefront is 0.25 mile from the main road.

28. Bear right for 1 mile to Plimoth Plantation entrance road on left.

29. Left for 0.3 mile to parking lot.

Directions for shorter ride

1. Follow the directions for the long ride through number 7.

2. Straight for 4.4 miles to traffic light (Route 3A). Notice the fine white church at the intersection.

3. Straight for 0.7 mile to Robbins Hill Road (unmarked) on left, shortly after Rocky Hill Road on left. If you come to the ocean, you've gone 0.1 mile too far.

4. Left for 0.6 mile to Warrendale Road (unmarked) on left, immediately after a large rock in the middle of the road.

5. Follow directions for the long ride from number 27 to the end.

cemeteries. Then you'll enjoy biking along Little Herring Pond and 2-mile-long Great Herring Pond. Just beyond the canal, you go through the tiny village of Bournedale (part of the town of Bourne), with a small, cupola-topped village hall and a charming country store.

The canal is a visual delight, curving gently between low hills with the graceful span of the Sagamore Bridge in the background. From the canal you'll head back to Plymouth, following the coast. Several small roads diverge from the main road to dip along the water's edge. In Manomet you'll go out to Manomet Point, which provides panoramic views of Cape Cod Bay. You'll go along White Horse Beach, a popular summer resort, and then rejoin the short ride just in time to pedal along the Manomet Bluffs.

The Cape Cod Canal Ride:
Bournedale–Buzzards Bay–Onset

Number of miles:	14
Terrain:	Flat, with one moderate hill at the beginning.
Food:	Groceries and snack bars in Onset and Buzzards Bay.
Start:	Herring Run Recreation Area, Route 6 in Bourne, on the north side of the canal, between the Sagamore and Bourne bridges. From I–495 South or I–195 East, take exit 2 (Route 6), which deposits you near the Bourne Bridge.
Caution:	The bicycle path along the Cape Cod Canal is very heavily used on weekends in good weather by both cyclists and noncyclists. Keep alert for walkers, joggers, in-line skaters, children, dogs, and people fishing. When passing, call out "Passing on your left" or "Coming through" in a clear voice. Keep your pace moderate. Start early so that you can enjoy the bikeway before it becomes busy.

This is a relaxing tour along the scenic Cape Cod Canal, the unspoiled woods and inlets just north of it, and the old beach resort of Onset. You'll start from the banks of the canal at the visitors center, where there's an exhibit on the canal's construction and history. Just inland

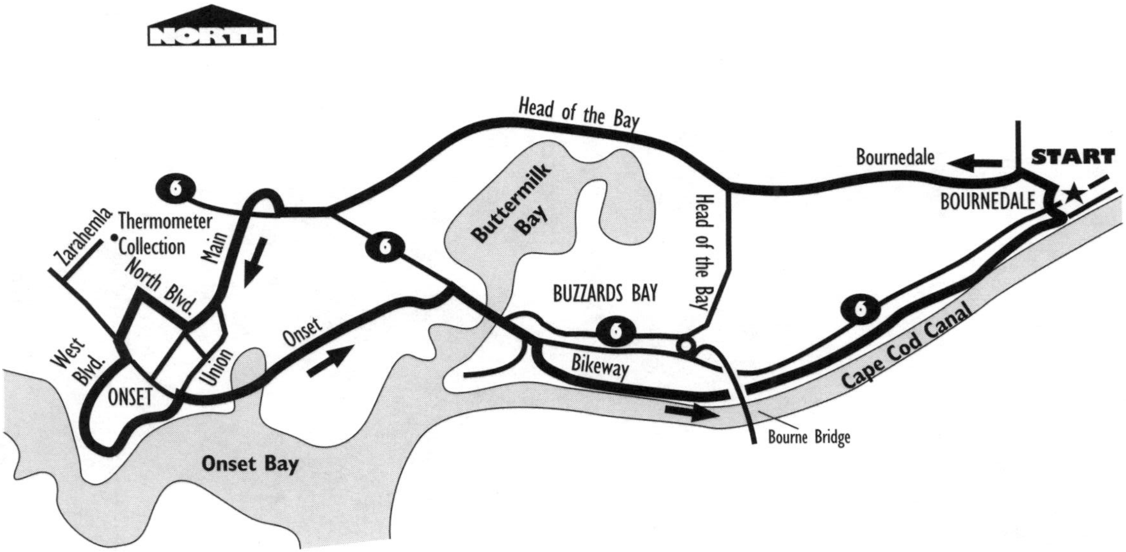

NORTH
Head of the Bay
Bournedale
START
BOURNEDALE
Buttermilk Bay
Head of the Bay
BUZZARDS BAY
6
6
6
6
Thermometer Collection
Zarahemla
Main
North Blvd.
West Blvd.
Union
ONSET
Onset
Bikeway
Cape Cod Canal
Bourne Bridge
Onset Bay

DIRECTIONS

FOR

THE RIDE

1. Go to the west end of the parking lot and cross Route 6 at the traffic light (**CAUTION** here). Go 100 yards to end, opposite country store. This is the village of Bournedale.

2. Turn left and just ahead bear left at fork on Bournedale Road. Go 2.2 miles to end (Head of the Bay Road), at a large, triangular traffic island. Shortly before the end, you'll pass a farm on the left with an unusual stone tower.

3. Bear right for 2.6 miles to end (merge right on Routes 6 and 28). You'll go along Buttermilk Bay on your left.

4. Bear right for 0.3 mile to traffic light (sign says TO ONSET BEACH, POINT INDEPENDENCE). Here you will turn left by making a jug-handle turn—you bear right just before the light, curve left, and cross Route 6 at right angles. **CAUTION:** Route 6 is very busy. If traffic is heavy, it's safest to ride through the parking lots alongside the road, dismounting when necessary.

5. Make jug-handle left turn. **CAUTION:** Bad railroad tracks as soon as you cross Route 6. Go 0.7 mile to fork immediately after metal-grate drawbridge. **CAUTION:** Walk across if the road is wet.

6. Bear right and just ahead turn right at crossroads on North Boulevard. Go 0.2 mile to end (main road turns left).

You'll follow Muddy Cove, an offshoot of Onset Bay, which is in turn an offshoot of Buzzards Bay.

7. Left for less than 0.2 mile to end (merge left). Here the ride bears left, but to see the thermometer collection, turn right for 0.25 mile to Zarahemla Road on right (immediately after house number 292 on left), and right for 0.3 mile to house number 49 on right.

8. Bear left and just ahead turn right on West Boulevard (after playground on right). Stay on main road for 0.9 mile to crossroads and stop sign in the center of Onset.

You'll follow the shore of Onset Bay and ride along Onset Beach.

9. Right for 1.9 miles to Routes 6 and 28, at traffic light. You'll pass an attractive stucco church on the right.

10. Right for 0.5 mile to rotary just after bridge over inlet, at yield sign.
CAUTION: Again, Route 6 is busy. If traffic is heavy when you cross the bridge, wait for a break in the traffic and then ride across quickly in the middle of the right lane. This forces traffic behind you to pass you in the next lane, rather than to squeeze past you by inches in the right lane.

11. Straight (don't bear left) for 100 yards to entrance to Buzzards Bay train station on right immediately after traffic light.

12. Turn right, passing train station on your right. The vertical-lift railroad bridge across the canal is in front of you. Just past the train station, the parking lot turns to dirt. Continue 100 yards to the canal, where you'll pick up the beginning of the bicycle path. Walk your bike around a barricade to keep out cars.

13. Curve left onto the bicycle path, following the canal on your right. Use **CAUTION** on the bikeway. See **CAUTION** notice after the Start section of the ride description. Go 3.7 miles until you come to several flights of stairs going up the embankment on your left. The stairs lead to the parking lot that you started from. (The bicycle path continues another 3 miles to Scusset Beach.)

---

from the canal is the tiny village of Bournedale (part of the town of Bourne), with a charming country store and the little Village Hall, an ornate old building with a cupola. From here you'll head a couple of miles inland along winding, nearly untraveled roads through woods and then along the shore of Buttermilk Bay, one of the many inlets along the edge of Buzzards Bay.

You'll then head south to Onset (part of the town of Wareham), an old beach resort with some fine Victorian buildings set on a peninsula surrounded by little coves and inlets. Onset is not Hyannisport—it's middle-class rather than elegant, and fairly congested. The views of neighboring peninsulas across the gracefully curving shoreline of Onset Bay, instead of just open ocean, give Onset a unique appeal. A private collection of thermometers, located in a house a half-mile off the route, is open to visitors; call beforehand (508–295–5504) to be sure that the owner is home.

From Onset it's a short ride to Buzzards Bay, which is a part of Bourne and the main commercial center for the southeastern corner of the state south of Plymouth. Here you'll get onto the bicycle path beside the Cape Cod Canal, one of the most enjoyable places to ride in Massachusetts. The bikeway is completely flat, and hugs the bank of the canal for its entire length. As a waterway the canal is beautiful, curving gently between low, wooded hills. The waterway is of uniform width (about 200 yards) and is crossed by the spidery steel spans of the Bourne and Sagamore highway bridges, as well as the striking vertical-lift railroad bridge that you'll see when you get onto the bike path. The railroad bridge, built in 1935, is among the highest of its kind in the country. In good weather the canal is alive with pleasure boats and some sleek yachts, and if you're lucky, you may see an enormous barge or cargo ship chugging along.

Appendix

Bicycle Clubs and Organizations

If you would like to bike with a group and meet other people who enjoy cycling, join a bicycle club. Most clubs have weekend rides of comfortable length, with a shortcut if you don't want to go too far. Usually a club will provide maps and mark the route by painting arrows in the road so that nobody gets lost. Joining a club is especially valuable if you don't have a car because you'll meet people who do and who'll be able to give you a lift to areas beyond biking distance from home. To find out about clubs in your area, ask at any good bike shop. Addresses of clubs and organizations active in eastern Massachusetts (subject to annual change) are as follows:

Charles River Wheelmen, 19 Chase Avenue, West Newton, MA 02165. The main club for the Boston area.

Carroll Center Bike Club, 770 Centre Street, Newton, MA 02458. This unique club, run by the Carroll Center for the Blind, pairs blind and sighted riders on tandems.

Hostelling International-American Youth Hostels, 1020 Commonwealth Avenue, Boston, MA 02215. Biking in the Boston area; also hiking, canoeing, cross-country skiing.

Appalachian Mountain Club, 5 Joy Street, Boston, MA 02108. Mostly hiking but some bicycle rides in the Boston area.

North Shore Cyclists, 18 Wheatland Street, Burlington, MA 01803.

Nashoba Valley Pedalers, Box 2398, Acton, MA 01720. Northwestern suburbs between Concord and Fitchburg.

Mass Bay Road Club, Box 791, Plymouth, MA 02362.

Northeast Bicycle Club, 559 Union Avenue, Framingham, MA 01702.

Granite State Wheelmen, 2 Townsend Avenue, Salem, NH 03079. Southern New Hampshire and nearby Massachusetts.

Narragansett Bay Wheelmen, Box 41177, Providence, RI 02940. Rhode Island and nearby Massachusetts.

Seven Hills Wheelmen, Box 114, Auburn, MA 01501.

Fitchburg Cycling Club, Box 411, Lunenburg, MA 01462.

Massachusetts Bicycle Coalition or *MassBike,* 44 Bromfield Street, Suite 207, Boston, MA 02108; (617) 542–2453; Web site: www.MassBike. org. A political action group devoted to improving conditions for bicyclists. MassBike has lobbied successfully to allow bicycles on many of the Massachusetts Bay Transit Authority lines on weekends and off-peak hours (see Introduction for details).

Bikes Not Bombs, 59 Amory Street, #103A, Roxbury, MA 02119. A grass-roots organization that aims to promote bicycling—especially cycling as a practical and nonpolluting means of transportation—in inner-city neighborhoods and Third World countries.

Most of these clubs are affiliated with the League of American Bicyclists, which is the main national organization of and for bicyclists. It publishes an excellent monthly magazine and has a dynamic legislative-action program. The address of the league is 1612 K Street NW, Suite 401, Washington, DC 20006.

There are certainly other clubs in the state that I'm not aware of. Your local bike shop will know about them.

Further Reading and Resources

Eastern Massachusetts is covered by other bicycling guides and maps if you'd like to explore new territory:

Nantucket, and the Vineyard, seventh editionm by Edwin Mullen and Jane Griffith. Guilford, CT: Globe Pequot Press, 1999.

Short Bike Rides in Rhode Island, sixth edition, by Howard Stone. Guilford, CT: Globe Pequot Press, 1999. Includes some Massachusetts rides.

New England Over the Handlebars, by Michael Farny. Boston: Little, Brown, 1975.

The Best Bike Rides in New England, fourth edition, by Paul Thomas, edited by Paul Angiolillo. Guilford, CT: Globe Pequot Press, 1998.

Exploring in and around Boston on Bike and Foot, by Lee Sinai. Boston: Appalachian Mountain Club Books, 1996.

Eastern Massachusetts Bicycle Map. Cambridge, MA: Rubel BikeMaps,

1997. Available at most bike shops. An excellent resource; keep one in your handlebar bag.

Boston's Bikemap. Cambridge, MA: Rubel BikeMaps, 1995. Available at many Boston-area bike shops and from American Youth Hostels. Shows suggested routes in Boston and nearby suburbs; also contains tips on safety and riding in traffic; lists bicycle shops.

Central Massachusetts Bicycle Map. Cambridge, MA: Rubel BikeMaps, 1998. Covers the outer western suburbs along I–495 west to the Quabbin Reservoir.

Claire Saltonstall Bikeway Map: Boston to Cape Cod, by American Youth Hostels, 1992. Available at AYH and many bike shops.

Cape Cod and the Islands, Cape Ann and North Shore Bicycle Map, by Andy Rubel. Cambridge, MA: Rubel BikeMaps, 1997.

MetroWest Bike Map. Natick, MA: MetroWest Growth Management Committee, 1996. Available at many bike shops.

MetroWest Local Cycling Routes, by Jacqueline R. Grocer. Natick, MA: The Author, 1998. Available at local bicycle shops or from the author, P. O. Box 817, Natick, MA 01760.

Pocket Rides: 5 Bike Rides, by Rosemary Jason. Cambridge, MA: Rubel BikeMaps, 1997–1998. Several packets, each containing five rides, with each ride on a laminated plastic sheet.

The Best Bike Paths of New England, by Wendy Williams. New York: Simon & Schuster, 1996.

Bike Paths of Massachusetts: A Guide to Rail-Trails and Other Car-Free Places, by Stuart Johnstone. Carlisle, MA: Active Publications, 1996.

Great Rail-Trails of the Northeast, by Craig Della Penna. Amherst, MA: New England Cartographics, 1995.

40 Great Rail-Trails in New York and New England, by Karen-Lee Ryan. Washington, DC: Rails-to-Trails Conservancy, 1996.

The Ride. A monthly magazine that covers all aspects of bicycling in the Northeast: recreational, racing, off-road, commuting, couriers, organized group rides, and advocacy. Available at many bike shops or by subscription. The address is 252 Main Street, Woburn, MA 01801.

Bicycle Shops (alphabetically by town)

Because there are too many shops for a complete listing, I have listed only those shops that advertise in bicycling publications or on the Eastern Massachusetts Bicycle Map, or that are members of the Massachusetts Bicycle Coalition.

Pedal Power Bike & Ski, 176 Great Road (Route 2A), Acton; (978) 263–3197

Peter White Cycles, 666 Massachusetts Avenue, Acton; (978) 635–0969

Bikeway Source, 111 South Road, Bedford; (781) 275–7799

Specialty Ski & Bike, Routes 140 and 126, Bellingham; (508) 966–5000

Belmont Wheelworks, 480 Trapelo Road, Belmont; (617) 489–3577

National Bicycle Shop, 393 Cabot Street, Beverly; (978) 922–8215

Back Bay Bicycles, 333 Newbury Street, Boston; (617) 242–2336

Beacon Street Bicycle, 842 Beacon Street, Boston; (617) 262–2332

Community Bicycle Supply, 496 Tremont Street, Boston; (617) 542–8623

Ski Market, 400 Franklin Street, Braintree; (781) 848–3733

International Bicycle Center, 89 Brighton Avenue, Brighton; (617) 783–5804

Ski Market, 860 Commonwealth Avenue, Brookline; (617) 731–6100

Burlington Cycle, 330 Cambridge Street, Burlington; (781) 272–8400

Cycle Loft, 28 Cambridge Street, Burlington; (781) 272–0870

Ski Market, Crossroads Shopping Center (Route 3A), Burlington; (781) 272–2222

ATA Cycle, 1700 Massachusetts Avenue, Cambridge; (617) 354–0907

Bicycle Exchange, 2067 Massachusetts Avenue, Cambridge; (617) 864–1300

The Bicycle Workshop, 259 Massachusetts Avenue, Cambridge; (617) 876–6555

Broadway Bicycle School, 351 Broadway, Cambridge; (617) 868–3392

Cycleville, 2228 State Road (Route 3A), Cedarville; (508) 888–5160

Bill & Andy's, 30 Chelmsford Street (Route 110), Chelmsford; (978) 256–8811

Chelmsford Cyclery, 7 Summer Street, Chelmsford; (978) 256–1528

Landry's Bicycles, 151 Endicott Street, Danvers; (978) 777–3337

Ski Market, Endicott Plaza, Danvers; (978) 777–3344

Western Cycle & Fitness, 22 Maple Street, Danvers; (978) 774–1685

Dedham Bike, 403 Washington Street, Dedham; (781) 326–1531

DEK Bikes, 260 Saint George Street, Duxbury; (781) 934–6900

Landry's Bicycles, 574 Washington Street, Easton; (508) 230–8882

Crosby Cycle Company, 397 Rhode Island Avenue, Fall River; (508) 679–9366

Landry's Bicycles, 303 Worcester Road (Route 9), Framingham; (508) 875–5158

REI, 375 Cochituate Road, Framingham; (508) 270–6325

Ski Market, 686 Worcester Road (Route 9), Framingham; (508) 875–5253

Franklin Bicycle, 22 East Central Street, Franklin; (508) 520–2453

Two for the Road, 74 East Main Street (Route 133), Georgetown; (978) 352–7343

Trek Stop Bicycles, Routes 140 and 30, Grafton; (508) 839–9199

Cycle Lodge, 1269 Washington Street (Route 53), Hanover; (781) 829–9197

Cycle Re Cycle, 263 Amesbury Line Road, Haverhill; (978) 372–0313

H.R. Sawyer Schwinn Bicyclery, 1 Ginty Boulevard, Haverhill; (978) 372–4981

Harbor Cycle, 55 Water Street, Hingham; (781) 749–1077

Yankee Pedaler, 141 Main Street, Hudson; (978) 568–9070

Ferris Wheels, 64 South Street, Jamaica Plain; (617) 522–7082

Jamaica Cycle, 667 Centre Street, Jamaica Plain; (617) 524–9610

Bikeway Cycle, 3 Bow Street, Lexington; (781) 861–1199

Steve's Bicycle Repair, 219 Massachusetts Avenue, Lexington; (781) 862–6038

Lincoln Guide Service, 152 Lincoln Road, Lincoln; (617) 259–1111

Seaside Cycle, 23 Elm Street, Manchester; (978) 526–1200

Marblehead Cycle, 25 Bessom Street, Marblehead; (781) 631–1570

Bikeway, Marshfield Plaza, Marshfield; (781) 837–2453

Ray & Sons Cyclery, 183 Main Street, Maynard; (978) 897–8121

Town and Country Bicycles, 67 North Street, Medfield; (508) 359–8377

Pro Cycles, 454 Main Street, Melrose; (781) 662–2813

Milford Bicycle, 71 East Main Street (Route 16), Milford; (508) 473–7955

Aries Sports, 100 Route 1, Newbury; (978) 465–8099

Riverside Cycles, 50 Water Street, Newburyport; (978) 465–5566

Centre Ski & Sports, 1185 Centre Street, Newton; (617) 964–3719

International Bicycle Center, 71 Needham Street, Newton; (617) 527–0967

Epicycle, 345 East Washington Street (Route 1), North Attleboro; (508) 643–2453

Sirois Bicycle Shop, 893 Landry Avenue, North Attleboro; (508) 695–6303

Pro Cycles, 20-A Main Street, North Reading; (978) 664–9762

Everybody's Bicycle, 168 Main Street (Route 20), Northboro; (508) 393–8087

Norwood Bicycle Depot, 85 Broadway, Norwood; (781) 762–2112

Bicycle Junction, 94 Washington Street, Pembroke; (781) 826–6385

Martha's Bicycles, 300 Court Street (Route 3A), Plymouth; (508) 746–2109

Peterson's Bike Shop, 421 Raynham Plaza, Route 44, Raynham; (508) 828–8851

Silver City Bicycle, 1470 New State Highway (Route 44), Raynham; (508) 828–9722

REI, 279 Salem Street, Reading; (781) 944–5103

Central Cycle, 195 Squire Road, Revere; (781) 289–0761

Buchika's Ski & Bike, 340 South Broadway (Route 28), Salem, NH;

(603) 893–5534

Northeast Bicycles, 124 Broadway (Route 1), Saugus; (781) 233–2664

Ace Wheelworks, 145 Elm Street, Somerville; (617) 776–2100

Park Sales & Service, 510 Somerville Avenue, Somerville; (617) 666–3647

National Ski & Bike, 102 Washington Street, South Attleboro; (508) 761–4500

Bay Road Bikes, 52 Railroad Avenue, South Hamilton; (978) 468–1301

Frank's Spoke 'n Wheel, 119 Boston Post Road, Sudbury; (978) 443–6696

Atlas Sporting Goods, 910 Andover Street, Tewksbury; (978) 640–0262

The Bicycle Shop, 17 Main Street, Topsfield; (978) 887–6511

Blackstone Canal Bicycles, 2 South Main Street, Uxbridge; (508) 278–3080

Wakefield Schwinn Cyclery, 16 Albion Street, Wakefield; (781) 245–2342

Frank's Spoke 'n Wheel, 887 Main Street, Waltham; (781) 894–2768

Farina's, 61 Galen Street, Watertown; (617) 926–1717

Saint Moritz Sports, 475 Washington Street, Wellesley; (781) 235–6669

T & S Cycle, 67 Main Street (Route 1A), Wenham; (978) 468–4488

Wachusett Cycle & Multisport, 71 Sterling Street, West Boylston, (508) 835–6100

Harris Cyclery, 1353 Washington Street, West Newton; (617) 244–1040

Bicycle Barn, 123 Boston Turnpike (Route 9), Westboro; (508) 366–1770

Landry's Bicycles, 1 Oak Street (Route 9), Westboro; (508) 836–3878

Fat Dog Pro Bicycle Shop, 940 High Street (Route 109), Westwood; (781) 251–9447

Overview of the Rides

		Historic Sites	Unique Spots	Ocean/Bay Views	Lakes, Ponds, Rivers, Dams
1	Nahant		●	●	
2	Saugus Ironworks	●			●
3	Woburn-Winchester-Arlington	L			●
4	Minuteman Bikeway	●			●
5	Newton-Brookline	●	●		L
6	Blue Hills	L			●
7	Lynnfield-North Reading				●
8	Lynn-Swampscott-Marblehead	●	●	●	
9	Estates and Estuaries		●	●	
10	Gateway to Cape Ann		●	●	
11	Cape Ann		●	●	
12	Ipswich	●		●	
13	Newburyport-Newbury-Rowley	●	●		
14	Newburyport-Byfield		●		●
15	Whittier Country	●			●
16	Middleton-North Andover	●			L
17	Topsfield-Ipswich-Wenham	●	●		●
18	Pedaler's Paradise	●			●
19	America's Stonehenge		L		●
20	Middlesex Canal	●	L		L
21	Reading Wilmington				●
22	Minute Man Ride	●			
23	Weston-Lincoln-Sudbury	●	●		●
24	Weston-Wellesley-Wayland		●		
25	Charles River				●
26	Upper Charles River				L
27	Plainville-Cumberland				●
28	Chelmsford-Carlisle-Westford				
29	Nashoba Valley	L	L		●
30	Wayside Inn	L	L		●
31	Holliston-Hopkinton				●
32	Westford-Dunstable-Tyngsboro		●		●
33	Covered Bridge		●		●
34	Shirley-West Groton-Townsend				●
35	West Boylston-Sterling		●		●
36	Apple Country Adventure		●		●
37	Triboro Tour		L		●
38	Upper Blackstone Valley	●	●		●

S – Short Ride Only
L – Long Ride Only

Mill Villages	New England Villages	Open land, Views	Easy	Hilly	
					1
	L		S		2
		L	S	L	3
			●		4
					5
		L			6
	●		●		7
	●		●		8
	L		S		9
			●		10
	L		S		11
	●		●		12
	●	●	S		13
	●	●			14
●	S	●			15
	●	●			16
	●		●		17
	●				18
	●				19
L					20
	●		S		21
	●	S	S		22
	●		S		23
	●				24
	L		S		25
L	●		S		26
	L	●			27
	●			●	28
	●	L		●	29
	●				30
	●				31
●	●				32
●	●				33
L	●	●			34
	●	●		●	35
	●	L			36
	●				37
●	L	●		●	38

Overview of the Rides

	Historic Sites	Unique Spots	Ocean/Bay Views	Lakes, Ponds Rivers, Dam
39 Purgatory Chasm		●		●
40 Hingham	●	L	●	●
41 Cohasset-Scituate		L	●	●
42 Scituate-Marshfield		●	●	
43 Duxbury-Marshfield	●	●	●	
44 South Shore Scenic Circuit		●		●
45 Canton-Stoughton-Sharon	●	●		●
46 Sharon-Easton-Norton				●
47 Foxboro-Mansfield-Plainville		L		●
48 Norton-Taunton		●		●
49 Bridgewater		L		●
50 Middleboro-Halifax		●		L
51 Seekonk-Rehoboth				L
52 Swansea-Somerset-Dighton			L	●
53 Profile Rock-Dighton Rock	L	L		●
54 Weston-Tiverton		L	●	●
55 Westport-Horseneck Beach		●	L	●
56 North Dartmouth-Westport		●		●
57 Dartmouth		●	●	
58 Land o'Lakes		●		●
59 Mattapoisett-Rochester			●	●
60 Marion			●	
61 Cranberry Cruise		●		L
62 Pilgrim's Progress	●	●	●	●
63 Southeastern Shore		●	●	L
64 Cape Cod Canal		●	●	●

S – Short Ride Only
L – Long Ride Only

Mill Villages	New England Villages	Open land, Views	Easy	Hilly	
●	L	●		●	39
	●				40
	●				41
	●				42
			●		43
	●		S		44
	L				45
	L		●		46
	●				47
	●		●		48
	●		S		49
	●	●	●		50
	●				51
	●	●	S		52
●	●		●		53
	●				54
	●	●			55
	●		●		56
	●	●			57
			●		58
	●		●		59
	●		●		60
	●		S		61
	●				62
	●				63
	●		●		64

About the Author

Howard Stone grew up in Boston, went to college in Maine and Illinois, and returned to his native New England, where he is now a librarian at Brown University. For many years Howard was the touring director of the Narragansett Bay Wheelmen, the major bicycle club for southeastern Massachusetts and Rhode Island. He is the author of the companion volumes *Short Bike Rides in Western Massachusetts* and *Short Bike Rides in Rhode Island,* both of which are also published by The Globe Pequot Press, and also bicycling guides for Maine and the Hudson Valley. Howard has done extensive bicycle touring, including a cross-country trip from Newport, Oregon, to Newport, Rhode Island, in 1978.